Millwater Publishing

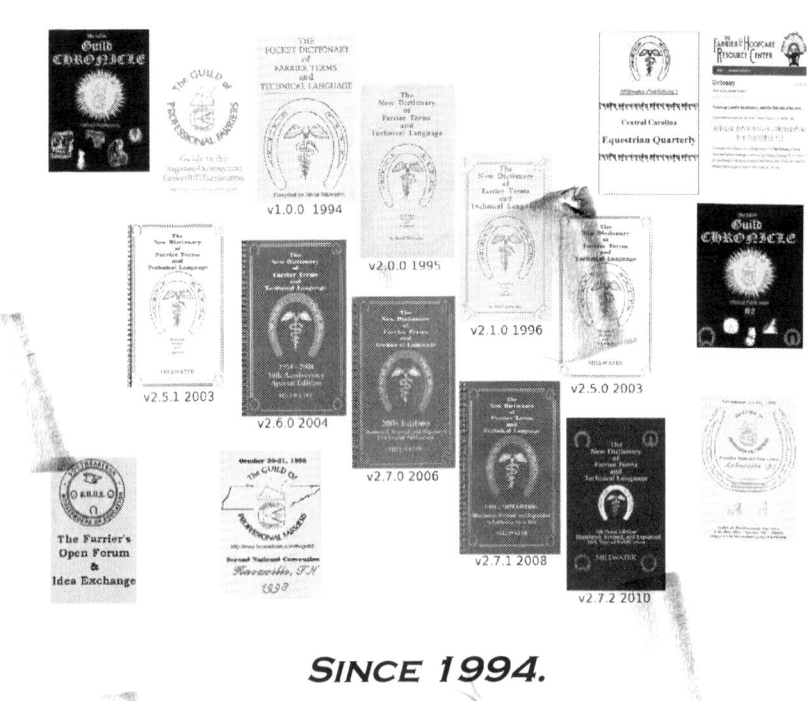

Since 1994.

Be Aware...

Horses are quite large, heavy,
and possess superhuman speed and strength.

Tools, nails, and metal stock have sharp points and edges.

Forge and welding fuels are flammable.

Hammering, filing, and grinding metal produces
eye-injuring sparks and fragments.

Sparks and radiant heat from forges and shoes can start fires.

Fire is very hot.

Working with horses, blacksmithing,
trimming, and shoeing hooves all
involve potential risk to people,
animals, and other property.

While great effort has been made to provide
useful and accurate information in this publication,
no book can replace competent instruction and supervision.

Proceed at your own risk.

Millwater's
FARRIERY:
The Illustrated Dictionary of Horseshoeing and Hoofcare.

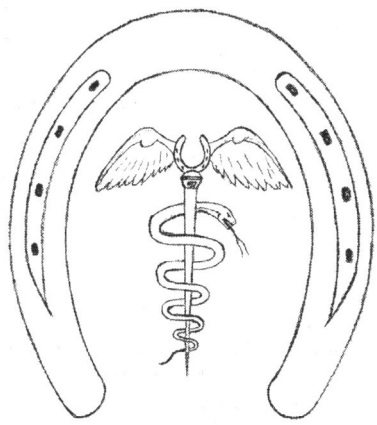

Encyclopedic reference for professionals, horseowners, and students.

• • • • •

by
Dave Millwater

With selected
Phonetic Guides and Etymologies

MILLWATER'S
FARRIERY:
THE ILLUSTRATED DICTIONARY OF HORSESHOEING AND HOOFCARE.

Copyright 2012
by MILLWATER.
All rights reserved.

ISBN: 1466444819
ISBN 13: 978-1466444812

http://www.MillwaterPublishing.com/

Millwater Publishing.
32306-C Hugh Road
Albemarle, NC
28001

Preface:

Farriery is one of America's last free professions. As such, there are many avenues to learning the trade. A multitude of schools with different course lengths and curricula. Apprenticeships formal and casual. Clinics, workshops, and symposiums. And individual study. Lots of it. All in all, education in the art and science is a unique experience for each farrier.

So there are always gaps in our knowledge to be filled, whether we are rookies or grizzled veterans. Always something new to learn.

Millwater Publishing's lexicon project started with **The Pocket Dictionary of Farrier Terms and Technical Language** in 1994. A humble little glossary to help farriers, horseowners, and researchers understand one-another better. Over the many print and virtual editions which followed, it evolved to include more extensive definitions and illustrations. With this, its 10th print incarnation, the lexicon makes the jump to being an *encyclopedic* dictionary.

The encyclopedic format is particularly suited to the free-form learning of farriery. Each article is designed to cross-reference with others, so that readers can easily fill in the basics required to comprehend a given topic, or follow on to more advanced information as needed.

This book is a collection and distillation of the ideas and observations of many farriers I've learned from over the years. Some I've had the privilege of knowing personally. Others, only through their work. The names of several appear within the entries. Many more have made contributions to the sum of hoofcare knowledge which have come down to me without attribution. Famous, anonymous, or somewhere in-between, these pathfinders are recognized and appreciated.

Dave Millwater, RMF.

If I have seen a little further, it is by standing on the shoulders of giants.

-Sir Isaac Newton

The difference between almost the right word and the right word is really a large matter. 'Tis the difference between the lightning-bug and the lightning.

-Mark Twain.

Knowledge is of two kinds. We know a subject ourselves, or we know where we can find information upon it.

-Samuel Johnson.

First among the evidences of an education I name the correctness and precision in the use of the mother tongue.

-Nicholas Murray Butler.

All words are pegs to hang ideas on.

-Henry Ward Beecher.

Knowledge is Power.

-Francis Bacon.

Using this book:

Each entry within this encyclopedic dictionary consists of its topic, which will be printed in **boldface**. This may be followed by a phonetic guide which will be enclosed (in parentheses) and/or etymological information enclosed [in brackets] with foreign root-words in *italics*.

The entry most relevant to farriery will be listed first. If additional entries are included, each will be preceded by a numeral in parentheses. Terms used within entries which are themselves covered elsewhere in this book may be printed in ***italic boldface***.

Where cross-referencing may clarify a word's meaning, **See:** or **See also:** directions are included.

The most commonly used terms and word forms receive primary listings. Common synonyms for these words are included at the end of primary entries with an **a.k.a:** denotation. These synonyms and alternate word forms often have their own separate listings with **See:** instructions.

x
. . .

abaxial (ab ́ ak ́ sē-əl)**:** Situated away from the center.

abscess, hoof: A localized infection of the sensitive tissues within the *hoof capsule*. May involve the sole, bars, *laminae*, and/or frog. Can be initiated by puncture wounds, *bruises* that go *septic*, and bacteria being allowed into fissures created in the laminae by swelling of the hoof capsule when the *horn* is wet, then being sealed-in when it dries and shrinks.

Abscesses often cause intense *lameness*. If a *horse* goes severely lame on one foot for no obvious cause, it is likely an abscess. Abscesses may also cause prolonged, low grade lameness, or no observable lameness at all. Intensity of lameness seems to be related more to the path of the pus and pressure within the foot than the amount, as *horses* in agony have been seen to gain tremendous relief by having a few drops of pus released, while others have had much greater quantities of pus erupt despite having shown little or no lameness beforehand.

If the location or path of an abscess can be ascertained, it may be possible to drain the pus and relieve the horse's pain by carefully cutting a small hole in the *solar* aspect of the hoof. It may also be possible to access the abscess by cutting through the hoof *wall*, which avoids the problem of leaving an open wound in the bottom of the foot. It is not always be possible to fully reach an abscess without compromising the hoof capsule to an excessive degree. A *pad* with *antiseptic* packing, *hospital plate horseshoe*, or bandaging of the hoof may be necessary to prevent re-infection through the drainage hole.

Soaking an abscessed foot in an *Epsom salt* solution may draw out the infection. The water should be as hot as a person can stand to immerse a hand in, with as much salt as will dissolve. The foot should be soaked to just above the hairline for around 20 minutes at the time, two or three times a day. A *sugardine* solar packing may also help draw out the infection.

Abscesses sometimes erupt at the *coronary band*, and may result in a *cleft*, which will grow out in time. Rupture may also occur at the bulbs of the heels.

Once the pus is drained, it may be advisable to continue Epsom soaks once a day for a few days to clear it out completely. If the opening heals over a still-active infection, the abscess may begin anew.

The intense pain of abscesses may tempt horseowners to administer *bute* or other *NSAIDs*. These may actually slow the abscess from coming to a 'head', and make it difficult to drain.

a.k.a: gravel; pus pocket. **See also:** hoof anatomy, basic; Page A-2; A-5: A-6.

Ace: Acepromazine maleate, a drug used for *chemical restraint*, administered via *IV* or *IM* injection. Despite being a legally controlled substance, acepromazine seems to be the most widely available tranquilizer to lay horseowners. This is particularly unfortunate, as acepromazine is often a poor stand-alone chemical restraint drug, and some *horses* react to it by becoming more unruly than they were to begin with. Experienced veterinarians often use acepromazine in conjunction with other drugs.

acetylene torch: A blowtorch which burns a combination of compressed acetylene gas and oxygen. Used for *welding*, *brazing*, and cutting metals.

acrylic: Any of numerous thermoplastic or thermosetting polymers or co-polymers of acrylic acid, methacrylic acid, esters of these acids, or acrylonitrile, used in horseshoeing to fill gaps or cracks in the hoof wall and sometimes to affix *horseshoes*.

acute: Coming about suddenly and severely, but persisting briefly.
See also: chronic.

adhesion (ad-hē zhə̇n): Sticking together. The abnormal joining of living tissues.

AFA: American Farriers Association. U.S. based organization of horseshoers and other people interested in farriery, founded in 1971.
 -Address:
  4059 Iron Works Pike
  Lexington, KY 40511

A.F.C.L.: Associate of the Farriers Company of London. Previous title for farriers at the level now designated *A.W.C.F.*

AHSA: See: USEF.

alligators: Colloquialism for *clinchers*.

alloy: A metal compound in which elements are added to the primary metal to impart new properties. *Steel*, for instance, is an alloy created by infusing a small amount of carbon into *iron* to make it possible to *harden* and *temper* the metal.

aluminum: A non-magnetic, conductive, metallic element. Atomic number 13, atomic weight 26.981526.98; melting point 660.2°C; boiling point 2,467°C; specific gravity 2.69; valence 3. It is abundant in impure form in the Earth's crust. Refined aluminum is very lightweight, workable, and easily recycled.

American Farriers Association: See: AFA.

AQHA: American Quarter Horse Association. The primary registry organization for pedigreed American quarter-horses, the AQHA also sanctions shows and races for these *horses* and sets rules and standards for these events. Established in 1940, the AQHA is the largest horse breed organization in the world, and has been used as a template for many other breed organizations which followed.

ankylosis [From Greek *angkylos*, crooked]: Fusing of a joint.

anneal [Anglo-Saxon *anaelan*, to set on fire.]**:** To render a given piece of *steel* as soft as it can be made. *Blacksmiths* traditionally do this by heating the steel up to a cherry red heat, then cooling it very slowly by packing it in the coals of a dying fire or some other insulating material. The effect of annealing is dependent upon the makeup of the steel *alloy*. Mild steel (such as is used in *horseshoes*) aren't much softer when annealed than they are when *hardened*. High carbon steels (like rasps) can withstand being bent double when annealed, but would snap into fragments if this were attempted while they were hardened.

annular ligaments: *Ligaments* which form sheet-like bands to hold *tendons* in place.

anterior: On or towards the front. **See also**: posterior.

antiseptic: Inhibits micro-biotic growth.

anvil [Anglo-Saxon *anfilt*; from *an*, on, and *fealdan*, to fold]: **(1.)** A block of steel against which metals are hammered. The *London pattern* anvil, which began it's evolution in the 13th century, has been the trademark of *farriers* and *blacksmiths* for three centuries. Shop anvils commonly weighed hundreds of pounds, with the largest known being 1400 pounds. Modern farrier anvils often have special features and usually weigh between 50 and 150 pounds.

(2.) In human anatomy, the middle bone {incus} in the ear.

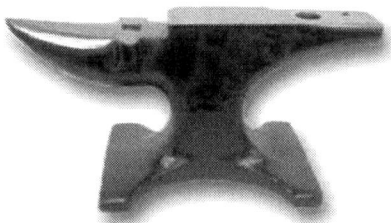

anvil (1.)

anvil shooting: (1.) A recreational practice in which an explosive charge (usually black gunpowder) is placed between two stacked anvils and ignited with a fuse, launching the top anvil as much as 100 feet into the air. a.k.a: Blowing the anvil.

(2.) Hammering a white-hot piece of *iron* against a wet anvil. This produces a pistol-shot like sound.

apron: Protective garment worn over clothing. The *blacksmith* or *fireman's* apron is traditionally made of leather and protects the front of the *smith's* body and clothes from sparks and hot *scale* from the chest down to the knees.

The *farrier* or *doorman's* apron, also usually made of leather, covers only from the waist down to the shins, is split to allow the *hoof* to be held between the knees, and is often reinforced to protect the farrier's legs and pants from *horseshoe nails*, sharp tools, and hooves.

farrier's **apron**

apprentice [From Latin *apprendo*, to seize or apprehend]: Traditionally, an individual whose primary reward for labor is the opportunity to learn a trade. The apprentice is usually bound to an established craftsman for a specified period of time and paid a modest salary. An apprentice cannot accept payment for his work directly from customers. Formal *farrier* apprenticeships traditionally run from 3 to 7 years in length.

arc welder: A device which uses high-current electrodes to generate intense, concentrated heat. Used to weld and cut metal.

Arm & Hammer: Brand of forged *anvils* from 1900 until 1950.

arteries: The thick-walled vessels which carry oxygenated blood from the heart to the tissues.

arteriovenous anastomoses: See: A.V.A.

articulation: The range of movement of a skeletal joint.

ass

ass: Member of the species *Equus asinus, Equus hemionus,* or *Equus kiang*. Asses tend to be smaller and slower than domestic *horses*, but are very tough and can survive well on a relatively poor diet and may carry proportionately larger burdens. Asses exist in truly wild as well as *feral* forms in addition to the domesticated population, which are more commonly called donkeys. Donkeys have been selectively bred to sizes from miniature up to over 16 *hands*. The *jenny* may carry her foal for up to 13 months. Asses have small, upright *hooves* with large frogs. They are most recognizable for their long ears, each of which may be more than half the length of the animal's head. Asses have a very distinctive bray which may be heard for several miles and which may be voiced continuously for an impressive length of time.
See: jack; mule.

Associate of the Farriers Company of London:
See: A.F.C.L.

association: A society whose members are united by mutual interests.
See also: guild.

atmospheric forge: A propane *forge* that requires no *blower*. Perfected by Donald Jones of NC Tool in 1982. This was the first gas forge in which good welds could consistently be made.

atrophy (**at** rə́-fe) [From Greek *atrophia*, not to nourish]: Shrinking or degeneration of tissues. Usually results from disuse or disease.

autointoxication: Poisoning from within. *Laminitis* may begin with excessive amounts of carbohydrate reaching the *cecum*, resulting in a population explosion of bacteria (which are beneficial at normal levels), then a massive release of toxins during the bacterial die-off that follows.
a.k.a: autotoxemia.

autotoxemia:
See: autointoxication.

A.V.A.: Arteriovenous anastomoses. Special blood vessels which act as bypass valves, diverting blood away from the tiny *capillaries* which nourish the *laminae*. Opening the A.V.A.s reduces blood flow resistance, thereby increasing the flow rate. This is thought to be a mechanism for preventing frostbite in *equine hooves*.

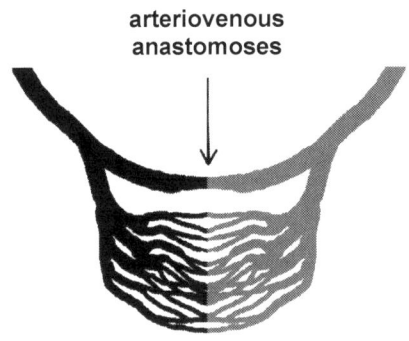

arteriovenous anastomoses

A.W.C.F.: Associate of the Worshipful Company of Farriers. A recognition of advanced skill and knowledge awarded by the *W.C.F.* Applicants must have achieved the *D.W.C.F.* at least two years prior. The two day A.W.C.F. examination includes three essay questions, to be answered fully and with color illustrations, live remedial shoeing, advanced shoe forging, and a 30 minute oral questioning period.

axial (ak sē-əl)**:** Situated toward the middle or center.

azoturia: Severe chemical imbalance in a *horse's* muscles due to lactic acid building up in the tissues faster than it can be carried away. This causes the horse's muscles to contract painfully and uncontrollably, sometimes rendering him unable to move. This most often happens when a horse is overworked for his condition, especially if he is high-strung and doesn't settle down when fatigue begins to set in. The horse should be kept as calm and comfortable as possible, and encouraged to remain still until a veterinarian arrives. Prevention is the best approach, and can be achieved by balanced diet, proper conditioning and turn-out, access to electrolyte and trace mineral salt block, plenty of fresh water, and beginning work with a gradual warm-up.

a.k.a.: tying-up; exertional rhabdomyolysis; Monday morning disease.

backwards shoe: A conventional *horseshoe* applied with the heels of the shoe at the toe of the hoof. This usually requires that extra nail holes be made. The backwards shoe acts as a *rockered toe eggbar*.

a.k.a: reverse shoe; open toe egg bar; Napoleon shoe.
See: Page A-9.

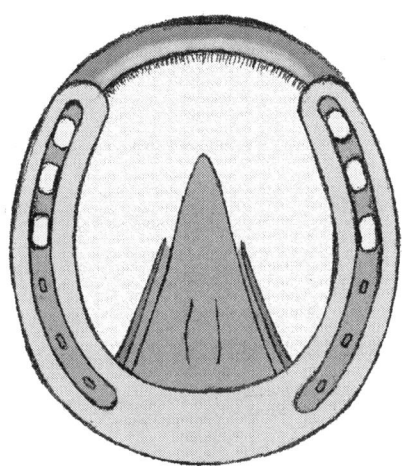

backwards shoe

bag of marbles: Multiple bone fractures in a small area.

balance: A subjective term used in reference to both *equine* conformation and *hoof* geometry. Balance describes a condition in which each part is in optimum proportion to all others.

balancing the horse's hoof:
Trimming the *horse's hoof* to its optimum form is not a matter of simple geometry. The hoof is a dynamic structure which loads, unloads, accelerates, flexes, wears, and grows. It is connected to the horse via a jointed *limb* which has its own deviations and eccentricities. So there is considerable variation between individuals, and even between limbs on the same horse when it comes to determining the correct form for each hoof.

Several aspects of hoof form need to be addressed simultaneously to achieve balance and optimum function.

Flares. Any attempt to balance a hoof without correcting deformed *walls* is futile. Even if the plane of the solar surface is perfectly perpendicular to the limb, the mediolateral balance will be functionally far from ideal when there is a flare on one side of the hoof. A toe flare can make the apparent *hoof angle* meaningless. Above and beyond making it impossible to achieve correct balance for the hoof, flares are a structural failure of the horn, and tend to pull the still-functional *horn* above the flare out of place.

The wall should be straight from coronary band down to the ground. Unless the horse is a *sinker* or is sloughing a hoof entirely, the first inch of wall below the coronary band will be parallel to the surface of the *P III*. This first inch can be used as a guide to dress away any flared wall below.

{See: two finger radiograph.}

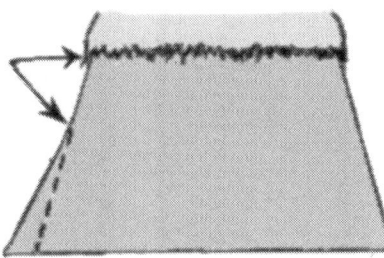

Dorsal view of hoof with lateral flare. Arrows indicate the part of the wall which can safely be assumed to be parallel to the PIII.
The dotted line indicates flare which should be dressed-off.

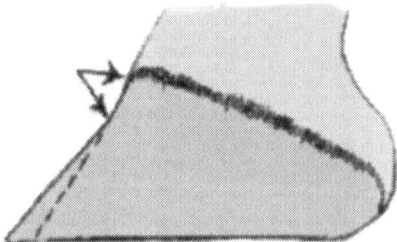

Lateral view of hoof with toe flare.

Hoof angle. Once all flares have been eliminated, the hoof angle can be evaluated. Hoof angle determines how impact and loading are distributed between the front and rear halves of foot, and has considerable effect on breakover speed and leverage. *{See: hoof angle.}*

Hoof angle can be measured with hoof protractors, which are available in various forms. But the normal range is more than ten degrees from slightly below 50° to slightly above 60° for horses of different types and conformation, so protractor measurements tend to be rather academic.

One of the most widely used means of determining the correct hoof angle for an individual horse is to use the pastern angle as a guide. The pastern angle changes inversely to changes made in the hoof angle, so it is usually fairly easy to bring the dorsal faces of the pastern and hoof wall into alignment. This alignment has proven to be a good indicator of correct hoof angle.

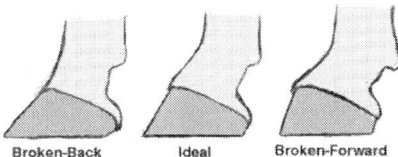

A supplementary guide to hoof angle is the angle of the shoulder and the overall conformation type of the horse. Shoulder angles are difficult to measure accurately, and are much steeper than any functional hoof angles on the whole. But a relatively steep shoulder angle (compared to shoulders of other horses) may suggest that the horse would do better with a hoof angle a few degrees higher than what is required to establish a straight hoof-pastern axis. Short-torso, compact body type horses tend to have such upright shoulders.

An important guide to achieving correct hoof angle is to consider the immediate dynamic balance effect. This is determined by watching the horse move. The hooves should land flat or just slightly heel-first. Toe-first landing suggests that the hoof angle is too low, or that the heels are in pain, which may also be the indirect result of a low hoof angle. Overly heel-first landing might suggest that the hoof angle is too high, and/or that the toe of the foot is in pain.

Because the hoof wall tends to grow faster where it bears less load (and vice-versa), minimal change in hoof angle in a shod hoof over the shoeing cycle due to even growth pattern can be an indicator of balanced loading.

Toe length. Taken together with the hoof angle, the toe length (measured from hairline to the bearing surface) provides an overall picture of how much total wall there is on a hoof. With the same hoof angle, a longer toe length increases the clearance of the sensitive structures of the foot from the ground, but also increases hoof's resistance to breakover. As a rule, any more toe length than is necessary for the protection of internal structures tends to reduce athletic efficiency. Unfortunately, any less length than necessary results in lameness.

The toe length is usually based on the level of the sole, with enough wall being left to extend slightly beyond the sole. This means that the method used to determine how much sole to trim has a direct impact on the toe length.

In temperate climates, the amount of sole to trim can be established in many horses by how much of the horn is easily removable. The sole naturally exfoliates excess horn, and there may be little that needs to be removed on some horses, especially those which are kept barefoot. What extra sole material there is can often be disposed of with little effort with a hoof knife or even a wire brush. On these horses, when the flaky, soft horn gives way to tougher, smoother material, the sole has been trimmed to the correct depth.

In dry climates the excess sole may be glass-hard and resist removal. In wet conditions, the sole may become soft all the way through, making it easy to cut too deep. Some horses retain solid-feeling sole to excessive thickness even in normal conditions. *{See: retained sole.}* In these cases, other means must be used to determine how much sole to trim.

The level of the frog is one guide to trimming the sole. In most horses, the frog should be recessed a fraction of an inch below the level of the sole. Unfortunately, the frog itself is a horny, exfoliating structure, and is not an entirely reliable indicator of appropriate sole level.

A more reliable, although not always advisable means to determining how much sole to take on an individual horse is to carefully trim the sole near the toe until it will yield to firm thumb pressure. At that stage the sole has been reduced in thickness a little too much, but not to a degree which would make injury likely. A measurement may be taken after this trim is complete, and the hoof should be left at least 1/4" longer in future trims.

Mediolateral. Uneven distribution of load between the inner and outer halves of each hoof can result in excessive strain on ligaments and wear damage to some joints. The overloaded side of the hoof is subject to stress failure, and the horse's **trueness of gait** is often adversely influenced as the animal moves his entire body in an attempt to shift weight away from the overloaded side of the hoof with each step.

The most common means to judge mediolateral geometry is to

lift the leg and hold it up as if to clean out the hoof. Holding the leg loosely just below the knee or hock, one "looks down the leg". The hoof is trimmed so that the solar plane of the hoof is perpendicular to the line of cannon as seen in the described palmar view.

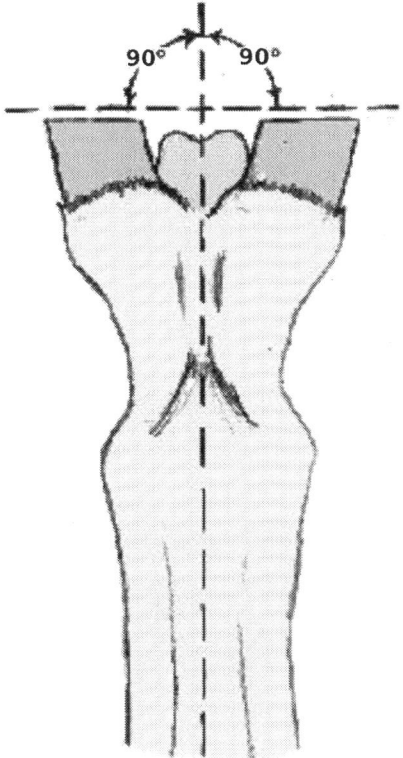

A method used to fine-tune mediolateral geometry which considers immediate dynamic balance is to have the horse walked or ridden on a flat surface so that the way the hooves land may be observed. If a hoof lands unevenly, the side of the hoof which lands first may be need to be trimmed more, or the other side of the hoof may have been over-trimmed.

A method that can be employed on shod horses which indicates how loading has been distributed between the halves of the hoof over several weeks is to observe the wear pattern on the shoe. If the shoe is being worn away faster on one side than the other, the fast wearing side of the hoof may need to trimmed more and the other side trimmed less.

Hairline. A warped coronary band, particularly one that appears "jammed" upwards in some areas, may indicate uneven loading of the hoof. The hoof wall below the areas where the coronary band deviates upward may need to be trimmed more.

Solar. The shape and symmetry of the ground-facing surface of the hoof has great effect on the functional mediolateral loading, breakover, and which internal hoof structures bear the greatest forces as the foot lands and loads.

The frog is an important guide in judging hoof geometry from the solar aspect. Because the frog itself is a horn structure which can shed, become overgrown, or distorted, only the fixed parts of the frog can be used for reference. The tip of the frog can be trimmed to determine its true apex, and the sides of the frog may be trimmed if they have been mashed into the commissures. Further trimming is not necessary for reference purposes, and is not advisable unless the frog horn is rotten.

A line envisioned through the center of the frog should bisect the hoof into equal inner and outer halves. If one side is substantially bigger than the other, there is a functional mediolateral imbalance even if the solar plane of the hoof is perfectly perpendicular to the cannon. It may be advisable to dress the bigger side of the hoof down, or to apply a shoe that extends the bearing surface of the smaller side of the hoof, or to do both at once in order to achieve a reasonably symmetrical bearing surface.

One may envision a spot on the frog about 3/8" behind its apex on typical riding-size horses. (Perhaps slightly closer to the apex on smaller hooves, and slightly farther back on draft-size hooves, as proportion dictates.) This spot is known as the *Duckett's Dot*, and corresponds with the center of mass of the coffin bone. The toe arc the hoof should be centered around this point.

A line envisioned crossing the foot somewhat behind Duckett's Dot, at the widest part of the hoof, should be equidistant from the anterior breakover line and a line crossing the buttresses of the heels. This line, which separates the front and rear of a properly trimmed hoof into equal halves, is directly below the coffin joint's center of articulation, and is known as *Duckett's Bridge*.

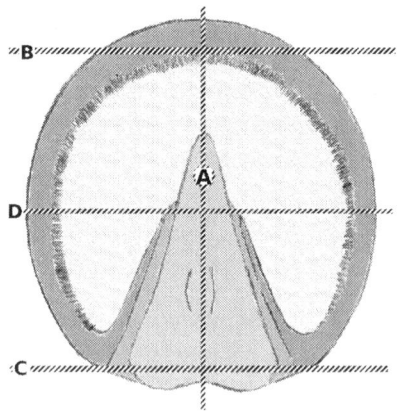

A. Duckett's Dot. B. Anterior Breakover.
D. Duckett's Bridge. C. Heel Buttresses.

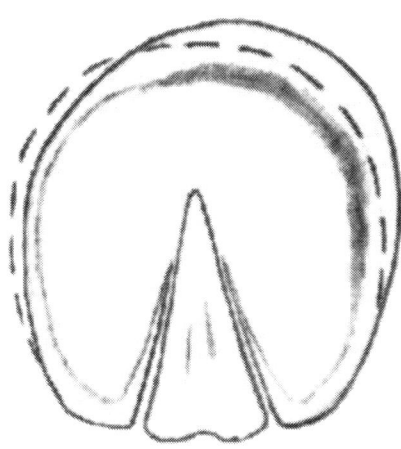

Solar view of a distorted hoof. The wall which extends beyond the dashed line needs to be dressed away. Where the wall does not reach the dashed line, the base of support may need to be extended with an appropriate horseshoe.

A line envisioned from one heel buttress to the other should cross the frog no further forward than its rear-most third. Even farther back, crossing the frog near its widest point, is desirable if practical. Even if a long-heeled or eggbar horseshoe is applied, the impact forces incurred when the foot lands are initially directed into the foot at the line of the buttresses. If the buttresses are allowed to extend forward so that a line connecting them would cross the middle third of the frog, those forces are directed into the navicular area. Such forward-placed buttresses are the result of heels that are functionally underrun, and will be crushed upward when loaded. It often requires the removal of only a thin wafer of horn at the heels to bring the buttresses back to the rear part of the frog. This results in the impact forces being directed into the digital cushion rather than the navicular area, and establishes more upright, structurally sounder heels.

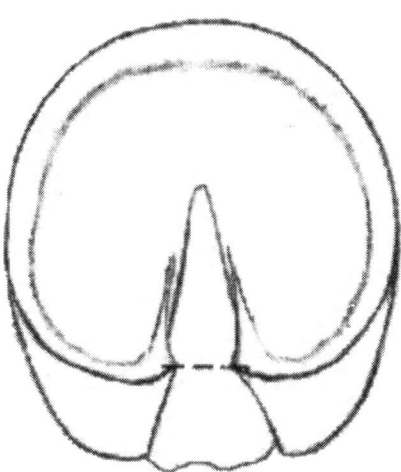

Crushed, underrun heels.

On a horse with near-ideal conformation, the various aspects of balance described above are complimentary. For instance, if all flares are dressed away and the solar plane of the foot is trimmed perpendicular to the cannon and the hoof angle is adjusted to establish a straight hoof-pastern axis, the foot will "automatically" be centered around Duckett's Bridge and neatly bisected by the mid-line of the frog.

In practice, few horses are near this ideal. Many have congenital or developmental conformation flaws, histories of injuries and disease, and other factors that affect the way their hooves function. In such cases, some means of establishing correct hoof form may contradict others, and it may not be possible to get the hooves to fit within the normal parameters of correct hoof geometry. The attempt may, in fact, be detrimental to the horse.

The practical experience of the qualified farrier provides him with the insight to take the particulars of each case into consideration and to decide which aspects and methods of determining hoof form to favor, and which aspects may need to be at least partially disregarded or adjusted due to the individual's peculiarities. This "eye for balance" is developed by the farrier as he fine-tunes thousands of hooves over the course of years and observes the results in horses with various conformation types and flaws. Because different combinations of adjustments can achieve similar positive results, and each farrier develops his own analog criteria for making these adjustments, it may be impossible to express the fine points of establishing overall hoof balance in explicit technical terms.

The ultimate test of hoof balance is how form facilitates function. Correct balance makes it possible for a horse to maintain optimum soundness and athletic performance over the course of years. Imbalance reduces efficiency and shortens the horse's working lifespan.

barefoot: An un*shod* horse. Many *horses* are able to meet the demands of their owners without *horseshoes*. This is frequently the case where sound horses are worked relatively lightly on surfaces which are not excessively rocky, hard, or abrasive. There is a great deal of difference between individual horses when it comes to how much work they can withstand on any given terrain. Horses subjected to moderate workloads often have their fore *hooves* shod and their hinds left barefoot, as the former carry the majority of the load. Many horses who require shoes for their regular use may benefit from going barefoot during the off season, during which time they can grow out old *nail* tracks and toughen their soles.

Barcus: Brand of shoeing *stocks* from around 1865 to around 1930.

bar shoe: Any *horseshoe* which is not interrupted by an opening between the heels. Various forms of bars are used to increase support surface, apply pressure, prevent pressure, or stabilize the shoe.
See: Page A-9.

bar shoe

bar stock: The metal stock from which *handmade horseshoes* are *forged*. Typical *steel* horseshoe bar stock is 5/16" by 3/4", but many other sizes are also used. Bar stock is usually purchased by the linear foot.

basal crack: A *sandcrack* which starts at the ground surface and splits upward.

basement membrane: The microscopically thin layer of connective tissue between the secondary horny and secondary sensitive *laminae* within the equine *hoof*. This layer is partially dissolved by regulated enzyme action to allow the horny laminae (and the *hoof wall* with it) to slide downward in relation to the sensitive laminae so that *hoof horn* growth can occur. The basement membrane is uniformly smooth and unbroken in healthy hooves, but breaks down and tatters with the onset of *laminitis*.

bear foot: See: clubfoot.

bellows [Ultimately from Anglo-Saxon *belg*, bag or belly.]: A device used to force air into a *forge* featuring a bladder of sorts which is squeezed between a pair of boards to push air out of the opening at one end. Large hearth-type *coal forges* typically used a fixed, double-chambered bellows which produced a continuous blast of air on the up and down strokes. This was often operated by a cord or chain which ran through an arrangement of overhead pulleys so that the *smith* could pull straight down on the cord to pump the bellows remotely. Such a system relied on a counterweight which would continue the air blast for a few moments after the cord was released. The electric *blower* replaced the bellows in most shops generations ago.

bench knee: A *limb* conformation defect in which the *leg* fits somewhat to the outside of, rather than directly below, the forearm at the knee.
a.k.a: offset knee.
See: Page A-3.

bifurcate [from Latin *bi*, twice and *furca*, fork]: To separate, split, or divide.

big knee: See: popped knee.

big lick: See: running walk.

bilateral: On both sides. Usually means both *hooves* of a *pair*.

biotin: A colorless crystalline B complex vitamin $C_{10}H_{16}N_2O_3S$, essential for the activity of many enzyme systems and found in large quantities in liver, egg yolk, milk, and yeast. Biotin is popularly believed to be beneficial to *hoof* growth and quality, and is often included in *horse* feed supplements.

blacksmith: A craftsman who works *iron* and *steel*. This term is sometimes inaccurately used as a synonym for *farrier*. Because modern farriers *forge* steel *horseshoes*, they are indeed blacksmiths. But not all blacksmiths are farriers.

blemish: A cosmetic flaw which does not affect *soundness*.

blind gut: See: cecum.

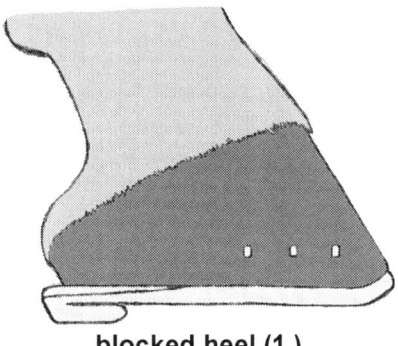

blocked heel (1.)

blocked heel: (1.) The heel of a *horseshoe* which has been folded down against the ground surface of the shoe. This can be done to raise the heels or to act as a *heel calk*. On thin shoes, the heel may be folded twice.
(2.) Large, square heel calks on manufactured racehorse shoes are sometimes called blocks, especially if the other heel is a *sticker*.

blower: A device, usually in the form of a housed fan, which forces air into a *forge*. Smaller, mobile forges often used hand-cranked blowers by the middle of the 19th Century. More modern designs use electric motors to power the blower, often with a multi-position switch or rheostat to adjust the force of the blast.

blowing the anvil: See: anvil shooting.

Bluegrass Laminitis Symposium: See: BLS.

BLS: Bluegrass Laminitis Symposium. A large conference of *farriers* and veterinarians covering a wide array of hoofcare and *lameness* topics. Sponsored by the International Equine Podiatry Center and held in the State of Kentucky.

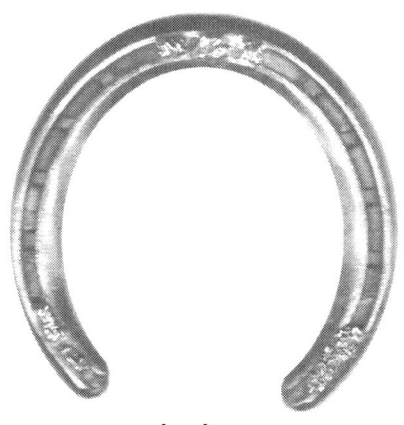

borium

borium: Common term for grains or chips of Tungsten Carbide in a *steel* or *brass* matrix. Applied to the ground surface of a *horseshoe* in the *forge* or with an *acetylene* *torch* before the shoe is cooled and *nailed* on, borium provides traction on hard, slick footing such as pavement. It also increases the wear life of the shoe.

Borium was originally a 1927 Stoody Company trademark for their chips in steel tube product, but the name has become generic in common usage. Brass matrix forms suited for forge application are commonly known as drill-tec/tech/tek, and are manufactured by various companies including Hartwell Industries (Carbraze) and B&W Metals (Kutrite). Tamcoloy TC Nuggets are small brass cups filled with chips and *flux* made for convenient horseshoe application.

Horseshoes with borium pre-applied are available, but not used by competent *farriers* as they cannot be modified to properly fit the *hoof*. Attempting to shape a shoe with borium will damage the hammer and *anvil*, while the borium is likely to crack off. Borium should be applied after the shoe has been made to fit the foot.

A thin layer, or a few small spots of borium at the toe and

heels are usually sufficient. Applying just enough borium to overfill the groove in a *swedged* shoe produces a long-wearing, relatively lightweight horseshoe that provides good purchase on a wide array of surfaces.

bowed tendon: Damage or rupture of the sheath of a *tendon*, most often the *SDF* of a foreleg. Bowed tendons usually occur in performance *horses* during hard exertion.
a.k.a: Tendinitis; peritendinitis; tendosynovitis; tendovaginitis.

bow legged: See: carpus varus.

boxed: Describes a *horseshoe* which has the outer edge of the *hoof*-facing side rounded or beveled. This is done to prevent a full-fit shoe from being pulled off should its exposed edge be stepped on by another hoof's shoe.

brand: A permanent artificial marking created by applying a red-hot iron to the skin. Brands are sometimes seen on *horses'* cheeks, rumps, and shoulders for identification purposes. While the act of branding does cause an animal momentary distress, there is far less pain than one would imagine due to the surface nerves being killed on contact with the iron. Brands appear as raised, slightly hard, and usually hairless designs on the skin.
See also: freeze brand.

brass: An *alloy* of *copper* and *zinc*. The color and properties of brass vary with its composition. When the alloy contains about 70% copper, it has a golden yellow color and is known as yellow brass, high brass, or cartridge brass. When it contains 80% or more copper, it has a reddish copper color and is known as red brass or low brass. Muntz metal contains 60% copper and 40% zinc. Alloys that have a high copper content are almost as soft as pure copper. But as zinc is added, they become harder. Compositions of 55% copper and 45% zinc can be somewhat brittle.
See also: braze.

brass hammer: A relatively soft hammer used primarily to drive hot stock onto a *hardie* so as to avoid damaging the cutting edge of that tool with a *steel* hammer face. Also used to avoid marring soft metals.

braze: To join metal surfaces using *brass*, *bronze*, or *copper* as a filler material.

break: To impart basic training to a *horse*. Training a horse to accept and obey a rider is 'saddle breaking'. Basic leading and ground handling training is called 'halter breaking'. Basic driving training is called 'harness' or 'cart breaking'. Some feel the term implies violence or excessive force, but to skilled horsemen breaking a horse is akin to breaking in a garment and certainly does not involve any breaking of spirit.

breakover: The action of the *hoof* as it leaves the ground.

breast collar harness: A simple form of *horse* harness which uses a wide, often padded, strap around the front of the chest to pull the load. This arrangement is relatively inexpensive and highly adjustable, so that the same breast strap may be used on horses of varying sizes.

Breast collar harnesses are popular for light cart and buggy work, but if used for heavy pulling, the strap will choke off the horse's windpipe and/or jugular circulation. Excessive work with a moderate moderate load will sore the animal's shoulders. A *collar and hames* harness is necessary for such pulling.

broken back:
See: hoof-pastern axis.

broken forward:
See: hoof-pastern axis.

bronze: An *alloy* made primarily of *copper* and tin. Usually less than 25% tin. Bronze is tough, relatively strong, and versatile. The development of bronze (around 3500 B.C.) was of such technological importance that historians and paleontologists use it as a major milestone in the history of mankind called the Bronze Age, which ended the Stone Ages.
See also: braze.

Brotherhood of Working Farriers Association: See: B.W.F.A.

bruise (brōz): The rupturing of blood vessels within sensitive structures resulting from trauma. *Hoof* bruises often result from the horse stepping on stones. Bruises can also occur in any sensitive structure, including the frog and the bulbs of the heels.
a.k.a: strawberries.

brushing: *Interfering* between paired hooves.

Buffalo: Maker of *forges* and blowers since 1879.

BUA: Barefoot Uber Alles. "Barefoot over all!" Used in reference to militant opposition to *horseshoeing*. The term was coined at a time when a

particularly harmful, radical *trimming* approach developed by a German veterinarian was in vogue among *barefoot* advocates on the Internet. BUA true believers may be referred to as BUAtistas.
See also: ferrophobia.

burro: A small *donkey*.

bursa (bėr′sa): Sac-like cushions which are found between anatomical structures which may place substantial pressure against one another. Bursae produce *synovial fluid* to ease movement.

bute: Phenylbutazone. A non-steroid, anti-inflammatory drug and painkiller usually administered in oral form to horses. Although legally restricted to veterinary prescription, this drug is widely available and often improperly used to mask *lameness* which could be corrected at the source through appropriate *farriery*.

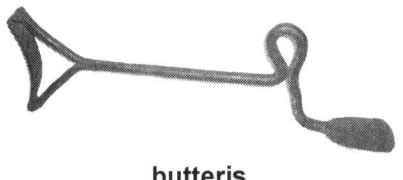

butteris

butteris: An ancient tool for *trimming horse hooves*. Essentially a long, sharp chisel which could be pushed with the *farrier's* shoulder. Rarely seen in the U.S. since the 1930s, the butteris is still common in some parts of the world.

buttress: Where the *hoof wall* turns in to form the bar on each side of the frog at the heel.
See: hoof anatomy, basic; Page A-2.

buttress foot: **See:** pyramidal disease.

B.W.F.A.: Brotherhood of Working Farriers Association. An organization run from a private horseshoeing school which has issued certifications ranging from low apprentice to "master" levels since 1989 and promoted these to the public as valid credentials, useful for identifying qualified farriers. Various requirements and examinations have been associated with these certifications, but the lower levels denote knowledge and skills no better than those of short-course shoeing school graduates, and the higher levels may be considered suspect due to a history of BWFA certifications being issued through inconsistent examinations and several incarnations of the "grandfather clause" which certified untested horseshoers with no previous formal credentials. The BWFA has also issued "horseowner certifications" and endorses short-course shoeing school instructors as "master educators", allowing them to certify their own graduates without regard to possible conflicts of interests. Regular membership with voting privileges is open to any dues-paying persons including non-farriers and students who pay reduced rates.

by: Refers to a *horse's* paternal parentage. For example: "Discovery is by Display" means that Display is Discovery's *sire* (father).

caecum: See: cecum.

calk [from Latin *calx*, the heel]: Any of several types of projection which may be forged on a *horseshoe*, welded or *brazed* onto a horseshoe, or inserted into a hole in the horseshoe. Calks are used to increase traction, alter movement, or adjust stance.
a.k.a: caulk; calkin; heel calk.

calkin: See: calk.

calking vise: A foot-operated variation of the *leg vise* with adaptations to facilitate the forming of *horseshoe calks* and bolt heads.

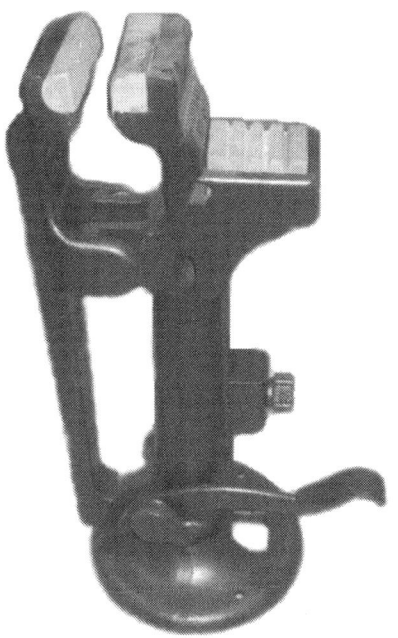

calking vise

cancellous: Loose bony tissue.

canker: Abnormal, vegetative growth of the frog. May also affect the sole. Caused by infection and the exposure of the *hooves* to harsh ammonia compounds. Effective management and prevention must include moving the *horse* to a clean, dry environment.
a.k.a: hoof cancer.

cannon: (1.) The third metacarpal in the front *leg*, or the third metatarsal in the hind.
(2.) The leg from the knee or hock down to the fetlock.
See: Pages A-3; A-4.

canted knee: A deviation similar in appearance to *bench knee*, but differing in that each row of carpal bones is offset from the bones above it, whereas bench knees have a relatively normal *carpus* with the metacarpals being offset at the carpometacarpal joint.
See: Page A-4.

canter [From *Canterbury gallop*, a gentle gallop such as was used by pilgrims riding to the town in Kent, England]: A fairly slow, collected version of the *gallop*. Used as a ground covering *gait* in general riding, and in the show ring in *English*-style classes.

Capewell: Horseshoe nail manufacturer since 1881. Based in the U.S.A.

capillaries [From Latin *capillus*, hair]: The tiny, often microscopic, vessels which nourish the tissues and transfer blood from the *arteries* to the *veins*.

capped hock: A bump under the skin at the point of the hock. This *blemish* may be of any size, and is often caused by direct *trauma* to the hock.
See: Page A-3.

capped knee: See: popped knee.

capsular rotation: The hoof wall rotates away from the *P III*, while the P III remains in alignment with the pastern. This condition can be due not only to *laminitic founder*, but also to overweight, too low a *hoof angle*, or use of *toe grabs*.

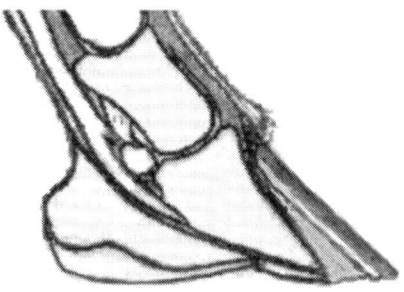

capsular rotation

Carbraze: See: borium.

carpus (kär′pus) [Latin]: The equine knee, or human wrist. **-carpal**, pertaining to the carpus.

carpus valgus: A conformation defect in which the fore *limbs* deviate *medially* above the knee, and *laterally* below the knee. This creates the appearance that the limbs are bent inward, under the *horse*.
a.k.a: knock-knees. See: Page A-3.

carpus varus: A conformation defect in which the fore *limbs* deviate *laterally* above the knee, and *medially* below the knee. This creates the appearance that the limbs are bent outward..
a.k.a: bow-legged. See: Page A-3.

cartilage: Flexible, somewhat elastic, skeletal structures.

CAT scan: Computerized Axial Tomography. Produces cross-sectional views of internal body structures.
a.k.a: CT scan.

cat walking:
See: rope walking.

caudal (kŏd′l): Towards the tail.

caulk: See: calk.

cecum [From Latin *cæcus,* blind]: A section of the large intestine which is open only at one end, forming a saclike cavity.
a.k.a: caecum, blind gut.

certified: One who has received a certificate which states, on the authority or reputation of the certifying body, that he has met the requirements or conditions associated with that document.
See also: CF; CJF; CTF; IC; registered; RJF; RMF.

CF: Certified Farrier. A recognition of knowledge and skill awarded by the *AFA*. The CF examination includes a one hour written test with 50 questions covering anatomy and general *farriery*, live shoeing one *pair* of *hooves* with *keg shoes* to strict requirements in one hour, and a basic *horseshoe* modification test.

Champion: Brand of *farrier* tools from 1895 until 1963. Champion developed the Channellock plier in 1933, quit making farrier tools in 1963 and became Channellock, Inc.

Charlier shoe: A patented *horseshoe* introduced by French veterinarian Henri Charlier in 1865 which enjoyed considerable popularity until the end of the 19th Century. It was a narrow, non-*fullered* iron shoe which was actually embedded into the *hoof wall*. A special knife was used to cut the outer hoof wall away to a prescribed depth, and the shoe was fitted into this groove. The supposed advantage of the Charlier shoe was that it did not raise the foot as high off the ground as conventional shoes did, so more frog and sole contact was maintained with the turf, which was thought to promote *expansion* and hoof flexing. This claim is countered by the fact that a hoof which has its entire perimeter locked within an *iron* band isn't likely to expand or flex at all. The removal of so much *hoof horn* at the junction of the wall and sole must have dangerously weakened the *hoof capsule*.

Cheap John: A colloquialism for a *horseshoer* who attempts to build up his business by charging low

prices. Because a Cheap John will have to shoe too many *horses* just to make a living, he will not have time to further his *professional* education or to provide quality care to his clients' horses.
See also: cowboy shoeing.

check ligament: A *ligament* which connects a *tendon* to a bone. Check ligaments are often considered to be parts of tendons.

chemical restraint: Use of drugs, usually injected *IV* or *IM*, to calm or relax a *horse* that would otherwise be inclined to resist a procedure such as shoeing. Chemical restraint should only be administered by, or on the direct instruction of, a veterinarian. Drugs are not a substitute for training, and should be used only when it is not possible to train the horse prior to having the procedure done, or to enable a horse to tolerate a procedure which causes discomfort. Chemical restraint has serious drawbacks in *farriery*, including the elimination of normal feedback from the horse during shoeing, and the possibility of a horse suffering sudden panic as it drifts in and out of awareness of its surroundings.
See also: Dormosedan; Rompun; Ace.

chondro- [Greek]: Having to do with *cartilage*.

chondrocoronal ligament apparatus: The *chondrocoronal ligaments*, the *collateral cartilages* which they attach to the short pastern bone, and the *laminae* which attach the collateral cartilages to the *hoof wall*. These structures work together to form a second system to suspend the *distal* end of the *limb's* bone column within the hoof. Even if the laminar connection between *P III* and the *anterior* hoof wall fails, the chondrocoronal apparatus will normally keep the short pastern bone from sinking down into the hoof. There are documented cases in which the P III has been completely removed or disintegrated without the bone column sinking.

chondrocoronal ligaments: *Ligaments* which extend *medially* and *laterally* from the short pastern bone just above the coffin joint, connecting the bone to the *collateral cartilages* which give form to the *posterior* portion of the *hoof* and the bulbs of the heels. These ligaments play a role in suspending the bony column within the hoof. They correspond closely with the center of *articulation* of the coffin join, and

appear to be the axis of coffin bone *rotation* during *founder*.
See: *hoof, basic anatomy*; Page A-5.

chondrocyte: A *cartilage* cell.

chronic [From Greek *Chronos*, Time]: Persistent. The long-term phase of many diseases and conditions.
See also: acute.

cinch, front [From Spanish *cincha*.]: In *western tack*, the strap which passes under the *horse's* torso just behind the elbows and connects to the saddle on each side. The cinch is the primary, and sometimes only, strap which holds the saddle on, and thus must be fairly tight before a rider mounts. Most cinches used to be made from many parallel strands of strong cord (such as mohair) with steel D-rings at either end. Padded cinches made of nylon and other modern materials are displacing the old design due to greater strength, durability, and a lesser tendency to gall the horse's skin.
See also: girth, flank cinch.

CJF: Certified Journeyman Farrier. The highest recognition awarded by the *AFA*. The CJF exam includes a written test with 80 true/false and multiple choice questions to be answered in two hours, live shoeing of a horse with *handmade, clipped* shoes in two hours, and forging a *fullered bar shoe* to fit a pattern in 35 minutes.

cleft: A horizontal *crack* in the *hoof wall*. Clefts are usually caused by damage to the *coronary band*, or the rupture of an *abscess* at the coronary band.
a.k.a: crosscrack.

clinch: The part of a *horseshoe nail* visible on the outside of a *shod horse's hoof wall*. This part of the nail is folded down against the hoof to form a clamp, and normally has to be straightened or removed before the horseshoe can be pulled off without doing damage to the hoof.
a.k.a: clench.

clinch block

clinch block: A solid piece of iron or steel used to seat a *clinch* after a *horseshoe nail* has been driven through the *hoof wall* and cut off. The block may be positioned against the bent-down and cut off end of the nail while the nail head is struck with a hammer, or the block may be held against the nail head while the hammer is used to tap down the cut end.

clinch cutter

clinch cutter: A hammer-driven tool which is used to shear off or bend up *clinches* to allow *horseshoe nails* to be pulled out of the *hoof* and/or the shoe to be removed.

clinchers: Tool designed to form a *clinch* after a *horseshoe nail* has been driven through the *hoof wall* and cut off. The straight jaw of the tool is placed against the head of the nail, while the curved jaw is used to roll down the cut end.
a.k.a: clinching tongs, alligators.

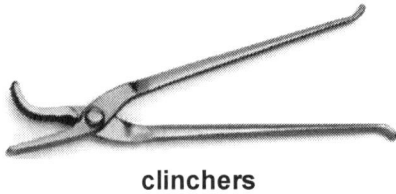

clinchers

clinch gouge: A hammer-driven tool used to remove a small notch of *horn* from the *wall* into which a *clinch* may be set.

clinch gouge

clinker:
See: forge, coal, operation of.

clip: Flat projections, usually triangular or semicircular, extending upward from the outer edge of a *horseshoe*. Clips are set into the outer surface of the *hoof wall*. Clips may be drawn from the metal of the shoe or welded on. They are used to prevent the shoe from shifting on the hoof, to stabilize the hoof wall, or sometimes as a purely cosmetic touch.

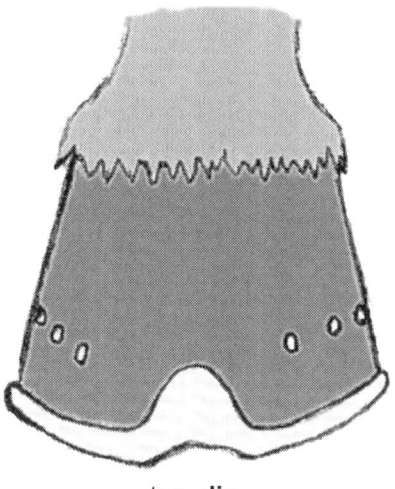

toe **clip**

clip forging and fitting: While there are an increasing number of clipped factory *horseshoes* available, and modern welding techniques make attaching clips to shoes a practical option, the traditional means of producing clips by drawing them from the metal of the horseshoe remains a popular method among *farriers*.

To start a clip, the yellow-hot shoe is placed on the *anvil* face ground side up, with the edge where the clip is to be drawn unsupported, either over the *hardie hole* or just off the anvil face. The unsupported part shoe is then struck, either directly with a hammer, or through a blunt bob-punch, to push down a bump of metal. The shoe is then flipped *hoof* side up so that it can be quickly leveled with overlapping blows everywhere but the bump. The shoe is then positioned with the hoof side alongside the body of the anvil and the bump at the top, so that it can be "hooked" on the edge of the face or *clip horn*. Hammer blows are then used to flatten the bump against the anvil face and draw it into shape. Care must be taken not to distort or excessively weaken the shoe in this process. The finished clip should be a rounded triangle with a base width and height similar to the shoe *web*. Once formed, the clip should be set at an angle to match the *hoof wall* where it is to be applied.

Hammering into the *turning hole* (alternative hardie hole) to establish a bump of metal for a toe clip. Note the reins of the tongs being used to stabilize the shoe, which tends to warp as the clip is forged.

Resultant bump, which is then flattened and pulled into a clip.

It may be easier to get a clip started at the midpoint of the face, where the anvil is most solid, and the edge will more readily "bite" into the shoe metal, then move to the heel or clip horn to finish the drawing process.

Traditionally toe clips have been used on the front shoes of riding horses and all four shoes of *draft horses*, as these shoes tend to be driven backwards on the feet during work. Quarter clips, placed between the first and second nail holes on each branch, were preferred on the hind shoes of riding horses, which tend to be subjected to more torque and *lateral* shifting forces. (When forging handmade shoes, extra space may be allowed between the relevant nail holes to allow for easier quarter clip drawing.) The current fashion is to use quarter clips on all four feet of riding horses. A common mistake is to place quarter clips too far back, at the widest part of the hoof, where they can restrict normal *hoof capsule* flexing, and do little or nothing to stop the shoe from shifting backwards.

The best way to set a shoe with *steel* clips is to *hot set* it. This is most easily accomplished with a good set of hot fitting tongs, like the W-Brand with locking ring. It can be done by tapping an old *pritchel* into a nail hole, but another tool will be needed to push the shoe backward on the hoof to press the clips into place.

Supporting the shoe on the anvil horn while the toe clip is adjusted to match the angle of the hoof.

The toe half of the shaped and clipped shoe should be heated bright red then quickly secured in the hot fitting tongs. The clips alone, being thin, will not hold enough heat. The shoe should be carefully positioned and very briefly touched to the foot to scorch-mark where the clip will go. The shoe is then set aside, toe-up to keep the clip hot. (The heels may still be hot enough to burn your toolbox or anything else they touch. Use caution.) A hoof knife and/or half-round file can then be used to cut out a seat for the clip. The shoe, cooled to low cherry or black heat by this point, is then pressed against the foot for several seconds, and pulled or pushed backwards to burn the clip into its seat. The shoe is then cooled for final application.

If the horse will not stand for hot fitting, or shoe materials other than steel are being used, it may be necessary to fit clips cold. A permanent marker or chalk (on black feet) can be used to trace around the clips to outline the placement of the seat notches. This will be somewhat difficult with quarter clips, which tend to prevent the shoe from being put into position until after the seats have been cut. A hoof knife, half-round file, and/or Dremel-type rotary tool can be used to create the seats.

Once the shoes have been applied, *clinched*, and dressed, the clips should fit smoothly into the wall and be virtually impalpable.

See also: horseshoe, forging; horseshoe, conventional application; keg shoe, fitting; Pages A-2, A-6, A-7, A-8.

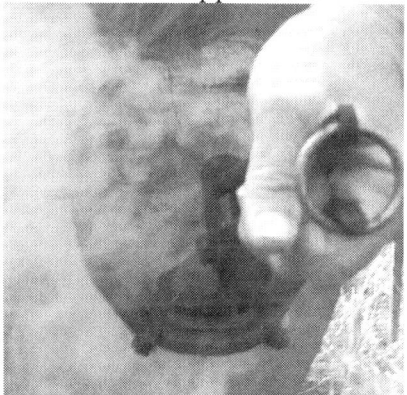
Hot fitting quarter clips.

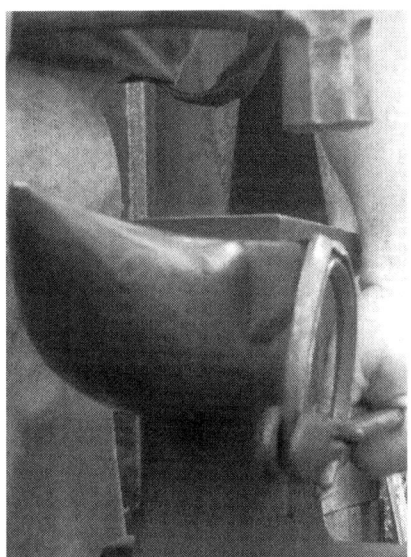
clip horn in action

clip horn: A small projection, usually found on the side of a *farrier's anvil* near the base of the main horn, which can be used to draw a *clip* from the metal of a *horseshoe*.
See: A-7.

close nail: A *horseshoe nail* that does not actually *quick* the *hoof*, but comes close enough to sensitive structures to create irritating pressure. It may take a few days for a close nail to cause the *horse* apparent discomfort.
a.k.a: hot nail.

clubfoot: An extremely upright *hoof* with a very broken-forward *hoof-pastern axis*. May be caused by *flexor deformity*. In extreme cases, the *digit* may be folded back, with the animal bearing weight on its *dorsal* surface. In *congenital* or developmental club feet, the slope of the heels is usually more upright than that of the toe.
See also: high-low hoof syndrome.

coal: Any of several related forms of dark-colored rock formed from ancient plant materials. Coal is made up primarily of carbon, and contains a great deal of energy which is released by burning. Coal is the traditional fuel for *blacksmith* and *farrier forges*, and is both cheaper and hotter-burning than propane, which is used in other popular modern forges. Bituminous coal is often used in forges, and must be cooked into *coke* on the perimeter of the fire before being pushed into the center to heat *steel*.

coarse punched: A *nail* hole in a *horseshoe* which is located towards the inner edge of the shoe *web*. Toe nail holes are often coarse punched.
See: Page A-8. **See also:** fine punched.

Coggins test: A routine test done to detect latent Equine Infectious Anemia in *horses*. A small sample of blood is drawn from the animal and sent to a lab for analysis. EIA is transmitted between *equines* by horseflies, and the virus does not survive long with the insect, so transmission is short-range unless an infected horse is transported. Thus a recent Coggins test is often required to haul horses interstate, move them to new boarding stables, or participate in events.

coke: *Coal* which has had impurities cooked out of it. In *blacksmith* and *farrier* coal *forges*, raw "green" coal is typically added to the perimeter of the fire, soaked with water, and patted into a bank. The coal on the inner face of the bank is cooked into coke, and eventually pushed into the fire as more wet, green coal is pressed into the outer face of the bank. When cooled rather than immediately burnt, coke looks and feels rather like black popcorn.

coldblood: Large-bodied, thick-boned, heavy-coated *horses* which developed in the cooler climates of upper Europe. Heavy *draft horses* and some Old World *ponies* are modern examples of the coldblood type. These horses are known for great strength, durability, and relatively stoic disposition.

cold shoeing: Horseshoeing without the use of a *forge*. *Horseshoes* are mild *steel*, and can be reshaped effectively while cold, especially with modern farrier's *anvils*. A skillful *farrier* can shoe most *horses* very well cold, and may choose to do so to save time in the field, or to avoid the hazards which accompany burning a forge in environments where he cannot control children, dogs, careless adults, and the proximity of flammable materials. Cold shoeing is physically more difficult than *hot shoeing* due to the relative rigidity of cold metal, and some horseshoe modifications require heat, so full-service farriers cannot rely exclusively on cold shoeing.

colic: Abdominal distress. In *horses*, colic can be a very serious condition, and is frequently fatal. Colic in horses is often caused by intestinal blockage due to impacted materials, parasites, or excessive gas build-up due to microbiological imbalance. Symptoms include loss of appetite, lying down, kicking or biting at the abdomen, with general discomfort and distress. Chances of colic are reduced (but not totally eliminated) by keeping horses on a regular feeding schedule with plenty of roughage, moderate carbohydrate intake, plenty of free exercise, unlimited access to clean, fresh water, and a good deworming program. Sand ingested by horses foraging in sparse, dry paddocks can cause very hard to clear blockages. First aid for colic involves keeping the animal as comfortable as possible. Afflicted horses should not be allowed to roll and thrash on the ground, as they may twist or rupture an intestine. Horses suffering from colic are traditionally kept walking to keep the circulation up and loosen the bowels while keeping the horse from lying down and thrashing. Veterinary assistance should be summoned as soon as possible. Treatment often involves administration of a laxative such as mineral oil via nasal stomach tube, injection of muscle relaxants to counter cramping, and a rectal exam to remove possible blockages. Gut noises are a good sign. Passing substantial manure, drinking water, and return of appetite are very good signs.

collar and hames: A thick, semi-rigid, usually leather-covered pad which fits snugly against the sides of a *horse's* neck (collar), providing a seat for a pair of curved wood or metal brackets (hames) which are connected at the top and bottom by straps, and provide the attachment points for pulling a load.

The neck collar design prevents pressure across the base of the windpipe and shoulder joints when pulling heavy loads.

Collar and hames type harness was one of the most important inventions in human history, as it allowed horses to pull at their full strength, and to pull relatively heavy loads for extended periods of time, neither of which was possible with earlier *breast collar harnesses*. This made the horse a viable source of farm traction. Being much faster and more versatile than oxen, farm horses greatly improved agricultural efficiency, reducing the percentage of the human population needed to produce food, and freeing them up for other endeavors.

The drawback to the collar and hames is that the collar must fit well to function properly, the amount of adjustment is very limited, and collars are relatively expensive. It is common for each *draft horse* to have at least one collar of its own.

The basic size of horse collars is expressed in inches from the inside of the top to the inside of the bottom. (Top of the crest straight through the neck to the base of the throat on the horse.) Because the curve/width of collars varies, the best way to fit them is to try them on. A collar should fit firmly against the side of the neck, and one should be able to slide a hand between it and the horse's throat. Oddly enough, measuring the circumference of the thickest part of the horse's forearm usually gives a good starting estimate for collar size.

collar and hames

collateral cartilages:
See: lateral cartilages.

colt: An entire male horse under 4 years old.

compromise pattern: The roughly oval pattern of most *keg shoes*, theoretically a compromise between the front *(Norman)* and hind *(Tag) hoof* shapes. Some *horseshoe* manufacturers have advertised that these shoes are suitable for use on front and hind hooves with little or no reshaping, but competent *farriers* treat compromise pattern *horseshoes* as blanks and modify them extensively to correctly fit each *hoof*.
See: Page A-8.

concave stock: *Horseshoe bar stock* which is pre-*swedged*, thus saving the *farrier* the effort of swedging or *fullering* the shoes as he forges them.

confluence: Flowing together, becoming one.

congenital: A characteristic present from birth.

contracted heels:
See: contracted hoof.

contracted hoof: Condition in which the posterior half of the *hoof* undergoes a significant reduction in width. This may result from other hoof or limb problems, improper shoeing, or both.
a.k.a: contracted heels; hoofbound.

contracted tendons:
See: flexor deformity.

contra limb: *Limb* opposite the one that suffered the original *lameness*. Sometimes becomes lame from compensatory stress.

controlled experiment: Trial or testing of a *hypothesis* under carefully managed conditions. All factors which might affect the outcome of the tests must be made as uniform as possible, except for the factor being tested. For an experiment to be considered valid evidence, it should involve a sufficiently large test group, and be repeatable with similar results.

contusion [From Latin *tundo*, to beat]: A *traumatic* flesh injury which does not break the skin.

cooling out: Because the *horse* is a large animal, it has relatively little surface area in relation to its mass. This makes it easy for a horse to become overheated when worked hard. It also has large, thick muscles which can become deoxygenated and build up lactic acid during work. If allowed to stand still after becoming winded and overheated, a horse often has difficulty recovering. Leading him at an easy walk keeps the circulation up so that the muscles get oxygen in and lactic acid out, keeps air moving over the horse's skin to cool him, and keeps his system from overreacting and cooling him to a chill.

coon foot: Very low *hoof angle* with an even lower pastern angle. May result from sprained suspensory *ligaments*, weak pasterns, or *chronic laminitis.*

copper [From Latin *cuprum*, from Cyprus, which was an ancient source for the metal]: A metallic, electroconductive element. Atomic number 29. Atomic weight 63.546. Melting point 1982.12° F or 1083.4° C. Copper was one of the first metals used by mankind. It was known to humans by around 8000 B.C. and was in widespread use by 5000 B.C. It is relatively easy to work hot or cold, resists deep corrosion, and can be *alloyed* with other elements to make stronger metals. Copper *horseshoes* have been applied to *equines* used in mines because such shoes do not create sparks and ignite gas pockets like *steel* shoes can.

See also: brass; braze; bronze.

copper, dietary: *Copper* is needed by the body to utilize *iron*, and to form and maintain strong bones, connective tissues, and blood vessels.

copper naphthenate: The active ingredient in popular *thrush* remedies such as Kopertox. The chemical is also widely used to treat lumber against rot.

corks: A rural colloquialism which may refer to *heel calks*, *blocked heels*, or turned down heels on *horseshoes*.

corn: A *bruise* located in the seat of corn. Sometimes caused by the heels of the *hoof* growing over the *horseshoe*.
See: Page A-2.

corium: See: dermis.

coronary band: The sensitive, vascular zone where the *horn* meets the skin at the top of the *hoof*. The coronary band produces the bulk of the *hoof wall*, and is protected by the *periople*.
See: Pages A-2; A-5.

coronary crack: A *sandcrack* which starts at the top of the *hoof* and splits down.

coronet: (1.) The area at the top of the *hoof* where it joins the haircoat-covered skin. The *coronary band* is included in this area.
(2.) White coat marking just above the hoof.

corrective: (1.) *Trimming* or shoeing a *horse's hooves* to counteract flaws in stance or *gait*.
(2.) Wrongly used as a synonym for *therapeutic*.

corrective and therapeutic farriery, basic principles: While *corrective* and *therapeutic farriery* have different objectives, a number of fundamental approaches to *trimming* and *horseshoeing* are common to both.

First consideration should be given to the question of whether or not remedial techniques are appropriate for a given *horse*. This is especially true of corrective farriery. Imperfect *gait* and/or stance may be the animal's means of adapting to flaws in conformation, and might have minimal negative effect on its usefulness. Attempts to force such a specimen's *legs* and movement to match a textbook ideal often do more harm than good. If it isn't broken, don't fix it.

It should also be kept in-mind that horses have various compensatory mechanisms. Efforts to push feet in one direction through farriery are sometimes met with such a mechanism which pushes back harder. As a result, attempts at remedial farriery occasionally achieve net results opposite of what was intended.

Adjusting the standing *hoof angle* through trimming, wedge

Page 35.

pads, wedge shoes, blocked heels, swelled heels, or *patten shoes* is one of the more common remedial techniques in farriery. Raising the hoof angle generally reduces tension of the deep digital flexor *tendon* and the pressure it puts on the *navicular bursa,* as well as giving the foot a mechanical head-start on *breakover.* Lowering the hoof angle reduces stress on the suspensory ligament and extensor tendons. The effects of altering the hoof angle are temporary, as the muscles the tendons connect to will eventually adapt and take up any "slack".

Adjusting the *mediolateral balance* by trimming one side of the hoof short (or lifting the other side up with asymmetrical shoe or pads) is rarely a good idea. Ideally, the foot should be trimmed to make the *solar* plane perpendicular to the cannon, to load both halves of the foot equally, or a happy medium between the two in cases where they don't fully coincide. When a *lateral* defect in stance needs to be addressed, it is usually best to do so by keeping the hoof form as close to normal as possible and employing an appropriate *medial* or lateral extension shoe to prevent the foot from "tipping" to the side.

Extending the solar plane of the hoof rearward, as may be done with an *eggbar* or *extended heels,* prevents the foot from rocking back and the heel from sinking into the ground. This *posterior* support has dynamic effects similar to raising the hoof angle without as much alteration to the form of the *hoof capsule.*

The solar plane of the hoof may also be extended forward via a toe extension shoe. This serves to impede breakover, which can be useful in severe *flexor deformity/clubfoot* cases to prevent the foot from knuckling-over onto the *dorsal* wall.

Many other situations call for easing breakover to reduce stress on the hoof capsule and leg, which can be accomplished with *rolled toe* or *half-round horseshoes.* As breakover has considerable influence on the flight path of the foot, *rockered toe, square toe,* or *set-back* combination square/rolled toe shoes can be used to direct breakover to the desired part of the hoof. This will usually be the center of the toe, but the breakover aids can be offset if needed.

Traction devices, such as *calks* and *fullering*, have a braking effect when the hoof lands. Asymmetrical application of such features can be used to turn the foot when the horse is in motion. This should be done in moderation, and with consideration for the surface the horse will be performing upon, as torquing the foot can be hard on connective tissues.

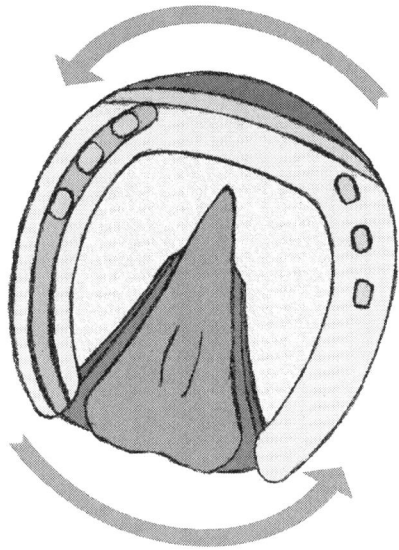

Half-swedged shoe with set-back, rolled toe used to turn a fore hoof on landing and breakover.

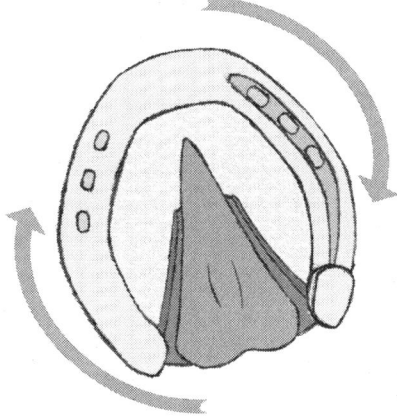

Half-fullering with heel calk shoe used to turn a hind hoof on landing.

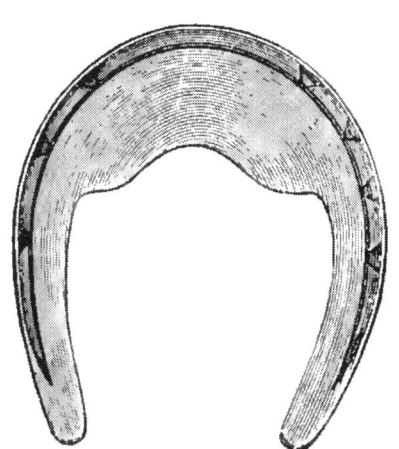

Toe-weighted horseshoe.

Weighted horseshoes can be used to enhance gait and action, and to alter the foot's line of travel while off the ground. Heavier shoes on fore hooves, especially with weight at the toe, tend to exaggerate the stepping action, as is often desired in some *gaited horse* shoeing situations. But each ounce on the foot is equal to pounds on the back, so horses thus enhanced will have effectively reduced stamina. Asymmetrical weight on the foot can cause (or correct) lateral deviation in flight, but is particularly unpredictable because some horses' locomotor reflexes will overcompensate for the side weight, yielding results diametrically opposed to what was intended. Trial and error is often required, and may be facilitated with weights temporarily affixed to the foot to test results before the final shoeing approach is decided.

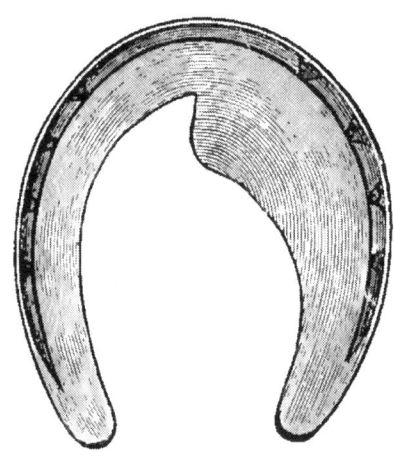

Asymmetrically weighted shoe.

One of the primary functions of horseshoes in general is the protection of the hoof. For therapeutic purposes, this function may be considerably expanded to protect compromised portions of the foot with wide-*webbed* shoes, pads, *bar shoes*, and *hospital plates*. Shock-absorbing materials may be employed to reduce concussion to injured structures.

Horseshoes can also be used to stabilize a weakened or damaged hoof capsule. This can be done with minimal weight using a bar shoe, as increasing the rigidity of a light shoe by connecting the heels with a bar requires less *steel* than achieving the same rigidity with an open shoe. Multiple *clips* on a bar shoe, when placed on opposite sides of a defect, or placed at the widest part of the hoof, can largely immobilize the hoof wall. (Immobilizing the entire wall is appropriate only in cases of severe internal damage, like *PIII* fracture.) A continuous clip around the circumference of the wall has sometimes been employed, but four or five separate clips will do the job, and are easier to set.

Transferring load from damaged parts of the foot to areas that can better tolerate it may be accomplished with horseshoes. *Heartbar* configurations, which shift loading from the wall to the frog, are particularly useful in therapeutic cases.

Transferring load from compromised wall can also be accomplished by removing *flares*, which is similar in concept to alleviating the discomfort of a hang nail by clipping it. Redirection of stress in the hoof wall can also be achieved by *grooving*.

Permanent correction of flaws in stance can only be achieved in developing horses before the skeletal structure has become fixed. This fact leads some to be overzealous in attempts to accomplish correction before it's too late. Growing horses have their own, inherent corrective mechanisms, so that it is commonplace to see *foals* with mild to moderate stance deviations grow into good, straight legged long *yearlings* without any special corrective measures by the *farrier*. In most cases, conservative trimming, good nutrition (not overfeeding concentrates), and free exercise are called for.

Remedial farriery in developing horses tends to be a matter of recognizing when something is getting too far out of hand and countering the problem. For instance, a fast-growing *colt* may be wearing the toes of his fore hooves down excessively due to long bone growth outpacing muscle/tendon adaptation (mild flexor deformity). In addition to adjusting the animal's feed, shoeing with tip shoes to stop the excessive *anterior* wear while allowing heel wear can prevent the development of a permanent club foot growth pattern.

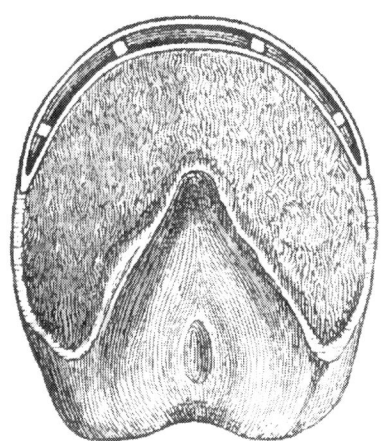

Traditional tip shoe for mild flexor deformity.

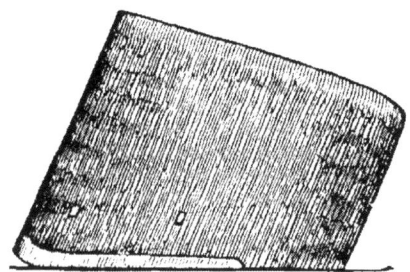
Tip shoe application on upright hoof.

One should always keep in-mind that the hoof is a dynamic unit with all parts interconnected. *Underrun* heels tend to be driven forward on landing, pushing the whole bottom of the foot forward, promoting a toe flare. The toe flare increases leverage against the hoof capsule during breakover, pulling the whole foot forward, aggravating the underrun heels. So management of underrun heels must include dealing with the toe flare, and vice versa.

It is also wise to remember that the farrier works on a whole horse, not just four individual hooves. Body type, size, age, work load, living conditions, and many other factors influence how a given animal will respond to trimming and shoeing approaches. What is done to one *pair* of a horse's feet will have an effect on the other.

Corrective, therapeutic, and general farriery often overlap. In fact, *soundness*, gait, and stance problems in many horses disappear after nothing more than well-balanced trimming and proper application of ordinary horseshoes.

See also: balancing the horse's hoof; hoof anatomy, basic; horseshoe, forging; trimming technique, basic; keg shoe fitting; horseshoe, conventional application; navicular disease; founder; L.H.L.T.; high-low hoof syndrome; cracks, hoof wall; underrun heels; epiphyseal plates; two finger radiograph; farrier's radiograph; Thera-Flex; Pages A-2; A-4; A-5; A-9; A-10.

cowboy shoeing: Shoeing done by an incompetent *horseshoer*, or a careless job done by a *farrier*. This poor quality work may not be readily apparent to non-farriers.
a.k.a: shoe-horseing; speed shoeing.

crack, hoof wall: a fracture in the *horn* of the *hoof wall*. May be *superficial, penetrating, basal,* or *coronary*. Cracks are usually a failure of the intertubular horn, allowing the wall to split along its grain. Passing injury to the *coronary band*, often from the eruption of *abscesses*, may cause a horizontal *cleft*. Permanent scarring of the coronary band can result in a *false quarter*, which may resemble a crack, but does not necessarily involve splitting of the horn.

Causes of hoof cracks include genetic predisposition, nutritional deficiency, rapid/frequent changes in moisture content, infected horn, unbalanced loading, and direct trauma. In most cases, some combination of these will be at fault.

Management of cracks should start with eliminating the causes, insomuch as it is possible to do so. The hooves should be *trimmed* into *balance*, with particular attention to unloading the compromised wall. If the horse is to be left *barefoot*, the wall needs to be beveled up to reduce leverage on the horn during *breakover*, both at the toe and at the sides of the hoof, as in the *four point* and *Natural Balance* trims.

Applying a *sealant* to the hoof wall may slow the changes in moisture content which weaken the intertubular horn. Rubbing a hoof dressing into the coronary band a few times a week may promote the growth of stronger horn, but application to the wall itself tends to be counterproductive.

Biotin, gelatin, and other feed additives may enable the *horse* to grow better hooves, but it will take months for the results to manifest.

A common remedy for superficial cracks is to cut or burn a horizontal *groove* into the wall just above the top of the crack. For this to be effective, the groove must be as deep as the crack. But care must be taken not to cut or burn the groove all the way through the wall into the *quick*. If nothing else, the grooves will provide a point of reference so that further splitting of the wall will be obvious.

Persistent cracks, and those which are sufficiently deep to compromise the horse's *soundness* either by exposing sensitive tissues directly, or by destabilizing the *hoof capsule*, usually require shoeing.

Clips set into the wall on both sides of the crack may be employed to reduce opening/closing of the crack when the foot loads/unloads. A *bar shoe*, such as a *heartbar*, may be used to transfer load from the cracked wall to the frog.

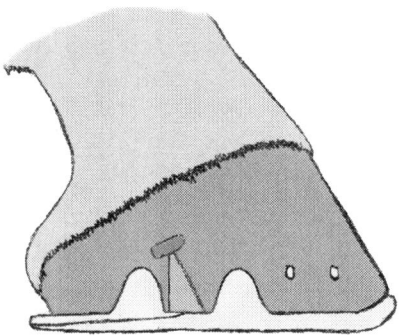

Clips set into the wall on each side of a crack to immobilize the defect.

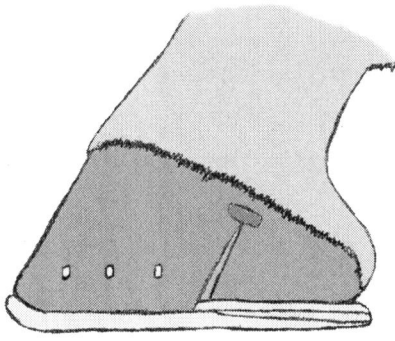

Heartbar shoe used to support the hoof after the wall from crack rearward has been unloaded.

A traditional direct approach to stabilizing the wall is to apply a steel strap across the cracked wall with shallow wood screws. (The screws must not be long enough to penetrate the full thickness of the wall.) The strap needs to be thick enough to prevent both opening and closing of the crack.

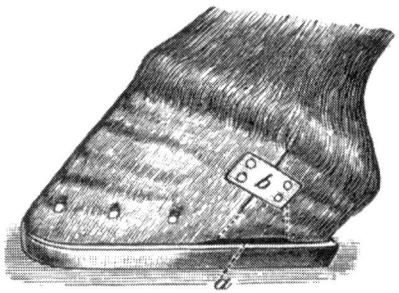

Old school screw-plate crack repair.

Modern *acrylics* can be used to fill hoof cracks, and generally do a good job of restoring the integrity of the hoof capsule. But any infection trapped in a deep crack under the airtight acrylic will likely get much worse. A drainage path, which can be created by placing a small, petroleum jelly-coated, rubber tube into the crack before the acrylic is applied, then pulling it out after hard-set, will allow antiseptic to be injected under the repair.

Cracks which bleed or cause *lameness* are open wounds which could leave a horse exposed to tetanus and other systemic infections. A veterinarian should be consulted to deal with this aspect of the problem.

See: Hoof anatomy, basic; balancing the horse's hoof; horseshoe, conventional application; Pages A-2; A-5; A-9.

cranial (krā′nē-əl): **(1.)** The front surface of the *limb*. Towards the head.
(2.) Having to do with the cranium of the skull.

crease: A groove cut into the ground surface of a *horseshoe* that has already been *turned*. Shoes are usually creased on the branches to provide a seat for the *nail* heads. Creasing creates mild traction, and allows the nails to be easily removed one at the time with crease nail pullers.
See: Pages A-6; A-8; A-9.

crosscrack: See: cleft.

crossfiring: A *gait* flaw which results in the collision of *diagonal* feet. This usually occurs at *lateral gaits*.

CTF: Certified Tradesman Farrier. The second highest recognition awarded by the *AFA*. The CTF exam includes a written test with 80 true/false and multiple choice questions to be answered in two hours, live shoeing of a horse with *clipped keg shoes* in 90 minutes, and forging a *handmade fullered horseshoe* to fit a pattern in 30 minutes.

curb: Swelling of the *plantar* surface of the hind *leg* just below the point of the hock. This is a *ligament* sprain, and may be caused by stress, poor conformation, or direct *trauma*.
See: Page A-3.

cursorial: Describes an animal (such as a *horse*) which can run fast for long distances. Such animals can be referred to as 'cursors'.

Cushing's disease: *Chronic* hormone imbalance caused by a tumor or enlargement of the pituitary gland at the base of the brain. Symptoms usually appear in middle-aged or geriatric *horses*. The coat becomes long, rough, and curly, and does not shed in the Spring. Weight regulation fails, and overall condition deteriorates. *Laminitis* and *founder* usually develop, often with very rapid, but distorted *hoof* growth.

Hormone levels may be treated with medication, but there is no cure. Secondary symptoms can be managed individually. Due to the founder and rapid *horn* growth, even regular *trimming*

may be something akin to dealing with a *flipper foot*. Body clipping the coat will be necessary in warm seasons, and may require sheep shears, as horse clippers are not designed for such rough hair. Care must be taken not to cut the horse's relatively thin skin with sheep clippers.
aka: ECD.

-cyte: Suffix meaning cell.

cyto-: Prefix meaning cell, or having to do with cells.

cytology (sī tol′ə-jē): Cellular biology.

dam: Maternal parent. Mother.

DDF: Deep Digital Flexor tendon. A major *tendon* which runs down the back of the *equine leg*, uses the navicular bone as a pulley, and inserts into the semilunar crest of the *P III*.
See: Page A-5.

dermis (dûr′mis): The sensitive connective tissue layer of the skin located below the *epidermis*, containing nerve endings, sweat and sebaceous glands, and blood and lymph vessels. The sensitive *laminae* of the *hoof* are dermal.
a.k.a: corium.

derotation: (1.) The distance between the outer surface of the *hoof* wall at the toe and the face of the *P III* is greater near the coronet than it is than it is near the ground. Often due to the *dubbing* of the toe.
(2.) Adjusting hoof *balance* to return the P III to its normal position relative to the short pastern and/or the dorsal hoof wall after it has rotated out of place due to *founder* or other affliction.

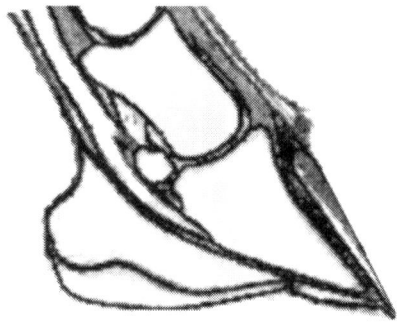

derotation (1.)

developmental orthopedic disease: A blanket term for various disorders in the bones, *cartilages*, and related muscles, *tendons*, and *ligaments* of growing horses, including *flexor deformity* and *OCD*. Genetic predisposition, overfeeding, insufficient free exercise, imbalanced nutrition (especially calcium to phosphorous ratio), systemic diseases and other stresses have been implicated as potential causes.
a.k.a: DOD.

Millwater's Farriery

desmotomy: The surgical cutting of a *ligament*.

diagonal gait: Each diagonal *pair* of *limbs* (off fore/near hind, near fore/off hind) move together. A natural *trot* is a good example of a diagonal gait.

diagonal pair: The fore and hind *limbs* on opposite sides of the horse. The *near* fore and *off* hind, or the off fore and near hind.

Diamond: Brand of *horseshoes* and *farrier* tools since 1908.

diaphysis: The shaft of a long bone.

digit [From Latin *digitus*, a finger]: The *equine limb distal* to the fetlock.
See: Page A-3.

digital cushion:
See: plantar cushion.

dimethyl sulfoxide:
See: DMSO

Diploma of the Worshipful Company of Farriers:
See: D.W.C.F.

distal: When referring to *limbs*, distal means away from the torso, or comparatively farther from the torso. Opposite of *proximal*.

DMSO: Dimethyl Sulfoxide. A solvent and penetrant so effective that it can be tasted in the mouth shortly after it is applied to the skin. DMSO is often used as an anti-inflammatory, free-radical scavenger, or mixed with *antiseptic* to treat localized infection.

DOD: See: developmental orthopedic disease.

donkey: A domestic *ass*.

doorman: When *farriers* work as a team to shoe a *horse*, as in traditional shop situations, the farrier who prepares the *hooves* and applies the shoes is called the doorman.
See also: fireman.

Dormosedan [® Pfizer inc.]: Detomidine hydrochloride, a drug commonly used for *chemical restraint*, administered via *IM* or *IV* injection. Considered one of the preferred drugs for the purpose because its use usually results in a fast, but not sudden, sedative response, little or no loss of balance, and a gradual, predictable return to normal as the drug wears off.

dorsal [From Latin *dorsum*, the back]: **(1.)** The front surface of the *equine hoof* and *leg*.
(2.) When referring to the entire animal, dorsal means the spine or center-line of the back.

double nail pad: A thick *pad* designed to be nailed directly to the *hoof* so that a package of additional pads and a *horseshoe* can be attached to the double nail pad with nails or screws. This is an extreme means of creating an artificially long and high foot that has been used primarily on Tennessee Walking Horses who do the *big lick* gait at shows.

draft horses: *Horses* bred for heavy pulling. These horses tend to be very large and heavy, with huge *hooves* and thick bone. Specimens have been documented at over 20 *hands* in height and a ton and a half in weight. Examples in excess of 17 hands and one ton are fairly common. A fit and well-trained draft horse may be able to drag weights in excess of his own body weight. A heavy-pulling draft horse differs from a riding horse in that he may shift his center of gravity forward of his front feet when leaning into the harness, using his front hooves as well as his hinds to drive his body. This makes drafters the only horses who actually derive much practical benefit from toe *calks* on the front shoes. Draft shoes are usually made of very heavy *bar stock* and frequently feature thick *clips*. Draft horses are normally worked at the *walk* and *trot* in harness, although they are perfectly capable of *cantering* or *galloping*.

Belgian **draft horse**

drill-tec/tech/tek: See: borium.

dropped sole: The sole of a *hoof* which has become convex rather than concave. As the sole protrudes below the *solar* plane of the *hoof wall*, it bears excessive weight and is subject to *bruising*. *Foundered horses* often have dropped soles.
See: Pages A-2; A-5.

dubbed toe: (1.) A hoof which has had the *dorsal* surface of its toe ground off. This may be the result of excessive rasping after a *horseshoe* was poorly fit, or of high *limb lameness* which may cause the *horse* to drag his *hoof*.
(2.) The intentional dressing back of the toe done to counter *founder* or a toe *flare*.
a.k.a: dumped toe.

Duckett's bridge: A *transverse* line across the *solar* aspect of the

hoof, crossing the frog an inch or so back from its apex in typical, riding *horse* sized hooves, passing directly below the center of *articulation* of the coffin joint. This line normally coincides with the widest part of the hoof, and the *anterior* extent of the bars. On a well *balanced* foot, Duckett's bridge will divide the hoof into equal front and rear halves. Concept developed by Dave Duckett, *FWCF*.
See: hoof anatomy, basic; balancing the horse's hoof; Pages A-2; A-5.

Duckett's dot: An theoretical point about 3/8 of an inch behind the apex of the frog, at the center of the toe arc of a properly dressed *hoof*. Named for Dave Duckett, *FWCF*.
See: hoof anatomy, basic; balancing the horse's hoof; Pages A-2; A-5.

dumped toe: See: dubbed toe.

D.W.C.F.: Diploma of the Worshipful Company of Farriers. The minimum requirement for being registered to practice *farriery* in England. The D.W.C.F. exam includes a written test with five essay questions which must be answered in full and with color illustrations, live shoeing with *handmade fullered horseshoes*, a test of forging skills, and an oral questioning period of at least 15 minutes.

eagle eye: The ability to *forge* or modify a *horseshoe* to fit properly after only a brief look at the *hoof*.

While eagle eye competitions are frequently seen in horseshoeing contests, the ability to correctly fit a shoe without repeated trips between the *horse* and *anvil* is useful in the field, as it saves the *farrier* time and labor, and helps prevent the horse from becoming impatient.

An effective approach to eagle eye fitting is to evaluate each foot for size (circumference or shoe size, depending on whether *keg shoes* are being used), width, and general shape. Inch marks on the farrier's hoof knife grip are handy for measuring the hoof width while trimming. Inch marks etched into the top of the anvil's horn can be used to measure the width of the shoe while forging or fitting it.

Most hooves fit into one of five basic shapes, or can be described as a combination of two of them. These five shapes have been named *Norman, Ralph, Tag,*

Spike, and *Stubby* by farriery instructor Scott Simpson

Etched marks on the anvil horn and hoof knife can be a handy aid in **eagle eye** horseshoe fitting.

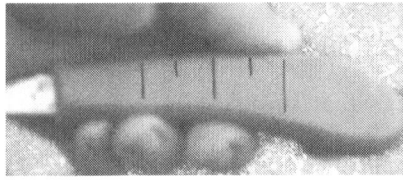

The eagle-eye measuring technique can also be used as shorthand instructions to allow the farrier to fabricate shoes ahead of time in the *smithy* to apply to a specific horse elsewhere.

See: horseshoe, forging; keg shoe, fitting; Pages A-6; A-7.

ECD: *equine Cushing's disease.* See: Cushing's disease.

eggbar horseshoe: A form of *bar shoe* designed to extend *posterior* support. Frequently used to manage *navicular disease, bowed tendons, flexor deformity*, and *sore suspensory ligaments*.

The eggbar brings the *solar* plane of the *hoof* parallel to the ground more quickly and positively during heel-first landing, and can prevent the hoof from flipping toe-up, loading on the bulbs and fetlock, as may occur in some *horses* under heavy stress. The eggbar also increases the load-bearing surface against the ground at the rear of the hoof, preventing the heels from sinking into the turf, and keeping the foot upright for an easier *breakover*, and provide some protection to the bulbs of the heels against rocks and other hazards on the ground.

Eggbars are primarily used on fore hooves. The shoes are usually fit much the same as conventional *horseshoes*, but with the curve of the branches at the heels continuing until they meet and merge. Ideally, the bar will extend back well back under the limb. Horses are less likely to step-off eggbars than one might imagine, as the support and breakover enhancement they provide tends to reduce *overreaching,* but the shoe should be well-*boxed* nonetheless.

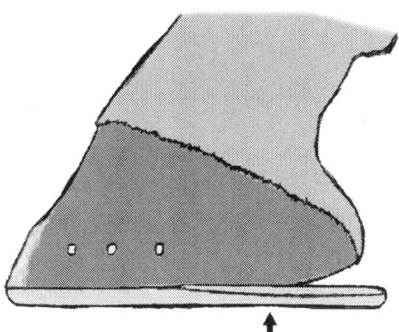

Even though the **eggbar** extends the support against the ground well-back, the heels of the hoof are still loading much too far forward.

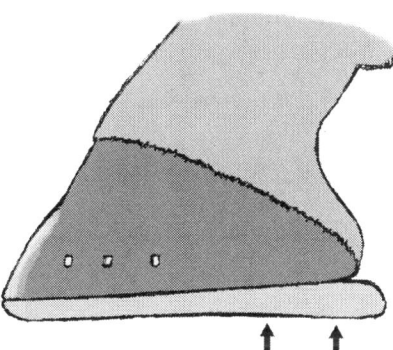

Taking a sliver of underrun heel horn off and adding a wedge eggbar allows the hoof to load against the shoe much farther back.

It is important that *underrun heels* be trimmed back towards the widest part of the frog before eggbars are applied. If eggbars are used on hooves with underrun heels, the heels may be crushed further by the nutcracker-like effect of the shoe projecting so far behind the sloping heels of the hoof. If trimming the heels back decreases the overall *hoof angle* too much, *wedge pads* or a wedge eggbar shoe may be used to compensate.

At this writing, a number of good, pre-manufactured eggbars are available in ***steel*** and ***aluminum***. *Farriers* who choose to forge their own shoes usually add a bit of length to their *bar stock* measurement, *turn, fuller,* and *pritchel* the shoe as usual, then scarf and *weld* the ends together rather than forming heels.

Eggbar made from oversized keg shoe. Note excessive weight and poor nail hole placement.

eggbar with poorly placed nail holes. A better way for a farrier to modify his preferred keg shoe into an eggbar is to weld an extra piece, such as the toe cut out of another shoe, into place across the heels of an appropriate sized horseshoe.

See also: balancing the horse's hoof; hoof, anatomy, basic; horseshoe, forging; Pages A-2 and A-8.

elbow hitting: Striking of the point of the elbow joint by the *hoof* of the same *limb* or its *horseshoe*. Injury from elbow hitting is possible, but is sometimes confused with injury caused while the *horse* is lying down with his legs folded beneath him.

English: A broad classification of equitation and *tack* styles which have their roots in European riding techniques and equipment. English saddles are relatively lightweight and may allow close contact between rider and *horse*, but may not provide as secure a seat for the former or as much weight distribution for benefit of the latter as some other saddle types. Most English riding is done with the reins held in both hands and the horse being cued with light direct reining with

Functional eggbar produced by forge welding the toe cut from one shoe across the heels of another.

A once-common approach to modifying **keg shoes** into eggbars is to choose a shoe two sizes larger than the hoof would usually take, then hook the heels in and weld them together. Because keg stock *web* and thickness increases with shoe size, this resulted in a very heavy

slight contact (no slack in the reins) at most times. Polo, which requires the player to have one hand free for the mallet, being an obvious exception. English riders typically use a somewhat shorter stirrup leather than *Western* riders, so that they ride with more bend to the knee and can raise out of their saddle seats more easily for posting. In addition to being a popular choice for leisure riders around the world, organized English disciplines range from tortoise-speed low-level dressage to athletic performance competitions like cross-country jumping.

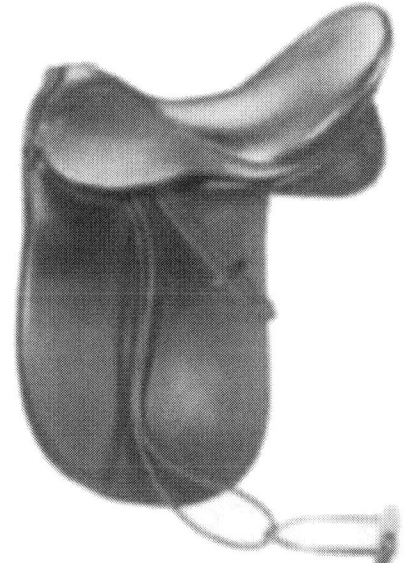

English saddle

epidermis (ep-i-dûr′mis): The outer, protective, non-vascular layer of the skin which covers the *dermis*. The *hoof wall*, horny *laminae* and other horny hoof structures are epidermal.

epiphyseal plates: *Cartilages* near the ends of bones which which allow them to grow lengthwise. As the *horse* matures, the plates *ossify* or close. The more *distal* plates close earlier as a general rule.
a.k.a: growth plates; epiphyseal cartilages.
See: Page A-10

epithelium (ep-i-thē′lē-əm): Thin membrane tissues covering most of the body's structures and organs, internal and external. Also describes the the first layers that heal over a wound.

Epsom salt: Hydrated magnesium sulfate. Most often dissolved into hot water which is used as a soak to draw infection out of an *abscessed hoof* in equines. Also can be used as an inflammation and tension reducing soak (particularly by humans), or taken internally as a purge.

etiology (ē-tē′ol-ə-jē): The study of causes.
a.k.a: ætiology.

Equidae: Family of mammals with only one extant Genus (Equus) which includes the nine species of *horses*, *asses*, zebras, and the recently extinct quagga.

equine: (1.) An animal of the family Equidae.
(2.) Having to do with *horses*.

Equus: Genus within the family *Equidae* which includes all extant *horses*, *asses*, zebras, as well as the recently extinct quagga. The members of the genus Equus are herbivorous mammals adapted primarily for a grazing lifestyle in open country. Their distinctive characteristics include the development of the third *digit* on each *limb* into a single *hoof*, with the other digits evolved out of existence. The third metacarpal/metatarsal in each limb has been developed into a long, strong bone with the second and fourth metacarpals/metatarsals in each limb diminished into support and *tendon/ligament* guide structures affixed to the third metacarpal/metatarsal. The nail of the single remaining toe on each limb has evolved into a load-bearing capsule that provides good traction on a variety of surfaces both for normal locomotion and high-speed evasion of predators. These hard *hoof capsules* are impervious to most natural surfaces, and can be used effectively as weapons to fend off predators. In their natural habitats, equines fit the herbivore niche between antelope and buffalo, being larger and stronger than the former, fleeter and more adaptable than the latter. Equines are herd animals capable of complex social relationships. All extant species have been successfully domesticated and breed well in captivity.
See: Page A-4; splint bone.

exertional rhabdomyolysis: See: azoturia.

exfoliate: To shed or flake off dead tissue. The sole of the *hoof*, for example, normally exfoliates as it grows down.

exostosis: Abnormal bony growth.

expansion: (1.) The very slight outward movement of the quarters of the *hoof* which may occur during weight bearing, and/or the increase in *solar* width which occurs as the hoof grows down.
(2.) In reference to a *horseshoe*, expansion describes the practice of fitting the *posterior* half of the shoe larger than the hoof to allow for hoof expansion.

extended heel: A long heel on a *horseshoe*. Usually fit parallel to the center-line of the *hoof*, and in line with the direction of travel.

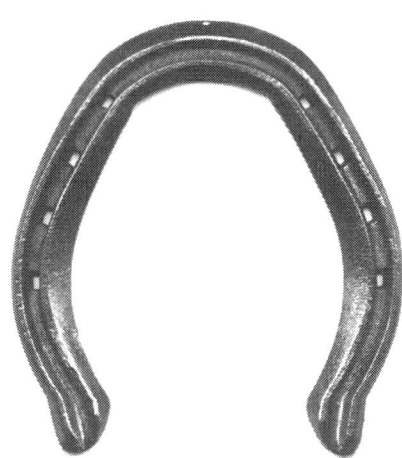
extended heels

extensor process: The point of insertion of the main digital extensor tendon into the *PIII*.

extensor process disease: See: pyramidal disease.

false quarter: A vertical indention in the *hoof wall* parallel to the *horn* tubules, resulting from a defect or injury to the *coronary band*.
See: Page A-2.

false sole: See: retained sole.

farrier [Old French *ferrier*, ultimately from Latin *ferrum*, iron]**: (1.)** While there are no legal restrictions on the use of this title in America, it properly describes only a *professional equine* hoofcare expert and shoer of *horses*.

(2.) In the past, farriers were charged with the full range of horse care.

farrier's radiograph: A worn *horseshoe*, which may give the *farrier* insight into the condition and function of the *horse's hoof* and *limbs* beyond what could be gained by external observation of the animal itself.

The horseshoe effectively records data about the way the hoof land, loads, and *breaks-over* during the weeks it is on the foot. This information can be used to fine-tune the *balance* of the hooves, and to recognize *chronic* or developing *soundness* problems before they become obvious.

The hoof side of the shoe may be polished by flexing of the *hoof capsule*. This polishing wear pattern can indicate whether the heels are crushing forward during landing/loading, or the heel quarters are expanding under load. No polishing at the heel quarters may indicate that the hoof has been immobilized by *clips* or *nails* placed too far back, or the development of *sidebone*. It may also mean the horse has an inherently rigid hoof capsule, which is usually a positive characteristic. Excessive polishing wear suggests a weak, almost rubbery hoof *wall*.

A tendency to bend or pull off one front shoe may indicate that the other front foot is in discomfort, causing the horse to protect the sore foot by keeping the sound hoof on the ground longer, where the hind can "catch up" and tread upon it.

See also: Page A-2; radiograph; two finger radiograph.

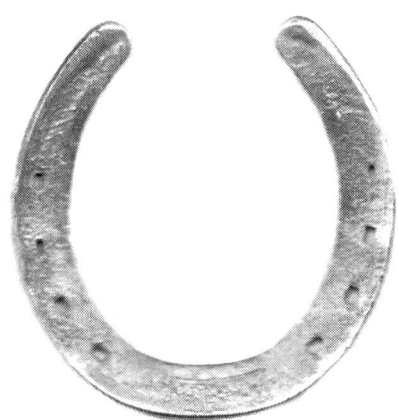

farrier's radiograph
A worn horseshoe can be a valuable source of information to the farrier.

farriery: The art and science of preserving or restoring *soundness*, enhancing *gait*, performance, and functionality in *horses* by *trimming* the *hoof horn* and affixing *horseshoes* and other devices as needed. Applied farriery requires an integrated knowledge of anatomy, biomechanics, gait mechanics, and *equine* behavior as well as specialized horsemanship, *blacksmithing*, and other fabrication skills not common to other equestrian professions. The organic nature of the hoof, being a mass of counterbalancing and ever-changing imperfections, demands an approach to farriery adapted to the individual horse, guided by the combined knowledge, skills and experience of a competent *farrier*. It is therefore impractical and unwise for anyone else to attempt to prescribe how a horse should be trimmed or *shod*.

Fellow of the Worshipful Company of Farriers:
See: F.W.C.F.

feral: Animals of domestic ancestry who have reverted to the wild state. American mustangs are feral, rather than truly wild.

ferrophobia: Fear of *iron*. Sometimes used in reference to militant critics of conventional *horseshoeing* who, despite identifying as "natural *horse*" or *barefoot* enthusiasts, advocate various artificial *hoof* protection devices affixed in a number of

ways, demonizing only metal shoes attached with *nails*.
See also: BUA.

fever rings: See: hoof rings.

filly: A female *horse* under 4 years old.

fine punched: A *nail* hole in a *horseshoe* which is located relatively close to the outer edge of the *web*. Heel nails are often punched fine.
See also: coarse punched; Page A-8.

fireman: When *farriers* work as a team to shoe a *horse*, as in traditional shop situations, the farrier who works the *forge* and produces the *horseshoes* is called the fireman.
See also: doorman.

Fisher: See: Mark Fisher

Fitzwygram's shoe:
See: Sir F. Fitzwygram's shoe.

flank cinch: In *western tack*, the strap which passes under the *horse's* torso and connects on each side near the rear-most part of the saddle. This strap is usually wide leather, and serves to keep the rear half of the saddle from rising up, especially when the horn is being pulled down and forward while roping. The flank cinch is not considered essential for ordinary riding, and is often omitted. Because it passes under the relatively sensitive belly of the horse, and is not needed to hold the saddle on, the flank cinch is never made very tight. Conversely, leaving the flank cinch so loose that a horse might get a rear *hoof* over it while kicking at a fly can be dangerous. The flank cinch should always be connected to the front *cinch* under the horse to prevent it from swinging backwards and causing the horse distress.

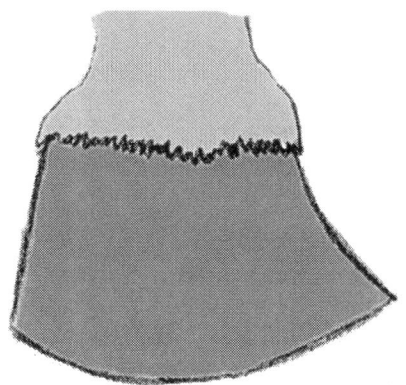

flare

flare: An outward distortion which may occur on any portion of the *hoof* wall. If left unremedied, they can alter functional *toe angle*, *mediolateral balance*, and hoof symmetry.

flexor deformity: Excessive tension on either the *DDF* or *SDF*. Can result from heredity, *malnutrition*, injury, or a combination of these. Can be managed with exercise, diet, *farriery*, and surgery.

a.k.a: contracted tendon.

flipper foot: An extremely overgrown, toe-*flared hoof*. Can result from *founder* or neglect. In severe cases, the *horse* may stand on the back of his pastern, allowing the *solar* aspect of the hoof to be seen from in front of the animal.

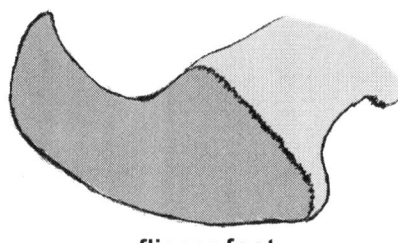

flipper foot

The sheer mass of excess *horn*, much of it tough scar material, presents some difficulty in *trimming* the flipper foot. Most horses with such hooves have difficulty standing with a foot up for extended procedures as well. So *farriers* often resort to a hacksaw to remove the bulk of the overgrowth.

One relatively safe approach is to use *nippers* to trim back the heels and bars, which will be severely *underrun*, crushed, and probably folded-over. Then the hacksaw is employed to take off the front of the hoof at an angle determined by *two finger radiograph*. This sawing can be done with the hoof on the ground for the most part, although standing the foot on a low block of wood will make finishing the cut easier. Lubing the cut and the saw blade periodically with cooking spray will ease the process considerably. The edges and corners left by the saw can then be trimmed and rounded with the nippers and *rasp*.

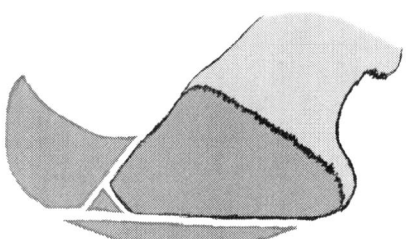

Flipper foot trimmed back to a nearly normal overall hoof form.

The exposed front of the hoof will be *laminar* scar material, often marked with *bruise* blood and *abscess* tracks. This should not be coated with a *sealant*, as it may serve as a release vent for still-active infections.

Horses with hooves in this condition are rarely inclined to be very active. If the animal has regained sufficient vitality to want to *trot* or *gallop* on his "new feet", as might be the case with a rescue horse, a few days stall rest may be advisable to allow the *tendons* and *ligaments* of the *limb* to adapt to the changes in the feet. Then gradually increase controlled exercise to avoid *suspensory ligament* soreness or *bowed tendons*.

See also: trimming technique; balancing the horse's foot; hoof anatomy, basic.

float: A tool used to file a *horse's* molar teeth, and the act of using said tool.

Because the *equine* lower jaw is somewhat narrower than the upper, the grinding teeth wear at angles. The upper teeth may develop a sharp edge on the outside, which can abrade the lining of the cheek. The lower teeth may develop a sharp inner edge, which can cut the tongue. This may cause a horse to go off his feed, drop grain while eating, or to swallow poorly chewed grain and hay, resulting in weight loss. Discomfort from such dental problems can cause the horse to alter his *gait* and carriage, which may be mistaken for *lameness*.

The dental float is essentially a small, housed *rasp* on a long handle, which is employed to periodically file away the sharp edges of the teeth.

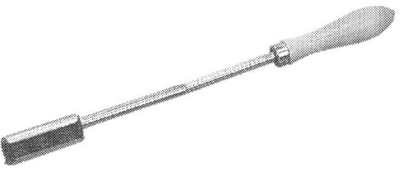

float tool

flux: A substance used in *forge welding* and *brazing* to reduce oxidation and aid the outflow of *scale* particles from the joint surfaces as they are pushed together. Usually a powder sprinkled onto the *steel* at red heat just before heating to yellow-white heat for welding. Traditional fluxes used by *blacksmiths* and *farriers* include borax and clean sand.

foal

foal: A very young *horse* of either sex. A pregnant *mare* is said to be "in foal". The birth process of horses is referred to as "foaling".

forge (fôrj): (1.) A furnace used to heat metal.
(2.) The workshop of a *farrier* or *blacksmith*.
(3.) To make something out of metal.

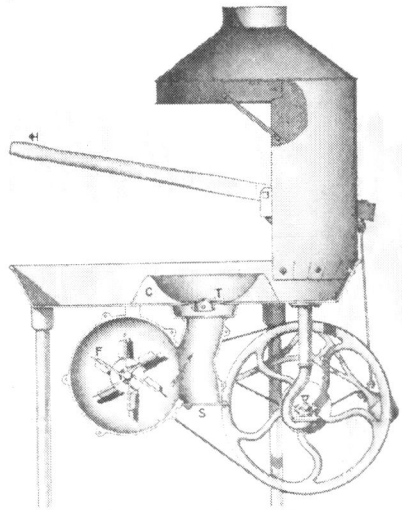
hand-powered **coal forge**

forge, coal: A device used to heat *horseshoes* and other metal stock. Some form of *bellows* or *blower* is used to force air into a burning pile of *coal* (sometimes charcoal), producing heat sufficient to incinerate *steel*. Coal fire is hotter and welds steel more easily than gas, but extra skill and effort are needed to build and maintain it. Coal forges are quieter and less expensive to operate than gas forges, but produce smoke and soot.

forge, coal, operation of: The core of a *forge* fire, where *steel* is heated, burns *coke*. But the fuel *blacksmiths* and *farriers* put into their forges is usually hard *coal*. (Ideally small chunks, called pea-coal.)

"Cooking" coal on the outer edge of the fire transforms it into coke, which resembles black popcorn. As the the coke is consumed in the fire, new coal is added to the pile on the outside. This is wet-down, and gradually pushed toward the center, driving fresh coke into the core.

The coal in the forge also serves as an insulator, keeping the core of the fire contained. Water is used to keep surface flames down, and to encourage slow coking rather than outright burning of raw coal.

Coke starts easier and burns cleaner than coal, and should be the only material in contact with the heated portion of steel in the forge.

To start a forge with coke, torn and crumpled paper can be

placed in a wad directly on the grate. Some coke should be pulled over the paper, but not enough to completely bury it. A small amount motor oil may be drizzled onto the paper and coke. The paper is lit and the fire allowed spread a bit before the *blower* is used to produce a low-powered air flow. A hard blast might burn-up the paper before the coke has a chance to catch, or blow-out the fire altogether. As the paper burns away and coke starts to burn, more coke is raked onto the flames. When the fire is first started, especially if there is a lot of "green" coal in with the coke, large amounts of thick smoke may be produced. This will abate when the fire starts burning properly. Do not stand in the thick smoke. Not only is it harmful to the lungs, it is also flammable... Sometimes the thick smoke momentarily, but dramatically, ignites as the forge suddenly transitions into a proper burn.

Starting a coal forge without coke requires a slow, hot fire to get the coal started. Not only are gasoline and kerosene dangerous, they burn far too fast and will be consumed before the coal is heated-up enough to start burning on its own. Building a fire with hardwood chips over the grate, with a small amount of coal mixed-in, and more raked-up around the edges, fed by a low power air flow from the blower, can begin the coking process.

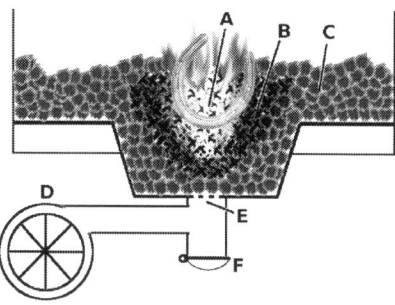

Anatomy of a coal forge fire.
  A. Core of fire.
  B. Coke.
  C. Coal bank.
  D. Blower.
  E. Grate.
  F. Ash dump.

Once a forge fire well started, the coal/coke in the first few inches above the grate will be cooled by the air blast from the blower. This keeps the grate from being burned-out. The burning coke above this zone will be the core of the fire, where metal to be heated will be placed. Heaping more coke over the top of the core will help contain and concentrate heat. Fresh coal is occasionally added to the outer edge of the pile, and a sprinkling can or squirt bottle is used to dampen it. As the fuel in the core is consumed, the smith may slap the sides of the pile with a shovel or other tool to push more coke into the core and fresh coal toward the center to be coked.

Mineral impurities in the coke and water used in the forge (silica, metals, etc.), along with oxidized traces of the steel being worked, melt and flow to the "cool" zone just above the grate, where they solidify into clinkers, which are hard, glassy lumps that block the blower blast and foul-up forge function. These have to be removed periodically during a smithing session.

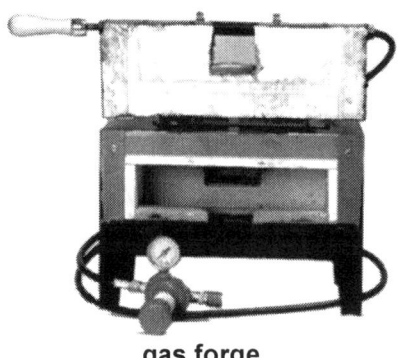

gas forge

forge, gas: A device used to heat *horseshoes* and other metal stock. Gas forges usually burn propane (sometimes natural gas) within an insulated *steel* or cast *iron* housing. Gas forges tend to be easier to set up and use than *coal forges*, but take longer to cool down after use. They produce little smoke and no soot, but are relatively loud and produce dangerous, odorless exhaust of which *farriers* need to be aware. Gas forges come in *blower* and *atmospheric* varieties.

forging: A fault in *gait* which results in the toe of a hind *hoof* striking the *solar* surface of its *lateral* fore hoof. Similar, but not identical, to *overreaching.*

fossa [Latin for ditch, plural **fossae**]: A pit, indention, or channel in a bone.

founder [Old French *afondrer*, to sink. From Latin *fundus*, bottom]: The biomechanical aftermath of severe *laminitis*. In most cases, with the anterior *laminae* compromised by the laminitis attack, the *chondrocoronal ligament apparatus* suspends the bone column within the *hoof capsule* by the short pastern bone, just above it's center of *articulation* with the coffin bone. Tension on the *deep digital flexor tendon* pulls the coffin bone into rotation around that point, swinging it downward at the toe. At the same time, *breakover* leverage on the *dorsal hoof wall* tends to peel it away from the coffin bone and weakened laminae. With the coffin bone and hoof wall rotating away from one-another, laminae that survived the initial laminitis are ripped apart. The gap between the wall and what's left of the *dermal* laminae is filled with scar *horn*. The *anterior solar* margin of the coffin bone will press down on the solar *corium*, usually producing *bruises*, and sometimes causing it to rupture through the horny sole.

have also failed. Instead of the coffin bone rotating around its point of articulation with the short pastern, the entire bone column will tend to descend into the hoof capsule. This is a *sinker*, and can be recognized by the *supracoronary depressions* running all the way back to the bulbs of the afflicted feet.

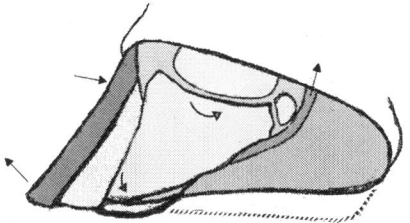

The general directions of forces in a foundering hoof. (Broken line indicates the extent of the wall. Note the raising heels.)

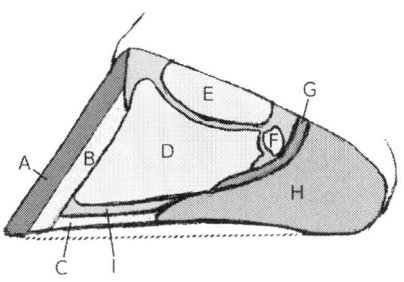

Simplified diagram of the hoof.
A. wall B. laminae C. horny sole
D. coffin bone (PIII) E. short pastern
F. navicular G. deep flexor tendon
H. frog/digital cushion I. solar corium

In cases where there was extensive inflammation and swelling of the anterior laminae during the initial laminitis, driving the coffin bone backwards into the hoof capsule, the *chondrocoronal ligaments* may

The separations, *necrosis*, and bruising throughout the laminae and sole make *abscesses* very likely in all cases.

Founder usually afflicts both front feet, but *unilateral* cases are possible. *Quadrilateral* cases also occur. Hind-only founder is rare, but not unheard-of.

Management of founder through *farriery* is based on attempting to directly counter the rotation of the coffin bone, relief of the forces that drive rotation, protecting compromised portions of the hoof capsule, and/or shifting loading from damaged parts of the foot to structures better able to support it.

Traditionally, foundered hooves are *trimmed* as low as possible at the heels, with the toe being radically *dubbed* back. The toe is not trimmed from below, and the anterior sole is left at full thickness. This trim brings the coffin bone back into more normal alignment with the pastern, takes peeling stress off the toe at breakover, and loads the frog. But it also increases standing tension of the deep digital flexor tendon. So, if the coffin bone's connection to the hoof capsule is insufficient, rotation will resume.

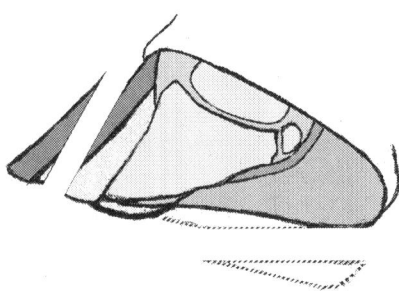

Traditional, derotation founder trim.

If *horseshoes* are applied, they must be well *seated-out* to prevent sole pressure, which foundered feet absolutely cannot tolerate. *Nails* have to be placed farther back than usual, as the anterior wall will be in no condition to hold a shoe.

Supporting the coffin bone and transferring load from the compromised hoof wall to the frog with a *heartbar* shoe, as popularized by the late Burney Chapman, *RMF*, has been a successful approach in many founder cases. The "arch support" from the frog plate of the heartbar prevents further sinking/rotation of the coffin bone and restores circulation within the foot.

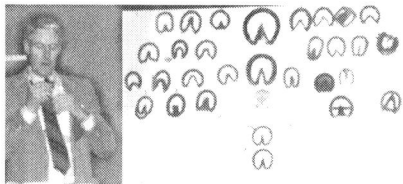

Burney Chapman and his collection of heartbar shoes (and unreasonable facsimiles thereof) in KY, 1994.

A variation on the heartbar technique is to employ *Thera-Flex* inserts carved to apply pressure to the frog, then fit with abbreviated shoes to float the heels and create dynamic frog pressure. This approach is somewhat more forgiving of imperfect application, but not as effective at holding together severely foundered hooves. It may be necessary to cut the flat part of the Thera-Flex insert into a *rim pad* configuration to avoid pressure on the convex sole that often develops in founder cases.

feel good to the *horse* short-term, but have negative repercussions later. After the appropriate support is confirmed, nailing can be completed.

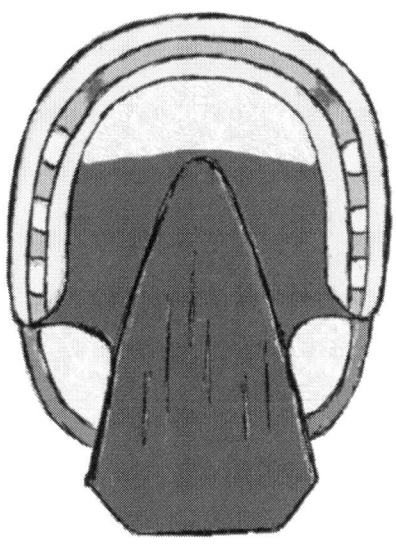

"Window" cut-out in pad section of a Thera-Flex insert to avoid sole pressure.

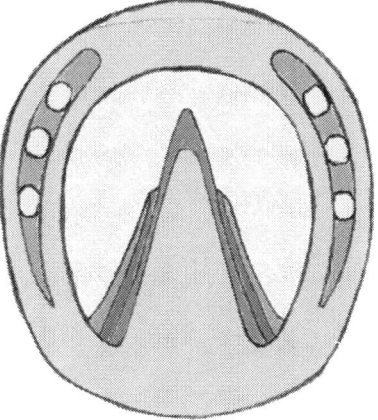

Applied full-support heartbar. Note that the load is spread over most of the area of the frog, but the tip and perimeter are not covered.

When applying heartbar type frog support in *bilateral* founder cases, it is usually advisable to attach the shoe with one nail in each branch, then let the horse put the foot down. If the frog plate is set correctly, the animal will quickly find the relief and stand down on the shod hoof, often visibly resting its mate. The goal is to apply just enough support to get this effect. More pressure may

Adjustable heartbars, with hinged frog plates and screws to increase/decrease pressure with the shoes still on the hooves, may be useful in clinical situations, but can be problematic in the field as well-meaning non-farriers may not be able to resist the "more is better" inclination to increase pressure beyond what is advisable.

Raising the heels to radically increase the *hoof angle* is an aspect of treatment popularized by R.F. Redden, DVM in the 1990s. This decreases the tension on the deep flexor tendon, one of the prime movers in founder rotation, but is diametrically opposed to the classic approach of lowering the heels to re-align the *phalanges*.

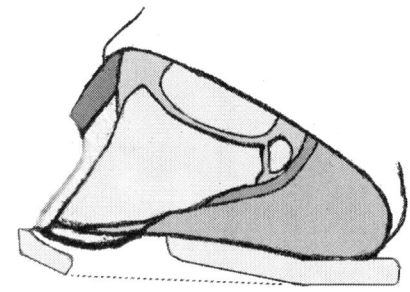

Dorsal wall resection and heartbar. (Broken line here represents the ground surface of the horseshoe.)

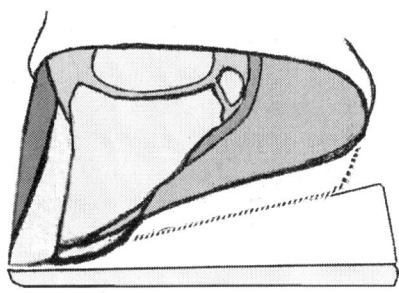

Breakover peeling leverage at the front of the foot can be eliminated by a dorsal hoof wall *resection*, which also creates an avenue of drainage for the abscesses which commonly develop in foundered hooves. A horizontal *groove* is cut across the dorsal wall at least an inch below the *coronary band*, then wall and wedge of scar horn *distal* to the groove is removed. The removal of this distorted material allows new hoof wall to grow down parallel to the face of the coffin bone.

Protection of the sole is often necessary in foundered hooves, especially when there is a prolapsed solar corium or severe bruising. **Hospital plates** are better suited to the task than flat pads, as they allow more clearance for the sole, and frequent inspection and disinfection of the bottom of the foot. When the horny sole is intact, well seated-out, wide-*webbed* shoes can provide protection for its perimeter.

In the immediate wake of laminitis, it can be very difficult for the horse to stand with one foot up for any length of time, and the hammering of nails can cause considerable discomfort. During the initial shoeing, standing the horse in deep bedding or placing a padded boot or bandage on the weight-bearing hoof may help.

When resetting, it may be wise to do one foot at a time so that the horse never has to stand on a *bare foot* during the procedure. A veterinarian may prescribe *chemical restraint* and painkillers to get through the process, but these have the drawback of partially eliminating the feedback from the horse which would guide the *farrier* in application. In some cases, alternatives to nailing, such as adhesives, can be a solution for early founder shoeing.

The prognosis for each case is dependent upon the severity of the initial laminitis, the character of the horse, and the willingness of the owner to do what is needed. It may take over a year of extra care and *therapeutic* farriery to get a horse from acute laminitis to a stabilized, new "normal". Even then, a full recovery cannot be assured.

Many foundered horses who do recover *serviceable soundness* will require special consideration from their farriers for the rest of their lives. Typically, the heels will grow down relatively fast, while the toe will tend to grow forward in a *flare*, so that trimming back the heels and dubbing the toe will be necessary. The anterior sole will need to be preserved. Breakover at the toe should be eased by beveling up the wall on bare feet, or applying a *rolled toe, set-back*, or combination horseshoe (like the *Natural Balance shoe*). *Rockered toe* shoes are usually not advisable, as they might pressure the apex of the sole on a foundered hoof. A *backwards shoe* is sometimes used for maintenance of fully stabilized cases with well-developed anterior solar callus horn, as it provides *posterior* support, easy breakover, and allows the flare-prone toe to wear back.

See: hoof anatomy, basic: horseshoe, conventional application; road founder; abscess, hoof; Pages A-2; A-5; A-8.

founder stance: The standing position often assumed by *horses* during *acute laminitis*. The hind feet will be placed far forward of their usual position, and will bear an inordinate amount of weight. The fore *hooves* will be placed out in front of the animal, and may bear weight only at the heels.

four point trim: A *hoof trimming* technique in which the heels are

trimmed back to the widest point of the frog, then the toe is beveled in a manner akin to what would be done in preparation for a *rockered toe horseshoe*. The quarters are then rasped until they would no longer bear weight on a firm surface. This leaves only four full-loading points on the *hoof wall*; one at each side of the toe, and one at each heel buttress. This method is based on observations of the hooves of *feral* horses, and its advocates claim that it results in the development of stronger hoof structure.
See: Page A-2.

fox trot: A broken *diagonal gait* performed by Missouri Fox Trotters and some Saddlebreds. Each hind *hoof's* timing is delayed by an extended loading phase, so that the hind foot lands after its diagonal fore foot is already on the ground, causing the fox trot to be a four-beat gait. The fox trot is done at the speed of a *jog* or *trot*, and is not tiring like the *rack*. Done well, the fox trot is a pleasant riding gait.

freeze brand: A permanent artificial marking created by applying a super-cooled iron to the skin. Identification freeze brands are most often found on *horses* necks, but may be placed on the shoulders, rump, or elsewhere. Some horsemen consider freeze branding more humane than conventional (hot) branding, or prefer the appearance of the freeze brand to that of the hot *brand*. Freeze branding causes the branded skin to produce white hair. Complex freeze brands, such as identification codes, can be difficult to read if the horse's hair coat is long.

frost nail: A special *horseshoe nail* designed to provide temporary hard surface traction. Made by Mustad, Inc.

frush: See: thrush.

fullering: (1.) In farriery; to cut a groove into the ground side of *bar stock* before it is *turned*. This may be done to provide traction for the shoe and a seat for the *nail* heads. Fullering allows crease nail pullers to be used to remove nails one at the time. **(2.)** In *blacksmithing*; to spread metal by forcing a wedge or semicircular edged tool into it. **(3.)** Wrongly used as a synonym for *creasing*.

fullering (AFA Certification and competition): A two phase process in which the stock must be worked prior to the groove being cut so that the **web** is the same width before and after fullering.

furlong: A 220 yard (1/8 mile) unit of distance often used for *horse* race measurement.

F.W.C.F.: Fellow of the Worshipful Company of Farriers. The highest recognition awarded by the *W.C.F.* A *farrier* must have achieved the *A.W.C.F.* at least one year prior to attempting the F.W.C.F. The candidate must submit a 2000-3000 word illustrated thesis 21 days before the examination. At the examination the candidate must make and apply a *fullered therapeutic horseshoe* to exact specifications and submit several handmade horseshoes for inspection. The oral portion of the exam involves an in-depth defense of the written thesis.

gait: The speed, order, and flight path of the *horse's hooves* and *limbs* in motion. The fundamental natural gaits of the *horse* are the *walk, trot, gallop,* and *run.* Horses have been trained, selectively bred, and specially *shod* to perform many other gaits.

gaited horse: A *horse* of any of several breeds which have been selectively bred to perform a *gait* or gaits other than those used by most riding and harness horses.

gallop: A fast, three-beat *gait* that is natural to most *horses*. One *diagonal pair* of limbs moves in unison, while the opposite diagonal pair does not. This results in the loading phase of both hind feet overlapping, so that the combined power of both hind *limbs* can drive the horse forward. The fore *hoof* on the non-unison pair is considered the lead foot, and is the last hoof to leave the turf before a relatively long phase in each stride when the horse is completely off the ground. Horses can easily gallop faster than any human can run on open terrain. A fit horse can gallop for several miles at a time, but will be winded by the effort. See: run.

gelding: A castrated male *horse* of any age.

get: A collective term for all of a given *horse's* offspring.

girth: The strap which passes under the *horse's* torso just behind the elbows and connects to the saddle on each side. The girth is the primary, and sometimes the only, strap which holds the saddle on, and thus must be fairly tight before a rider mounts. The term "girth" is normally used by *English*-style equestrians and occasionally by *western*-style horsemen as well. See also: cinch, front.

gouge: See: clinch gouge.

Millwater's Farriery

graded temper: To impart varying degrees of *temper* into different areas of the same piece of *steel*. This is often done on hand-forged cutting implements like axes and bowie knives to provide maximum toughness by virtue of a nearly *annealed* back or striking surface, with edge-holding hardness on the nearly *hardened* cutting edge. One means of accomplishing this is to slowly apply heat to the back or striking surface of the hardened and polished piece and let the oxidation colors run like a rainbow until the desired color (usually pale straw) reaches the cutting edge. Since the colors continue to run for some seconds after the piece is removed from the *forge*, it takes some practice to get the timing right. As with all heat treating, the makeup of the steel *alloy* determines the effectiveness of the temper. Mild steels (such as *horseshoes*) are little effected by tempering. High carbon steels (like rasps) can have their hardness/toughness levels greatly altered by the process.

granny stand: See: hoof stand.

gravel: See: abscess.

grooving: Cutting or burning a horizontal groove across the fibers of the *hoof horn* to alter the way in which stresses are transferred up the *wall*. This may be done when managing *founder, flares, basal cracks*, and other hoof maladies.

growth plates: See: epiphyseal plates; Page A-10.

growth rings: See: hoof rings.

guild: An organization of persons of the same trade or *profession*, formed to promote mutual interests by establishing and maintaining standards of competence and practice.

Guild of Professional Farriers: A U.S. *guild* of farriers established in 1996. The organization accepts only full-time *farriers* who qualify for the *RJF* credential as members, and is dedicated to promoting farriery as a true *profession*.
-Address:
P.O. Box 4541.
Midway, KY
40347

half-round horseshoe: A *horseshoe* made of stock which has a semi-circle cross-section, with the flat side of the stock facing the *hoof*, and the round side facing the ground. These shoes allow the *horse* to *breakover* at any point on the hoof with relatively little resistance, and are considered very easy on the hooves and *legs*, but they do not provide much traction.

hand: A unit of measure equal to 4 inches, used to measure the height of a *horse* at the highest point of the withers. The number of whole hands is properly followed by a hyphen, then the remaining height in inches. Thus a horse who measures 5 feet and two inches at the withers would be designated "15-2 hands". This is sometimes written with a decimal point replacing the hyphen, which is inadvisable because the decimal point is, on some rare occasions, used to designate following tenths. Hence the 15-2 hand horse might also be designated either "15.2 hands" or "15.5 hands".

handgallop: A controlled *gallop*. Generally a bit faster than a *canter,* but not fully extended or overly demanding on the *horse*. Used to cover fairly short distances in a hurry over open terrain.

handmades: *Horseshoes forged* from *bar stock* with hammer and *anvil* rather than those produced by machines.
See: horseshoe, forging.

harden: To bring a particular piece of metal to its hardest (and most brittle) condition. *Blacksmiths* do this to *steel* by heating it to cherry red in a *forge,* then suddenly cooling it by *quenching*. The effect of hardening varies greatly with the composition of the steel. The low carbon content in the mild steel *alloy* used in most *horseshoes* causes hardening to have very little effect, so that even quench-hardened horseshoes are fairly hard to break, but easy to bend or grind away. The much higher carbon content of rasps means that, when hardened (as they usually are except for the tang), they are easy to break, but resist bending or wearing away.

hardie: A *steel* tool with a square shank that fits into the *hardie hole* of an *anvil*, holding a cutting edge upward so that hot metal pieces may be driven down upon it with a hammer. A *brass hammer* is often used to avoid damaging the hardie. A simple hardie resembles a chisel. Hardies used by *farriers* to cut the heels of *horseshoes* usually have a cutting edge in a rounded "V" or semicircular shape.
See: Page A-7.

hardie for cutting horseshoe heels

hardie hole: The square hole, usually found in the heel of an *anvil*, into which may be fit the shanks of hardies, *swedge blocks*, and other tools. Such tools usually remain stationary in the hardie hole while metal is hammered down onto them from above. Hardie holes are often used as *turning holes* by *farriers*. Some modern farrier's anvils have larger, round turning holes in the heel, and have relocated the hardie hole to the step area of the horn.
See: A-7.

Hay-Budden: U.S. brand of forged *anvils* from 1893 through 1927.

head bob: When a *horse* is *lame* in a forelimb, it will tend to throw its head upwards as the *hoof* of the sore *limb* lands to reduce the impact. This bobbing motion of the head, especially evident at the *trot*, is used to recognize lameness and identify the afflicted limb.

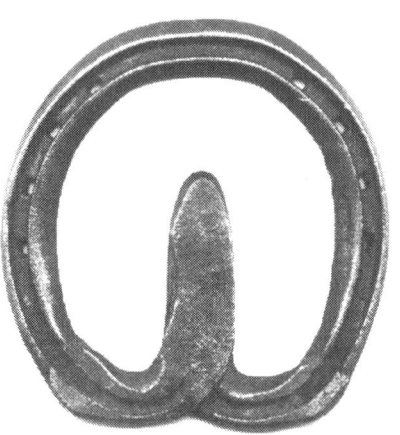

heartbar

heartbar [from the shape of this shoe, which vaguely resembles a Valentine heart when viewed heels-up]: A type of *bar shoe* in which the bar takes the form of a frog plate that can be used to either protect the frog from damage or to transfer weight bearing load from the *wall* to the frog. The latter application, sometimes called a pressure heartbar, is useful in managing major *hoof capsule* damage from direct injury, *founder*, or other causes. Heartbars must be made in such a way that they only load the frog, and do not touch the bars or the sole. The very tip of the frog should not be covered by the frog plate, which should be wide enough to spread the load over most of the frog, but not so wide that the perimeter of the frog is covered. The amount of pressure to be applied through the frog plate is a subjective matter. Too much may cause pressure *necrosis* and *abscess* in the frog. If the plate is applied so that it rests flat against the frog without pressure, it will take some of the load when the foot is on the ground. Some *farriers* find that the optimum heartbar pressure in support shoeing cases is achieved when the shoe can be held flat against the foot with only mild thumb pressure before nailing.

See: hoof, anatomy, basic; corrective and therapeutic farriery, basic principles; crack, hoof wall; Page A-2.

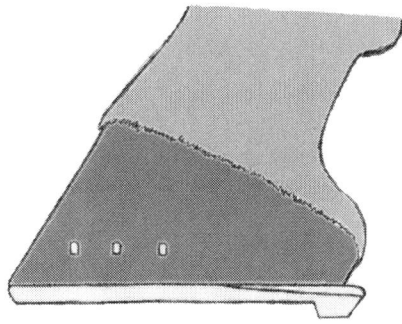

heel calk

heel calk: A projection forged from or welded onto the ground side of the heel of a *horseshoe*. Heel calks provide braking traction as the *hoof* lands, but no grip at *breakover*.

Heller: Brand of *farrier* tools from 1836 to around 1965.

Hephaestus: God of fire and *blacksmithing* in classical Greek mythology. Physically homely (at least by Olympian standards) and *lame*, he made himself invaluable to the other gods by virtue of his forgework. He wound up married to Aphrodite, goddess of feminine beauty and love. Hephaestus is analogous to the Roman god *Vulcan*.

high-low hoof syndrome: Significantly mismatched fore hooves, with one foot being upright and *atrophied*, while the other is relatively flat and spread-out. As the upright *hoof* is the more obvious deformity, this condition is sometimes perceived as *unilateral clubfoot*.

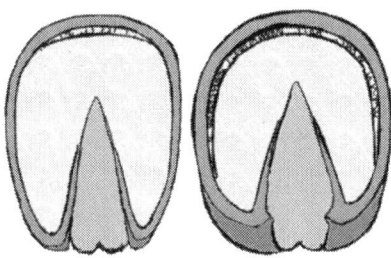

Solar view of high (on left) and low (on right) mismatched hooves.

The "high" foot typically develops steep heels which raise the narrow frog far off the ground, straight heel quarters, and a low, abrupt toe *flare*. The overall circumference or *horseshoe* size prior to *trimming* may be substantially smaller than its mate's.

The "low" foot will usually have sloping heels, a wide frog that bears weight, full *wall* flaring that starts relatively high on the hoof, a flat sole, and much stretching distortion at the *white line*.

This syndrome appears to have become more common in recent decades, leading some to believe that the trend towards taller *horses* who have to stand with one forefoot forward and the other back in order to reach the ground to graze may be a cause. *Draft horses*, however, have always had the long legs and short neck combination, and are not prone to mismatched hooves. It may be more likely that a long-term, low-level soreness during the development of fast-growing horses, from hard to detect injuries such as *palmar process* fractures, causes *chronic flexor deformity* and clubfoot in the affected *limb* while the other foot, constantly overloaded in compensation, suffers something akin to a mild *road founder*.

Preventative measures include not feeding excessive concentrates to developing horses, as is too often done in an attempt to get maximum early growth. Attentive monitoring of growing foals and yearlings, with prompt recognition and management of even subtle soundness issues, may also be helpful.

Mild cases of high-low syndrome may be managed by trimming both hooves into *balance*, which will mean lowering the heels of the high foot quite a bit, and dressing the low foot back into shape, while taking only as much heel as is necessary to remove *underrun*, crushed *horn*. If the animal is to be *shod*, the same size shoe should be applied to both feet, albeit fuller-fit on the high foot, especially through the heel quarters.

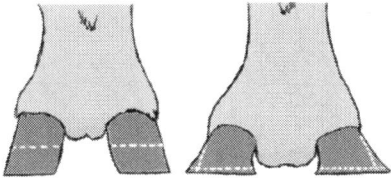

Palmar view of high-low hooves. Broken lines indicate what needs to be trimmed or dressed off.

Side view.

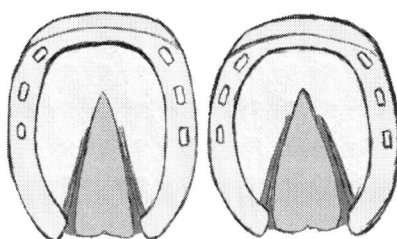

Trimmed and flat-shod. Note same-sized shoes.

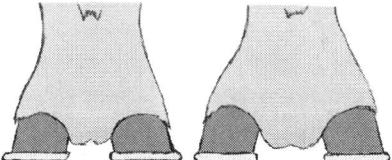

Note fuller fit on high (left) hoof.

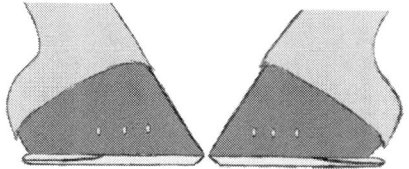

Here an acceptable, albeit imperfect match has been achieved with conservative trimming and shoeing.

Severe cases may be managed with *therapeutic* horseshoeing. After the hooves are trimmed as described above, some means may be employed to promote spreading of the high foot. One effective approach is to fit an abbreviated shoe with the *posterior* of the foot supported by a *Thera-Flex* or similar *pad* carved to transfer loading to the inner faces of the bars, gently driving the heels apart each time the foot bears weight.

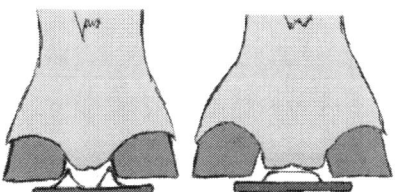

The insert on the high foot has been carved to gently drive the heels apart. The low foot insert functions as a dynamic heartbar.

Concavity can be promoted by applying a *heartbar* to the low foot to transfer loading from the walls to the frog, which may be visualized as pushing the middle of the foot up. An abbreviated shoe with a Thera-Flex pad carved in heartbar style can perform this function while matching nicely in weight and appearance with the package applied to the high foot.

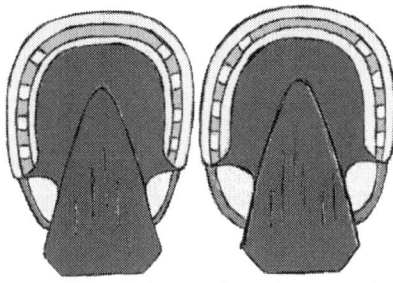

Abbreviated shoes allow the posterior of the hooves to be supported by the inserts. Note the symmetry in size, weight, and appearance despite the differing functions of the package on each foot.

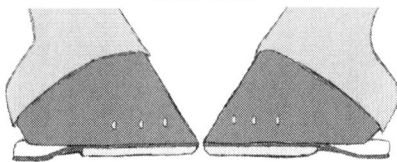

A shortened shoeing cycle may be called for while the therapeutic shoes are in use. Usually after two *resets* or replacements over twelve to eighteen weeks total, the horse can transition to conventional shoeing with nearly matched feet. High-low syndrome can be persistent, however. So there may be a slow regression to mismatch over time which can be addressed by re-applying the therapeutic shoes during the horse's off-season.

Any time a dramatic change is made in a horse's functional *hoof angles*, two or three days rest is advisable, followed by a gradual build-up to normal workload, to allow the muscles, *tendons*, and *ligaments* to adjust.

See: hoof anatomy, basic; hoof-pastern axis; corrective and therapeutic farriery, basic principles; Page A-2 and A-5.

hinny: A *hybrid* produced by breeding a *stallion* to a *jenny*, as opposed to breeding a *jackass* to a *mare*, which produces a *mule*. Hinnies are rarely produced due to their physical inferiority to both mule and *horse*.

hipposandal: A metal plate roughly the shape of a *hoof's* sole with extensions, hooks, or rings used in ancient times, particularly associated with ancient Romans. It is thought that they were used as a form of strap-on *horseshoe*. If this is the case, they must have been a temporary measure used on immobile or slow-working *horses*, since the awkward design could not withstand regular use.

hipposandal

histology (his-tol′ə-jē): Study of the microscopic structure of tissues.

hoof [Anglo-Saxon *hóf*]: The equine foot, includes the *coronary band* and all parts *distal*. Sometimes refers to only the *horny* parts of the foot. See: Page A-2.

hoof, anatomy, basic:

The *equine* hoof includes the *coronet*, the *horny* structures *distal* to the *coronary band*, and all the structures enclosed by them. Although the hooves are analogous to the human middle fingertips and toe nails, they are extremely well developed to endure the loads and stresses applied by a relatively large animal maneuvering at high speeds over various terrains.

As a general rule, the front hooves are developed to support a load. They tend to be larger and rounder than hind hooves, which are more spade-shaped to drive the horse's body forward. While standing still on firm ground, a typical domestic *horse* subjects the bearing surfaces of his hooves to a load over 55 pounds per square inch, compared to under 7 pounds per square inch for a typical man. *Running* and other activities can increase this load several times over.

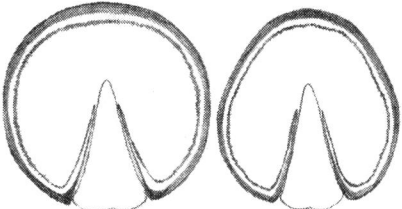

The fore hoof (on the left) is designed for load-bearing while the hind hoof (on the right) is made to facilitate driving the horse forward.

There are three bones within the equine hoof, including the coffin and navicular bones, which are situated completely within the hoof, and the lower end of the short pastern bone.
[See: Page A-5]

The short pastern bone (also called the PII, os corona, second phalanx, and middle phalange) enters the hoof from above and forms the *proximal* face of the coffin joint (also called the distal interphalangeal joint). The short pastern is considered a long bone, with *epiphyseal cartilage* at its proximal end to facilitate lengthwise growth in the early months of the horse's life.

The coffin bone (also called the *PIII*, os pedis, pedal bone, third phalanx, and distal phalange) is roughly hoof-shaped and gives form to the *anterior* half to two-thirds of the hoof. Its proximal aspect forms the distal face of the coffin joint. The coffin bone does not have a physis, and has a low density, actually being porous. When removed from the hoof and dried, it can be crushed almost to powder with relative ease. Within a living hoof, the pores are filled with vascular tissue and fluids, making the bone somewhat more durable, although still subject to fracture. The advantages of this design include the ability for the bone to be adapted through remodeling more extensively than most other bones.

A large mass of cartilage extends from each side of the *palmar* face of the coffin bone. These *lateral cartilages* give shape to the *posterior* third of the hoof and the bulbs of the heels. They allow a small degree of flexibility to the hoof. In many cases the lateral cartilages *ossify* as the horse matures.

[See: sidebone]

The navicular bone (also called the distal sesamoid) is the smallest bone in the foot, and is shaped a little like a canoe. (Navicular means "little ship".) The "canoe" fits sideways in the hoof, and makes up the palmar surface of the coffin joint. It is denser than the coffin bone, but still somewhat porous and given to remodeling.

The equine hoof is encased by tough, horny structures which are collectively referred to as the *hoof capsule*. These structures: the hoof wall, bars, sole, and frog make up most of the outwardly visible hoof. They are non-vascular and insensitive, much like human hair and nails.

The hoof wall is the most obvious external hoof structure, extending from the coronary band at the top of the hoof all the way down to the ground. The wall is typically between 3 and 4 inches in length at the *dorsal* face, where it usually forms an angle of between 50° and 60° with the *solar* plane of the hoof. Although there is considerable variation among individuals, a typical wall is around 3/8" thick at the toe, and is somewhat thinner at the quarters.

The hoof wall is considered to be the primary weight-bearing structure of the foot, and conventional *horseshoes* ideally touch only the wall. Horseshoe *nails* are driven through the wall and *clinched* into its exterior surface.

The wall is tubular in composition, and can be

visualized as a bundle of drinking straws (tubular horn) with the spaces between the straws filled with wax (intertubular horn) which holds them together. The horn tubules start at the top of the wall and extend downward. Like all tubular (column-type) support structures, they have great strength when vertical and straight, but can fail readily if bent or loaded too far off vertical.

The greatest factor affecting the material strength of hoof horn is moisture content. Like most organic materials, hoof wall is strongest and toughest when relatively dry. Excess moisture can lead to distortion of the wall, separation of tubules, and general structural failure. The normal moisture content of hoof wall is said to be around 25%. But the moisture content of hoof wall should not be constant throughout. The hoof wall seems to be at its most resilient when a moisture gradient is maintained, with the inner wall relatively wet compared to a dryer outer surface.

Hoof walls may be pigmented black, unpigmented, or anything in between including vertical stripes. Although various studies indicate that pigmentation makes no significant difference to hoof strength, *farriers* and horsemen traditionally hold that dark hooves are stronger and tougher than light-colored ones. Pigmentation does not go all the way through the thickness of the hoof wall. When seen from the solar viewpoint, the inner, unpigmented layer of hoof wall is called the *water line*.

The hoof wall grows downward from the top towards the ground surface where it is gradually worn away unless the horse is *shod*. Healthy hooves usually grow rapidly enough to replace the entire wall in six months to a year, and tend to grow faster in the spring and summer than in the winter. Nutrition, exercise level, age and general health can affect overall hoof wall growth rate. The hoof wall also tends to grow faster where it bears less load.

The periople is a thin, tough coating which protects the coronary band. It usually extends down the hoof wall an inch or so before being worn away. The periople has often been cited as being important to maintaining hoof wall moisture. This role seems to have been exaggerated, particularly in texts intended for horseowners.

The sole covers the majority of the bottom of the hoof. It's a surprisingly thin layer of protection for the sensitive structures above it, and can easily allow them to be punctured or *bruised*, especially if the sole is rendered even thinner by excessive *trimming*. A healthy sole should be at least slightly concave so that it does not bear weight when the horse is standing barefoot on pavement. The sole exfoliates in the form of white powder or flakes as it grows down. Some horses produce sole of such quality that it does not readily exfoliate and can become very thick. This is considered a beneficial trait, although the farrier may have to trim the old sole growth to allow the wall to be brought into balance.

The normal moisture level for soles is said to be around 33%. Excess moisture makes soles soft and weak, rendering them especially vulnerable to bruising, punctures, and knife quicks. Extreme dryness, especially following over-hydration, can make soles glass-like in hardness.

On sand, soft turf, and other deformable surfaces, the sole bears some weight. The amount of load the sole can or should be subjected to, especially in therapeutic situations, remains a subject of controversy.

The frog is a leathery horn structure that covers a pie slice shaped "hole" in the sole. The tip of the frog points to the center of the toe of a normal foot, and a point about 3/8" back from the tip marks the center of the arc of the coffin bone (and therefore the the concentric arc of a properly dressed anterior hoof wall). This point is called the *"Duckett's Dot"*.

The primary function of the frog appears to be to provide a break in the more rigid horny structures of the hoof capsule. An expansion joint of sorts, which allows the hoof to be wider at its base than it is at the top. It also allows some slight distortion in the hoof capsule under stresses which might cause fracture if the entire structure was rigid.

The frog may be shed two or more times a year, but rarely sheds all at once, so this process often goes unnoticed.

In many sound horses the frog does not bear weight on firm ground. But it can be used to support a considerable portion of the hoof's load in therapeutic situations, provided that care is taken not to compromise circulatory structures.

The frog is said to have a moisture content of about 50%. Excess moisture renders the frog very soft, and it may be mashed out of shape. It may also become too weak to provide protection to the structures above it, including the navicular area.

The bars are extensions of the wall along each side of the frog.

They are generally considered weight-bearing structures. The trench between each bar and the frog is called a commissure.

The horny parts of the hoof are each produced and constantly replaced by corresponding sensitive structures. These structures are well supplied with blood vessels to provide the nutrients needed to build the hoof horn.

The hoof wall is produced by the coronary band, which is located at the top of the wall near the hair line. Injury to the coronary band often results in a great deal of bleeding. Damage to the coronary band causes it to produce distorted hoof wall from the affected area. A permanent scar to the coronary band will result in a distortion or fault in the wall which will eventually continue all the way down to the bearing surface. **[See: false quarter]** Stimulation or mild irritation of the coronary band can increase hoof wall production.

Just above the coronary band, at its junction with the normal, hair-growing skin of the foot, is the perioplic ring, which produces the periople.

Beneath the coffin bone lies the solar corium and the sensitive sole, which produces the horny sole. The solar corium is very soft and heavily blooded, and may protrude through ruptures in the horny sole.

The sensitive frog, which produces the horny frog, is essentially an extension of the *digital cushion* above it, but has considerably more blood supply than the digital cushion proper, which is a fibro-fatty shock absorber within the posterior of the hoof.

The hoof wall is attached to the coffin bone and lateral cartilages by a complex arrangement of tissues called *laminae*. These laminae provide many times the attachment surface area than would be attained through a flat, face-to-face adhesion while allowing the hoof wall to "slide" down in relation to the internal structures as it grows. When seen from the solar viewpoint, the laminae are called the *white line*, although they tend to appear slightly yellow compared to the water line, which is just outside the white line.

The primary horny laminae appear as a continuous series of fine ridges extending from the inside surface of the hoof wall. Each "ridge" runs all the way from the top of the wall at the coronary band down to the bottom of the wall. With magnification, one can observe smaller ridges on each of the primary horny laminae. These smaller ridges are the secondary horny laminae.

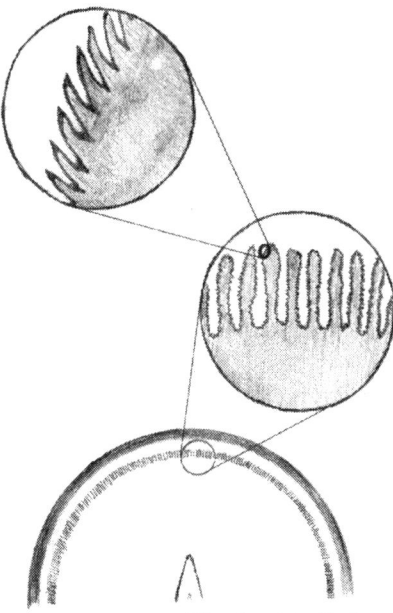

Bottom center: The front half of a hoof, showing (from the middle outward) the apex of the frog, the sole, the white line, the unpigmented wall known as the water line, and the pigmented outer wall.

Middle right: Magnification of the white line showing the primary horny laminae (light) and the primary sensitive laminae (dark). In reality, you would have to trim the horse into the quick to see the sensitive laminae, since they don't normally reach down to the ground surface.

Top right: Magnification increased to show the secondary horny (light) and sensitive (dark) laminae, separated by the basement membrane.

The sensitive laminae extend outward from the coffin bone and lateral cartilages. They are exact reverse images of the horny laminae, right down to the secondary laminae, and fit against them perfectly. The sensitive laminae are well supplied with blood, and can produce scar horn material if they are exposed by wall removal or separation.

Between the sensitive and horny laminae is the *basement membrane*, which can be thought of as a special kind of glue. Apparently there is some chemical mechanism which periodically causes the basement membrane to enable the laminae to slide against each other vertically, thus allowing the wall to grow down from the coronary band, yet provides a very strong bond between the laminae in other circumstances.

Most of the non-horny structures of the hoof are thoroughly permeated with blood vessels, ranging from the relatively large circumflex *veins* and *arteries* down to the countless tiny *capillaries* that feed the tissues. As in all parts of the body, blood flow in the hoof is used to carry oxygen and nutrients to the tissues, to carry waste chemicals away, and to help regulate temperature.

The hoof is equipped with some special circulatory adaptations which allow it to withstand long exposure to freezing temperatures. ArterioVenous Anastomoses *(AVAs)* are vessels which allow blood to flow from arteries directly into veins, bypassing the fine capillaries. Because the AVAs offer less flow resistance than the capillary beds, warm blood is allowed to rush through the foot, keeping it from being frostbitten. Normally, the AVA bypasses open when the foot is cold, and periodically close to force blood back into the capillary beds to nourish the sensitive laminae. The sensitive laminar tissue can withstand long periods of *ischemia* when cold.

One of the only parts of the internal hoof that is not heavily blooded is the plantar cushion above the sensitive frog, which tends to contradict the popular belief that the frog acts as an "auxiliary heart" which must bear weight to function. But the hoof as a whole may actually act as an auxiliary pump to enhance circulation. The slight movement caused by the bony column driving down into the hoof capsule can act as a piston pump when the foot is loaded. The flexing of the hoof capsule can act as a bellows pump as well. But the value and importance of these blood circulating aids in the hoof can be overestimated and do not justify the hoof flexibility enhancing treatments often used to increase their supposed function. Such treatments usually weaken the horn and do more harm than good.

The fluid mass of blood being moved within the hoof is also thought to act as a hydraulic shock absorber.

The internal structures of the hoof are bound and animated by many *ligaments* and *tendons*. As a general rule, ligaments attach skeletal structures to one another and hold the skeleton together. Tendons attach muscles to bones to facilitate movement.

There are different kinds of ligaments within the hoof. Among them are collateral ligaments which hold the short pastern to the coffin bone to form the coffin joint. The coffin joint is sealed by capsular ligaments, which produce and contain the *synovial fluid* which lubricates the joint. The navicular bone is held in its place at the back of the coffin joint by its own sling-like suspensory ligament which originates from the long pastern bone (also called PI, the first phalanx, and the proximal phalange) above the hoof, and by the distal navicular (also called the impar or navicular interosseous) ligament which inserts just under the coffin bone.

There have been a number of cases in which the laminar connection between the coffin bone and hoof wall has been eliminated, either through laminitis or the surgical removal of the coffin bone. When the bony columns failed to drop down into the hoof capsules subsequent to the loss of laminar bonds, some began to question the traditional view that the limb was entirely supported through the coffin bone's attachment to the wall. Current research indicates that the *chondrocoronal ligaments*, which extend from the sides of the distal end of the short pastern bone into the lateral cartilages provide at least a secondary means of suspension for the bony column. These ligaments also appear to provide the pivot point for rotation in founder cases.

The deep digital flexor tendon originates in a muscle above the knee, runs down the back of the leg, under the navicular bone and its bursa, then inserts into the underside of the coffin bone (a place called the semi-lunar crest). When the muscle is contracted, the tendon pulls the coffin bone down and back, causing the toe of the hoof to drive downward while the heel is raised off the ground.

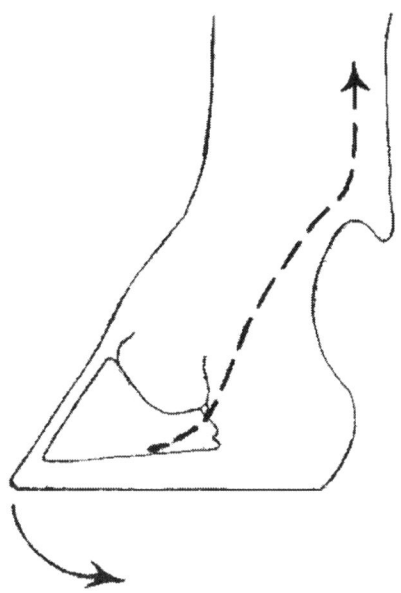

Path of the Deep Digital Flexor tendon shown by dashed line. Direction of movement facilitated by tendon shown by solid line.

The main (or common) digital extensor tendon inserts into the dorsal face of the coffin bone just below its joint with the PII (a place called the *extensor process*). Its function is approximately opposite to that of the deep digital flexor tendon. It pulls the toe of the hoof forward and up as the limb swings forward, allowing it to land flat or slightly heel-first. Because branches of the suspensory ligament tie into the main digital extensor tendon above the hoof, the tendon plays a role in keeping the fetlock from sinking as well.

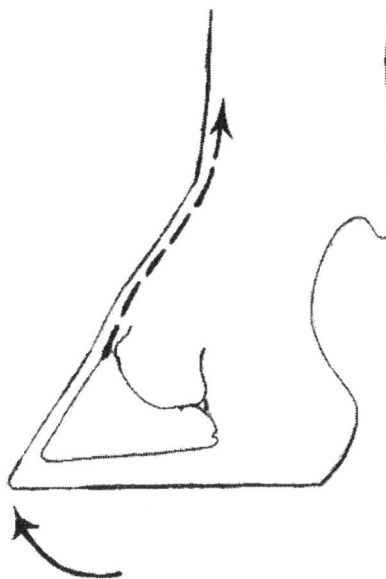

Path of the Main Extensor tendon shown by dashed line. Direction of movement facilitated by tendon shown by solid line.

Overall, the equine hoof is a far more complex, dynamic, and adaptable system than its static outer appearance might lead one to believe. It is designed to continuously repair damage and replace wear, withstand heavy stresses, and is equipped with back-up features which allow it to survive extreme overloads intact. Its structure is also such that it can be reinforced artificially through shoeing without impeding its physiological functions. Properly maintained, the horse's hooves are amazingly well-suited to carrying the horse and his human-imposed burdens over a remarkable diversity of ground surfaces.

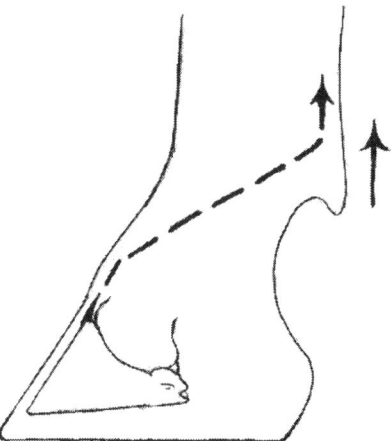

Path of Suspensory Ligament which joins the Main Extensor tendon from each side.

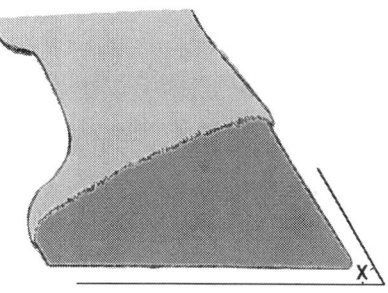

"x" = **hoof angle**

hoof angle: The angle at which the *dorsal* line of the *hoof wall* intersects with the plane of its *solar* surface. Hoof angle can be

measured with a tool called a hoof gauge or hoof protractor.
a.k.a: toe angle.

hoofbound:
See: contracted hoof.

hoof cancer: See: canker.

hoof capsule: The *horny*, external parts of the *hoof* which form a capsule-like container for the sensitive and skeletal structures of the foot.
See: Pages A-2, A-5.

hoof horn: The tough, insensitive parts of the *hoof*, such as the *wall*, are made of horn. The wall is composed of fibers which grow downward from the *coronary band* called tubular horn. These are cemented together by intertubular horn. The approximate moisture content of hoof horn is 25% for the wall, 33% for the sole, and 50% for the frog.
See: Page A-2.

hoof-pastern axis: The slope of the *dorsal hoof wall* compared to that of the pastern. The slope of the pastern changes inversely to alterations in the *hoof angle*. When the hoof angle is steeper, the slope of the pastern becomes shallower. When the hoof angle is made shallower, the slope of the pastern becomes more upright. Hoof angle is traditionally considered ideal when it has been adjusted so that the slope of the hoof and pastern are the same, which is called a straight hoof-pastern axis. When the slope of the dorsal hoof wall is steeper than that of the pastern, the axis is said to be broken forward. When the slope of the dorsal hoof wall is shallower than that of the pastern, the axis is said to be broken back.

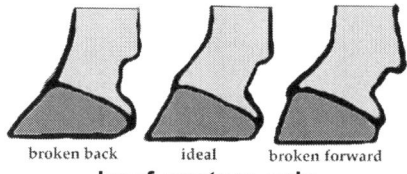

hoof-pastern axis

hoof pick: Tool used to remove dirt from the bottom of the *hoof*. It is carefully inserted into the commisure at the heel, then pulled towards the toe. Doing this on both sides of the frog usually eliminates the bulk of detritus from the foot.
See: Page A-2.

hoof pick

hoof rings: Roughly horizontal distortions on the *hoof wall* which may be caused by changes in diet, environment, season, or by illness. Uneven hoof rings may

indicate that the *horse* has been *foundered*.
a.k.a: growth rings; fever rings.

hoof sealant: Any of a number of artificial varnishes which impede the transfer of moisture between the *hoof* and the environment.

hoof spring: A spring, usually "V" shaped, which is placed between the bars of the hoof in an attempt to promote *expansion* or combat *contracted hoof*.
See: Page A-2.

hoof stand: A device designed to provide an elevated place where a *horse's hoof* may be rested while it is being worked upon by a *farrier*. It is usually employed when the hoof is brought forward for *clinching* and finishing or dressing of the outer *wall*, but some designs can also support the *leg* in the shoeing position. The common design features some sort of base, upon which the farrier can place his foot for added stability, with an upright pole emerging from the base up to around knee-height. At the top of this pole there is generally some sort of small platform upon which the middle of the horse's hoof can be placed. Some hoof stands have mechanisms which allow for easy height adjustment. Since a horse can put as much weight as he likes straight down onto a good hoof stand, standing in the dressing position upon one requires little effort. Counter-intuitively, many horses seem more comfortable with the hoof stand set somewhat high rather than low for the fore limbs.
a.k.a: shoeing stand, granny stand.

hoof stand

horn: See: hoof horn.

horse: Member of the species *Equus caballus*. Horses are arguably the most useful beasts of burden in human history, possessing the optimum balance of strength, speed, endurance, size, and tractable nature.

Although early humans hunted horses for food, men have domesticated horses for riding and driving since the dawn of recorded history. Selective breeding has produced horses ranging in size from seven *hands* up to twenty-one hands in height, and from below one hundred pounds to well over a ton and a half in weight. Most horses used for riding and light driving are in the fifteen to sixteen hand range in height and around a half ton in weight.

Under a light rider and tack, horses have averaged speeds of over thirty miles per hour for distances in excess of a mile. Sprinting speed may be on the order of forty-five miles per hour. Well conditioned horses can cover over one hundred miles in a day, and cavalry units could average as much as forty miles per day. A single horse can pull a large trolley with thirty or forty people on board at walking speeds without difficulty on level streets.

Millennia of human-directed selection have resulted in horses developing extremely good rapport with people. They quickly learn to respond to even the subtlest of cues, and may even learn to respond to cues that the handler is not aware of giving, resulting in communication that extends below the level of conscious awareness. Selection has also resulted in horses developing some human-like predatory behaviors. Horses often show courage, even fierceness, that would not usually be expected from a grazing, prey species.

The gestation period for horses is a little over eleven months. *Mares* are usually bred in the early spring so that the *foals* will be born before the insect season and so that there will be plenty of summer grass for mares and foals during *weaning* around four months later. (Some breeders attempt to have foals born in January so that they will be as mature as possible for their official competition age, which many organizations calculate from January first of the birth year.)

Horses achieve most of their adult height before two years of age, and their mature weight by about five years. Most breeds are trained for riding between two and three years old. Light driving may begin earlier. *Colts* and *fillies* often reach reproductive maturity before two years of age, but it is advisable to put off breeding until colts have completed basic riding or driving training (for the sake of discipline in the *stud*) and until four years of age for the mare (for the sake of allowing full physical development before the burden of carrying a foal). A normal lifespan for a horse is twenty-five to thirty years, with well cared-for specimens remaining capable of work well into their twenties.

horse

horse holding: One of the first jobs with which an *apprentice farrier* may be tasked is holding *horses* for *horseshoeing* and *trimming*. It may seem like a simple thing, but few people really do it well. Learning the basics of good horse holding can make you a valuable asset to the farrier.

Pay attention. It may get boring standing there for an hour or more at a stretch, but don't lose focus or get careless. Things can come unglued with little warning.

Stay in front of the horse's nose. Your main job is to keep the horse from leaving. So don't let him get his nose over or past your body. He can effortlessly drag you by the halter, or shove you with his neck, chest, or shoulder. But *most* horses will stop if you stay in front of their noses, unless they are really panicked.

Stay on the same side of the horse as the farrier. That way, if the horse becomes unruly, you can pull his nose toward yourself, which will swing his rump *away* from the farrier and his toolbox. Exceptions to this rule include the dressing of the front hooves, when the farrier will be in the position usually occupied by the holder, and when the holder may need to briefly switch sides to discourage a horse from swinging away from the farrier.

Hold your ground. Horses can be sneaky, and may encroach on

you a little at the time. Before you realize it, you may have moved ten feet from where the farrier wanted to work.

Don't play tug o' war. If the horse moves backwards, there's really nothing you can do except calmly ask him to stop. If he seriously backpedals, you should try not to make it worse by "chasing" him. Feed out the rope, let him easily pull you along, try to keep him pointed in the right direction, and look at his feet (thereby avoiding glaring at his face, which may frighten the animal). Since the farrier is working under and behind the beast, backing is rarely a problem if the horse is trying to get away from him.

Don't hang on the horse's head. Keep the horse from leaving. Keep him from biting the farrier. But don't try to keep his head immobile. He'll wrestle with you, and in so doing, will wrestle with the farrier.

Keep the horse's feet still when the farrier is away at the *anvil*. We don't want him pawing and messing-up the trim job before the shoe can get nailed-on, or walking around and shifting the shoes before they get clinched tight, or grinding dirt into the feet to make the farrier spend time and effort re-cleaning them.

Don't fight with the horse during shoeing. Your job is to keep things easy and calm. Not to add conflict.

Don't feed fingers to the horses. Some people insist on holding horses in such a way that their hands or arms are pretty much in the horse's mouth, then are somehow surprised when they get nipped. Don't do that.

Use discipline and restraint techniques only under the farrier's direction. The last thing a farrier trying to focus on steering a *nail* through a tricky *wall* needs is the horse suddenly dancing around in response to a swat on the neck or trying to duck an ear-mug.

Keep the horse (somewhat) awake. A really mellow near-doze is a good thing while a horse is being *shod*. But sometimes they will actually fall asleep, which can lead to them startling awake in a panic.

Keep the horse happy. If he likes to chew the lead rope, don't fuss with him over it. Bring a worn-out rope for him to chew on.

Distraction is often better than restraint. When a horse is getting too worried about what the farrier is doing, it often helps to speak to him, or even tap lightly on his forehead with your fingertips. Just enough to get him to swing his ears toward you.

horse mule: A male *mule*. Sterile due to being a hybrid, usually *gelded* for easier management.

horse nail: See: nail, horseshoe.

horseshoe: (1) A device affixed to the equine *hoof* to protect it from wear and damage, provide support, and/or alter its traction characteristics. Most modern horseshoes are made of *steel* or *aluminum* and affixed with *nails* driven through the *hoof horn*, but there are some types which are made of other materials and attached in other ways.

(2) Any thing possessing a shape reminiscent of a conventional horseshoe.
See: Page A-8.

horseshoe

horseshoe, conventional application: For some centuries, the standard means of affixing a *horseshoe* to the *equine hoof* has been by driving multiple *nails* through holes in the shoe into the bottom of the hoof, and out through the side of the *wall*, where the nail tips are cut-off and formed into *clinches*, allowing the nails to function as rivets, holding the shoe firmly in-place. If done properly, the nails pass only through insensitive *horn*, causing the animal no discomfort.

After the hoof has been properly *trimmed* into *balance*, a suitable shoe must be selected or *forged* then correctly fit for the hoof. It is considered good form to remove all hoof *flares*, then fit the shoe precisely to the perimeter of the wall around the toe and quarters. But, in practice, many *farriers* will leave some flare on until after the shoe has been nailed to maintain structural integrity of the wall during the nailing process and provide extra horn under the clinch. The experienced eye can assess where the base of support should be, and place the shoe accordingly.

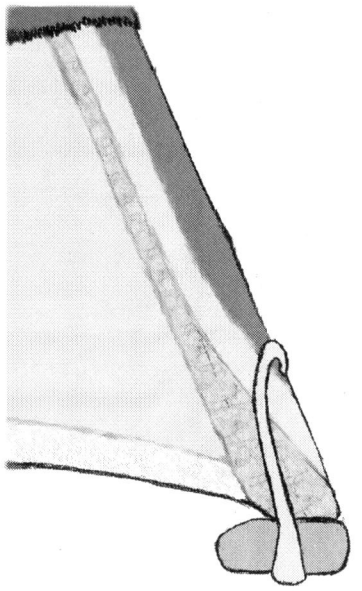

"Proper" shoeing approach has flare dressed away, then shoe applied. Note that the nail passes through scar laminae and soft inner horn, with little purchase in solid outer wall.

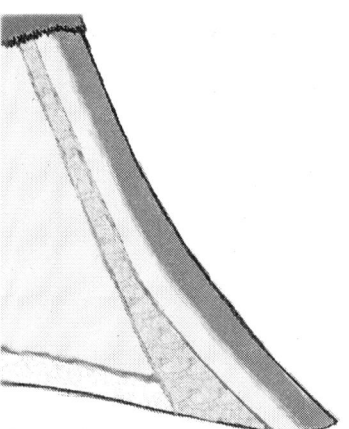

Cross-section of a badly flared hoof wall before shoeing..

Despite it's cosmetic flaws, applying the shoe before dubbing-off most of the flare allows the nail to pass through and be clinched into more solid material. Shoe placement is identical in both approaches.

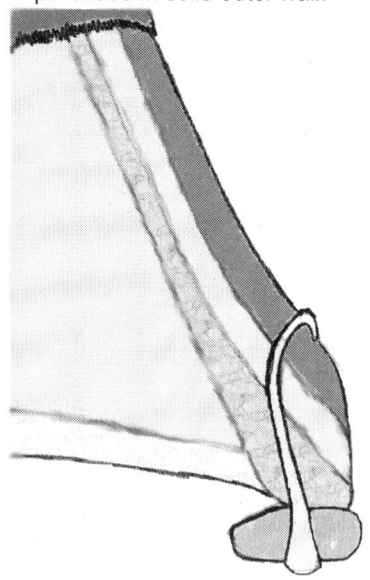

Millwater's Farriery

In most cases, it is advisable to fit the shoe slightly wider than the hoof from the quarters back to the heels to allow for *expansion*, and a little long at the heels to provide *posterior* support. *Boxing* wide/long fit heels will help prevent the shoes from being stepped or pulled off.

Horseshoeing nails are patterned or trademarked on one side of the head, and beveled at the point on the same side. Always inspect nails to make certain of this, as there is occasionally a manufacturing error, and driving a nail with the bevel on the wrong side of the point will likely cause a severe *quick*. Nails are driven with the marked facet of the head oriented towards the frog.

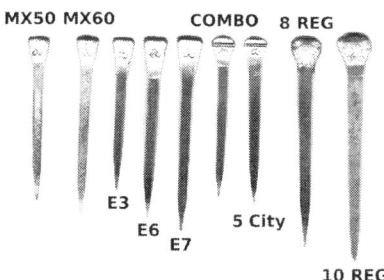

Assorted horseshoe nails.

There are a wide variety of horseshoe nails currently on the market. The most popular *keg shoes* for riding *horses* are punched for #5 City head. *Pony* shoes and *training plates* may take #3 1/2 or #4 1/2. Heavy *draft horse* shoes are often punched for #8 Regular head. Larger sizes are used for shoeing through thick pads on gaited horses. E or MX headed nails work well with hand-forged shoes. Slim blades and combo nails have become popular for use on thin-walled hooves. In all cases, the nail head should seat solidly into the hole, and project just slightly beyond the ground surface of the shoe.

It is often stated that nails must be started at the outer edge of the *white line* of the hoof, as any farther out will split the wall, and any farther inward will result in a quick. The latter is not actually true. Inspection of hooves immediately after shoes have been pulled will reveal that farriers often start their nails inside the white line, into the sole. (As the foot is largely covered by the shoe during nailing, the *horseshoer* doesn't have much of a view when starting his nails anyway.) These coarse-started nails will only quick the horse if they fail to traverse into the inner wall before reaching the level of the sensitive sole. If an appropriate shoe has been selected and correctly fit, the nail holes will probably be placed so as to be safely usable.

Nails are generally driven through the shoe into the foot at an angle slightly less sloped than the hoof at each point in the wall. This means the third nail back in each branch will be driven almost perpendicular to the plane of the shoe, while the toe nails should be driven with a bit more *pitch* inward. The hoof wall is wetter/softer on the inside and dryer/harder on the surface. When the tip of the nail begins to move into the relatively hard outer wall, it is possible to get the bevel to "bite" and turn the nail outward with a sharp, slightly off-center driving blow. With practice, one learns to hear and feel the way the nail drives, and can become proficient at steering it through the wall to consistently emerge at the desired height.

Unless the nail is disproportionately long for the foot, it is possible to drive the full length of the shaft into the hoof without quicking the horse. This is not done intentionally, as it would not allow for a clinch to be formed. But, if it is done accidentally, the nail can be removed, and another driven in its place, either at a more upright pitch, or with the tip slightly pre-bent to make it easier to turn at the desired height.

The nail on the right has had its tip bent to make it easier to "turn" and emerge through the wall.

Ideally, all the nails will emerge through the outer wall at the same height, so that the clinches will be in an even line around an inch up from the shoe. In practical terms, each nail needs to emerge high enough to have enough wall below to support a tight clinch, but not so high that there isn't enough nail left to form the clinch properly. Perfectly even clinches are a sign of good workmanship, but may need to be sacrificed in order to place clinches securely in a damaged hoof wall.

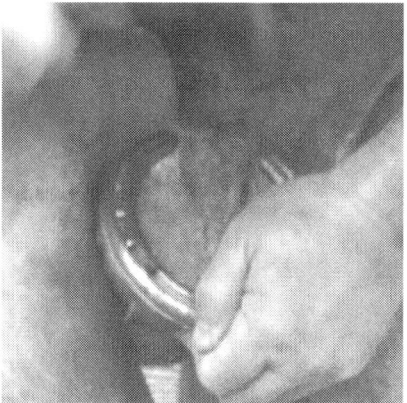

Each nail driven tends to shift the shoe inward. Driving the *medial* toe nail shifts the shoe towards *lateral* heel. Driving the lateral third nail shifts the shoe towards the medial side of the hoof. The greater the pitch of the nail driven, the more noticeable the effect. Each nail driven partially secures the shoe, and reduces the shifting effect of subsequent nails. Understanding the way the shoe tends to shift during nailing can enable a horseshoer to make minor corrections in shoe placement by altering the order in which he drives his nails.

Immediately after each nail is driven, its tip should be bent-down or wrung-off with the hammer to reduce the hazard the exposed point presents to the horseshoer and the animal.

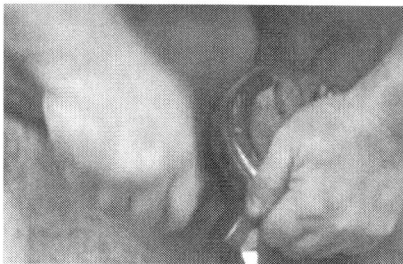
Nails should immediately be bent-down or wrung-off after driving.

One effective approach to nailing on a shoe is to place the shoe precisely into position, then push the tip of the third nail on one side firmly into the foot. Concentrate on keeping the nail from slipping against the foot until it can be driven about halfway in, and don't be concerned if the shoe slips a little out of place. With the first driven nail acting as a pivot point, swing the shoe back into place and start the third nail on the other branch. (The third nails are in the relatively upright quarters of the hoof, so seating the nails there will move the shoe least.) When the third nail on each side is partially driven, quickly evaluate which direction the shoe needs to go to be perfectly centered. If the shoe needs to shift medially, drive the lateral nail home first, or vice versa. Then drive the opposite nail home.

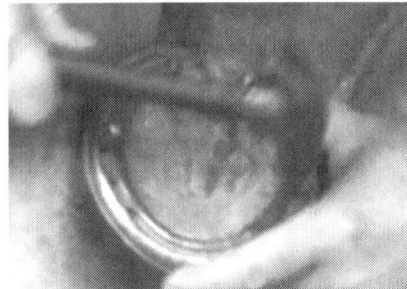

Starting with the third nails back.

When using clipped horseshoes, it may be advisable to start with the toe nails, as this will push the shoe back on the foot, pulling the clip(s) tightly against the wall.

After at least one nail has been driven home in each branch, it is possible to set the foot down if necessary. But do not allow the horse to walk around much, or paw the ground, as the shoe is not fully secured at this point.

Riding horses are usually shod with at least three nails in each branch of the shoe, although two may be sufficient in some cases. To allow for expansion, it is usually preferable to place nails forward of the the widest part of the foot, which means one or both heel nail holes may be left empty, especially in front shoes. (The most popular light horse keg shoes are punched with four nail holes per branch. #000 and pony shoes have three. Draft shoes often have five or more.)

Until all nails are in-place and bent-over or wrung-off, they should only be driven until the heads are lightly home in their holes. The harder blows needed to fully seat the heads may annoy some horses, so wait until you're just about ready to set the foot down and seat all the heads at once.

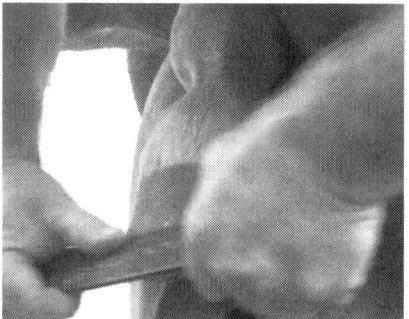

Undercutting the nails with the corner of a rasp before clinches are formed.

If the nail points were not wrung-off, they may now be snipped off with nail nippers. (Hoof *nippers* should not be used for this purpose, as nails will quickly ruin them.) A small, horizontal notch should be cut into the wall just below each nail's exit point with either the corner of a *rasp* or a driven **clinch gouge**. This discourages hoof wall splitting during the clinching process, and allows the clinch to be seated into the wall.

the wall if the clinchers are used too aggressively. Alternatively, a clinch may be started by holding a **clinch block** or heavy **pullers** firmly against the wall and the cut-off nail end while the nail head is struck with a hammer.

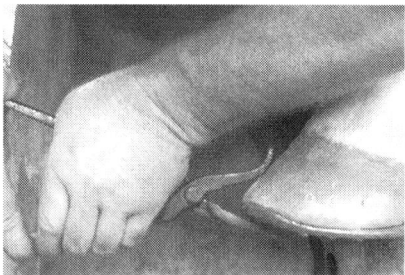
Clinch being made with clinchers.

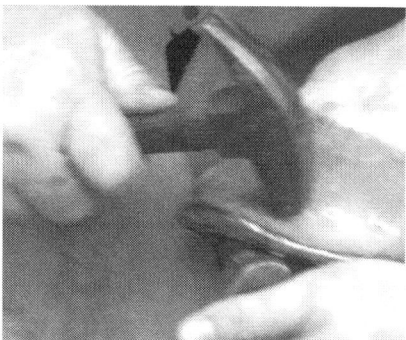
Tightening the clinches down.

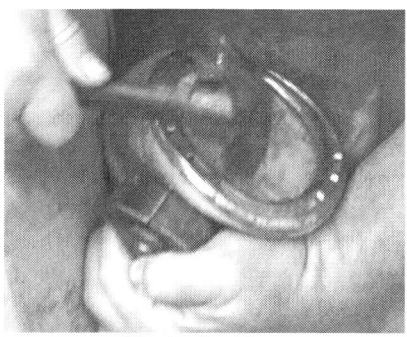
Block clinching.

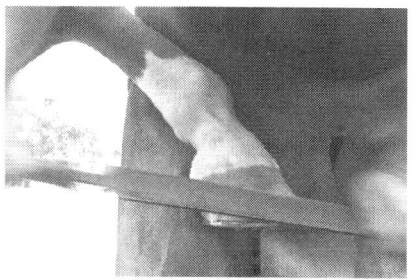
Smoothing the clinches and finishing the hoof.

The clinches are usually formed with a pair of **clinchers**, with the straight jaw positioned against the nail head, and the curved jaw being used to roll down the cut-off end of the nail. This task requires some finesse, as it may be possible to rip the nail through

The clinches may be tightened by placing a clinch block or heavy pullers under the nail heads and lightly tapping the clinch into the face of the wall with the hammer. Care should be taken to strike the nails, not the wall itself. The clinches should then be rounded and smoothed with the fine side of a rasp, but not thinned too much, lest they become too weak to keep the shoe tight. The rasp may also be used to remove wall that hangs out over the shoe at this point.

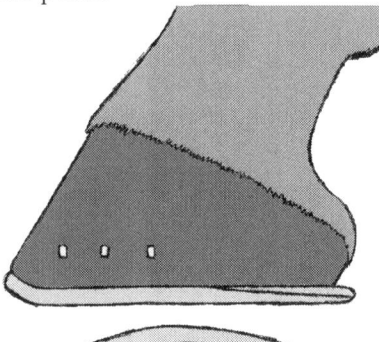

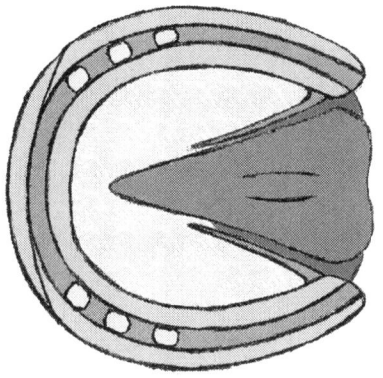

Theoretically ideal horseshoe application with centered shoe placement, even clinches, shoe heels extending beyond buttresses without covering frog, all nails forward of the widest part of the hoof, allowance for expansion, breakover eased, and heel quarters well boxed

Wax or a modern *sealant* may be applied over the clinches to help prevent the nails from providing a point of entry for fungi and bacteria into the wall.

All horseshoers occasionally quick a horse while nailing. It is usually sufficient to remove and omit the offending nail and flush the hole with a syringe of Betadine or similar mild iodine solution. The owner or caretaker should be informed so that the horse can be kept out of mud and other conditions which may cause infection for a few days.

See: balancing the horse's hoof; keg shoe, fitting; horseshoe, forging; horseshoe, removal; Pages A-2, A-6, A-8.

horseshoe, forging: With the wide availability of many brands and types of premanufactured *horseshoes*, most modern *farriers* rarely find it necessary to produce *handmade* horseshoes from *bar stock*. But the ability to *forge* good handmade shoes is still considered a requirement for *journeyman* farriers, as the skills needed to do so are also essential to modifying *keg shoes* for proper application. Some farriers still use handmade horseshoes for all their shoeing.

There are many effective approaches to forging a horseshoe. Some of these are based on completing the shoe in the minimum number of "heats", but this is less important when forging shoes in *pairs* or *sets*, as the farrier is always busy with one shoe as the others are being heated in the *forge*, so there is little time wasted.

One approach to forging a shoe is as follows; Measure and cut a piece of appropriate bar stock to length. A rule of thumb for estimating the length of stock needed is to measure the circumference of the *hoof* from one heel around to the other, then subtract two inches for most riding-sized horses being shod with typical (around 3/4" wide) stock. It is, of course, better to err on the side of too long than too short, as the shoe can always be cut down if needed.

Fullering or *swedging* can be done while the stock is still straight. Fullering can be cut from *coarse* at the middle (which will be the toe) to *fine* at the ends (which will be the heels), but many farriers prefer to fuller straight down the center of the *web* and accommodate the relative thicknesses of different parts of the *hoof wall* by *pitching* their *nail* holes later. The shoe can instead be *creased* after being *turned*, but if fullered while straight, the stretching effect of the turning process tends to minimize the appearance of flaws in the fullering.

After fullering or swedging (if used), the turning of the shoe begins with the toe bend. It is often useful to think of the toe bend as two bends, one near each side of the toe, and allow the broader arc of the toe between these two bends to happen as a by-product.

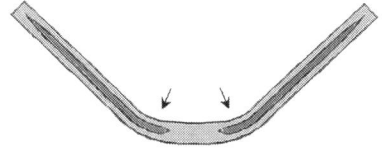

On a fore shoe, the two toe bends are farther apart and the overall toe bend is broader than on the hind.

Next, the heel of one branch is hammer-formed, then the branch is turned.

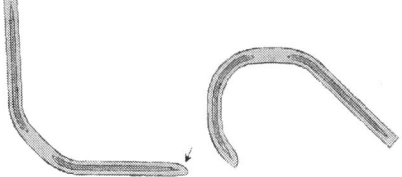

Order is important here, as it is difficult to properly form a heel after the branch is turned, and virtually impossible to do so after both branches are turned. The curve of the branch and heel tend to be more gradual on fore hooves than on hinds, where the branch is often nearly straight and the heels may turn inward more abruptly.

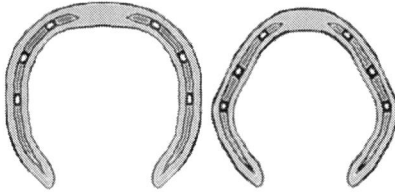

After the second heel is formed and its branch turned, the nail holes can be punched. Even if the shoe is fullered or swedged, it may be advisable to start the nail holes by stamping them with a forepunch before punching them through with a pritchel over the *pritchel hole* of the *anvil*. The heel nail holes should be placed at the widest point of the shoe and made nearly perpendicular. The toe nails are usually best placed at each toe bend, near the front of the quarter area and given the greatest pitch. One or two additional nail holes are usually punched in each branch, evenly spaced between the toe and heel nail holes and given an intermediate pitch. Nail hole position may be adapted to allow for quarter *clips* or to avoid damaged sections of hoof wall.

As the shoe is being leveled, the inner edge of the hoof-facing side should be hammer beveled, especially at the toe, to prevent the shoe from pressing against the sole of the hoof, and the heels and heel quarters of the shoe should be *boxed*.
See: Pages A-2; A-7; A-8.

horseshoeing: See: horseshoe, removal; hoof anatomy, basic; balancing the horse's hoof; trimming technique, basic; horseshoe, forging; keg shoe, fitting; eagle eye; horseshoe, conventional application.

horseshoer: Any person who applies *horseshoes* to *horses' hooves*. This term does not imply any particular level of skill, and may refer to a very good *farrier*, an incompetent hack, or anyone in between.

horseshoe, removal: First the *clinches* need to be eliminated, lest they damage the *hoof wall* while being pulled-through. This may be done by filing them off with the fine side of a *rasp*. Each clinch should be filed individually, to avoid excessive removal of hoof surface which may occur when one attempts to rasp across multiple clinches with each stroke.

The clinches may instead be sheared-off or straightened by placing the edge of a *clinch cutter* against the wall, just under the clinch, then driving it upward (toward the *coronary band*) with a hammer.

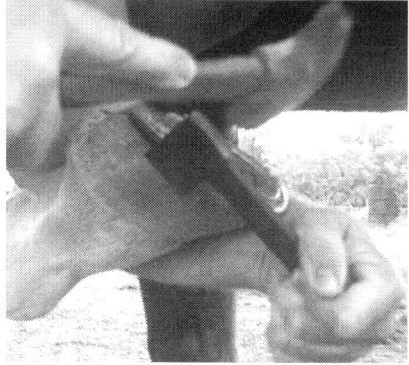

Clinch cutter shearing off clinches.

The hoof is placed between one's knees (forelimb) or across the lap (hind) so that both hands may be employed for shoe pulling. The jaws of the *pullers* are closed around one branch of the horseshoe at the heel. The jaws sliding between the hoof and shoe start the loosening process. Once the jaws are closed, one hand should support the toe of the hoof while the other swings the puller reins forward, further loosening that side of the shoe. The process is then be repeated at the other heel. Alternate from side to side, moving the pullers a bit towards the toe each time. Caution should be taken to avoid biting through the *nails* with the puller jaws, as they should come away with the shoe. Do not attempt to pull the shoe with a few mighty yanks. "Walk" it of with many mild lever swings, always supporting the hoof with your free hand to avoid causing the *horse* discomfort.

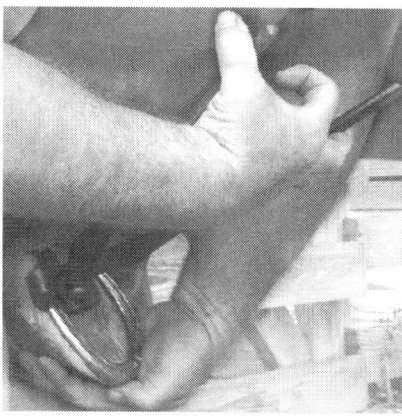

Supporting the toe while employing pullers... If you need more than one hand to lever off the shoe, you are pulling too hard.

Pads, heartbars, and other shoe packages may make using the pullers problematic. In such cases, a crease nail puller can be used to remove the nails one at a time. This may be the preferred approach for inexperienced persons pulling ordinary shoes, as it is easier, if slower, than using pullers.

In cases where the pullers should not be used in the usual

way, and the crease nail puller won't work (perhaps due to worn nail heads or shoes without *fullering, creasing,* or *swedging*), the clinch cutter blade may be carefully driven between the hoof and shoe package from the side, near the heel, to slightly loosen the shoe. Tapping the shoe back against the bottom of the hoof should then raise the nail heads enough to allow them to be pulled one at the time with the pullers.

Ideally, the nails will be removed with the shoe. If any are left behind in the hoof, they should be removed before trimming, as they will damage *nipper* blades.

See: Page A-6; A-8; horseshoe, conventional application.

horseshoe, repair: The best shod horse can still manage to step-on or snag a *horseshoe*, pulling it partially or completely off. Fortunately, it does not take the skills or tools of a competent *farrier* to do a serviceable job of putting the hoof back to right until a *professional* is available.

The tools required are a *rasp, pullers,* wire brush, light driving hammer, heavier hammer, and something to use as an *anvil*. A section of railroad track, piece of heavy steel plate, or a machinist's vise are adequate anvil substitutes for this task. All that is needed is something solid with a reasonably flat top surface. Chaps, sturdy boots, and safety glasses are recommended. A small supply of appropriate *nails* (#5 City Head for most riding horses) will be needed.

A handy "anvil" for the lay-horseman.

First the shoe will need to be removed, if this has not already been done by the horse. (See *horseshoe, removal*.) Any nails left behind in the foot will need to be removed as cleanly as possible.

Pulled shoes are usually bent away from the *hoof* on the stepped-on or snagged branch. The fit of the shoe is usually retained, so it only needs to be re-leveled. After removing the nails from the shoe and wire brushing the dirt off of it, place the bent-down branch hoof-side up onto your "anvil". The bent shoe should form an arch supported by the anvil at two points. Strike down on the shoe between these points with the heavy hammer to drive the top of the arch down. Move the shoe around on the anvil face, driving down high spots, until the shoe is as level as you can get it. When held against the foot, the toe and both heels of the shoe must make contact with the hoof. A slight gap at the quarters, while undesirable, may not prevent the shoe from being adequately secured.

Wire brush the bottom of the hoof clean and hold it in the shoeing position. (Between your knees with fore hooves, across the lap for hinds.) Set the shoe onto the foot and place a nail through the third hole back in one branch of the shoe, being sure to orient the nail with the trademark facing inward. Search around until you find the hole left by the original nail with the tip of your new nail, then push it in with your thumb. Do the same on at the third hole back on the other branch. Use your light hammer to tap one nail home. It should easily follow the path established by the original nail. Bend the protruding nail tip over, then do the same with the nail on the other side. Now the remaining nail holes in the shoe should be directly over the established nail paths in the hoof, so tapping nails through should be a simple matter. See *horseshoe, conventional application* for nail seating and the block method of *clinching* and tightening.

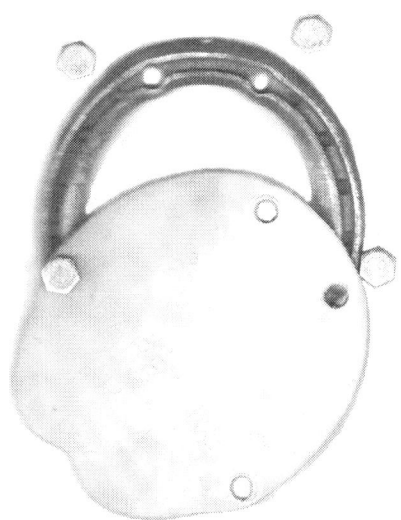

hospital plate

hospital plate: A plastic or metal plate which is affixed to the ground-facing surface of a *horseshoe* after it is nailed to the *hoof*. Because the plate can be removed without pulling the shoe, the sole and frog can be easily treated or disinfected between shoeings. Because the thickness of the shoe separates the plate from the sole of the hoof, great protection can be provided without the risk of sole pressure that can sometimes occur with conventional *pads*.

hotblood: Athletic, fine-boned, thin-coated *horses* which developed in the warmer climates of the Middle East. The classic Arabian is a modern example of the hotblood type. Although *thoroughbreds* have some *coldblood* in their ancestry, they are usually classed as hotbloods as well. Hotbloods are known for speed, elegance, beauty, and excitable disposition.

hot nail: See: close nail; quick.

hot set: To briefly press a hot *horseshoe* against the bottom of a *horse's hoof*. This is traditionally done as an aid to leveling the hoof and shoe, and to burn *clips* into the hoof *wall*. Hot setting has also been recommended as a way to kill surface germs and to seal the perimeter of the sole. A healthy hoof with normal thickness of sole can withstand a horseshoe at dull red heat for several seconds without the horse feeling any discomfort, but uninitiated horses may react to the sound and smoke generated during a hot set.

hot setting

hot shoe: Horseshoeing with the aid of a *forge*. May involve fabricating the *horseshoes* from *bar stock* and/or *hot setting*.

hyaline (hī'ə-lēn): Glassy or transparent. Particularly the substance which covers the ends of bone at a joint.

hybrid: The offspring of parents who are of different species. The most common *equine* hybrids are the *mule* and *hinny*, both of which are normally sterile.

hydrated lime: See: lime, hydrated.

hypertrophy (hī-pûr-trō'fē): Increase in tissue volume resulting from the enlargement of existing cells.

hypothesis (hī-poth'i-sis): An educated guess that seems to fit the available evidence.
See also: Scientific process.

HYPP: Hyperkalemic periodic paralysis: A genetic disease among American quarter *horses* and associated breeds. The gene is dominant, so either parent can pass it and the disease on to a *foal*. The disease causes tremors, weakness, collapse, and occasionally sudden death, but the frequency and severity of symptoms varies greatly between individuals. The HYPP gene is closely associated with Impressive, an enormously popular *AQHA* sire of the 1970s and 80s. Genetic testing can identify the mutant gene, and is required by some registries for Impressive descendants.
a.k.a: Impressive syndrome.

IC/ICF: Intern Classification (or Certification) Farrier. An *AFA* recognition for student and novice horseshoers. The IC examination was similar in format to the *CF* exam, but had longer time limits and no forge work. Sub-passing scores on the CF exam could be accepted as part of the IC exam. Now replaced with "AFA Farrier".

IM: Intramuscular. To inject deep into a muscle.

Impressive syndrome:
See: HYPP.

improver: Used is some European *smithies* to describe a *farrier* whose status within the trade is between that of an *apprentice* and a *journeyman*.

interdigitate: To fold or lock together, as when the fingers of one hand are laced between those of the other. This term describes the manner in which the *horny* and sensitive *laminae* interlock within the *hoof*.

interfering: (1) Generally describes any *hoof* which strikes another of the *horse's legs* in movement as a result of a fault in *gait*.
(2) Specifically, collision between paired legs.

intern: One who completes a specified academic requirement, then embarks on a formal *apprenticeship*. Spelled "interne" as a verb.

in vitro (in vē'trō): In the glass. Describes an experiment or procedure done outside of the animal's body, often in a test tube or petri dish.

iron [Ango-Saxon *iren* or *isen*; Sanskrit *ayas*]: **(1)** A metallic, electroconductive element. Atomic number 26. Atomic weight 55.847.
(2) Wrought iron was a common form of impure iron with a fibrous structure. It was workable cold, resisted burning, and forge *welded* easily.
(3) Mild *steel*, which replaced wrought iron in general use during the 20th Century, is often called iron.

iron age: The development of *iron* smelting and *blacksmithing*, which occurred circa 1200 BC in Europe, was of such technological and social importance that historians and archaeologists mark it as the start of the final era of antiquity prior to the collapse of the Roman Empire and subsequent Middle Ages.

iron, dietary: *Iron* is essential to the transport and storage of oxygen within the body. Severe and/or prolonged iron deficiency will cause anemia.

ischemia (is-kē′mē-ə): Lack of oxygenated blood flow to the tissues.

-itis: Suffix meaning inflammation or disease.

IUJH: International Union of Journeyman Horseshoers. A *farrier* trade union started in 1874 as the Journeyman Horseshoers National Union. The name was changed to its current form in 1893. In 1934 the primary emphasis of the IUJH shifted from *draft horses* to track horse shoeing.
a.k.a: JHU; Platers Union.

IV: Intravenous. To administer (as with a drug) directly into the vein.

jack: A male *ass*.
a.k.a.: jackass.

jammed heel: One heel appears to be jammed up into the foot, with its bulb and *coronary band* correspondingly distorted.

jar calk: Short, narrow *calks* that are riveted, *brazed*, or *welded* onto the ground face of a *horseshoe*. Jar calks may be installed at any point on a shoe, and are often placed across the *web* to achieve asymmetrical *gait correction* in race *horses*. Jar calks are also used at the heels of jumping horses' front shoes, placed either in-line with the direction of travel or the middle of the web, to function in a manner similar to the rudder of a boat, preventing the *hoof* from sliding side-to-side on landing.

jar calks (jumping type)

JEB: Junctional Epidermolysis Bullosa. A genetic disease among Belgian *draft horses* and American Saddlebreds. The gene is recessive. If both parents are carriers, the *foal* has a 25% chance of developing the disease, a 50% chance of being a recessive carrier, and a 25% chance of not inheriting the gene at all. The disease results in the sloughing of skin and *hooves*, and is fatal within two weeks of birth. Genetic testing is available to allow breeders to avoid mating carriers to one-another. A foal with only one carrier parent has no chance of developing the disease, and only a 50% chance of inheriting the gene.

jenny: A female *ass*.
a.k.a.: jennet

JHU: See: IUJH.

jog: A slow, relaxed *trot*. The term is used primarily by *western*-style riders and in western pleasure show classes. Although this is specifically cautioned against in the *AQHA* rule book, it is not uncommon to see western pleasure horses moving in a non-*diagonal gait* when they are supposed to be jogging. *Walking* in the back and jogging in the front in an attempt to move forward as slowly as possible.

john mule: A male *mule*. Sterile due to being a *hybrid*, usually *gelded* for easier management.
a.k.a.: Horse mule.

journeyman [French *journée*, a day's work. From Latin *diurnus*, daily]: **(1)** A person who has completed an *apprenticeship* and is free to sell his labor to the *master* of any shop willing to hire him. Due to the mobile, independent nature of the modern horseshoer, the traditional journeyman *farrier* is rare today.
(2) A fully competent workman.
See also: RJF; CJF.

Juniata: Brand of *horseshoes*. *Handmade* from 1824 to 1859, then machine made until 1925.

keg shoe: A conventional, factory made *horseshoe*.
See: Page A-8.

keg shoe, fitting: Most common factory *horseshoes* are manufactured in a *compromise pattern*, and sometimes advertised as being ready to apply to both front and hind *hooves* with little or no modification. In recent years, front and hind pattern shoes have become more widely available, but competent *farriers* will always treat keg shoes as blanks to be custom-fit to each *horse*.

Most brands of keg shoe are sized on a scale which makes #1 appropriate for a typical, average-sized riding horse. Larger hooves take higher number sizes, with #3 or #4 being large *warmblood* to small *draft horse* sizes. Below #1, keg shoes are sized #0, #00, and #000. (Usually spoken as "aught", "double-aught", and "triple-aught".) Sizes below #000, when available, switch to *"pony"* size numbers.

A shoe which amply covers the full perimeter of the trimmed hoof should be selected. There is often a slight size difference between hooves in a *pair*, so the shoe size that fits the larger of the hooves should be used on both. It is not uncommon for the hind hooves to take a size smaller than the fronts. If the *off* and *near* hooves of a pair cannot take the same size shoe, *high/low syndrome* is indicated.

Once the appropriate size has been determined, the shoe can be shaped either *hot* or *cold*, usually with a hammer and *anvil* or *stalljack*. There are several basic techniques for manipulating shoe shape.

Straightening is done by resting two points on the inner edge of the shoe against the anvil, then striking the outer edge. Hooking/bending is done by positioning the larger portion of the shoe below a *turning hole or cam*, with the branch or heel to be bent protruding up and through to be hammered. Opening is done by resting the shoe heels on surfaces of the anvil (the side of the body and the face) with differing slopes and striking the toe. Closing is done by setting the edge of one branch on the anvil and striking the opposite branch, driving them towards one-another.

which would necessitate re-punching.

Straightening a shoe branch on the anvil's heel.

Opening the shoe.

Using the turning hole to add bend to the heel quarter of the shoe.

Closing (narrowing) the shoe.

Care should be taken to direct hard hammer blows and sharp bends between *nail* holes to avoid crushing them out of shape,

The common front pattern can be made by straightening the center of the toe (to make it broader), adding bend at each side of the toe, usually just before and behind the toe nail holes, and slightly hooking the heels.

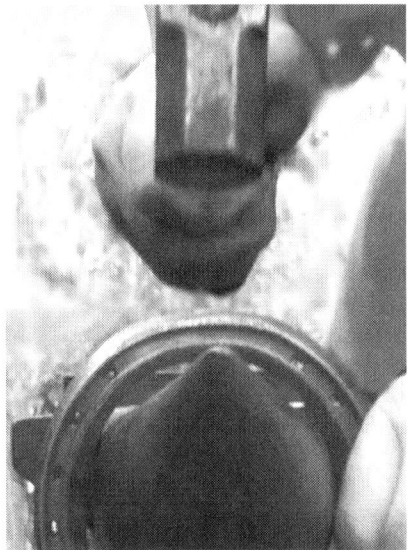

Straightening (emboldening) the toe of a front shoe on the anvil's horn.

The common hind pattern can be made by straightening the toe quarters, hooking the heels a bit, then closing the shoe to width.

Leveling the shoe can be done by observing the shoe with the hoof-side up to determine which branch is bowed downward. Place that branch, and as much of that side of the shoe as will fit, against the anvil face and strike with overlapping blows on the hoof-facing side of the shoe until that branch is slightly bowed-up. Then shift the other branch onto the face and work its hoof-facing side until it's back to even with the first side.

Focusing the leveling blows to the inner *web* of the hoof-facing surface of the shoe from the heel nails forward will seat the shoe web away from the sole, reducing the chance for harmful sole pressure. It will also tend to *pitch the nail holes*, which are usually punched perpendicular on keg shoes out of the box.

Light horseshoes, especially *training plates*, may be more securely applied if they are not perfectly level, but rest on the toe and heels of the hoof with a slight gap between the shoe and quarters.

Shoe fitting can be practiced extensively without supervision at no risk to any horses, and with no cost beyond a pile of mangled horseshoes, which can be straightened and re-turned repeatedly. So there is no excuse for the aspiring horseshoer's skills in this area to be lacking, even early in his career.

See: horseshoe, forging; balancing the horse's hoof; eagle eye; Pages A-2; A-7; A-8; A-12.

Page 108.

keratin [Greek *keratos,* horn]: The tough protein component in horn, hair, skin, and *hooves.*

keratoma: A tumor of the horny *laminae.* Often seen as an inward distortion of the *white line.*
a.k.a: keraphyllocele. See: Page A-2.

knee hitting: *Interference* in which the fore *hoof* strikes the inside of the knee of the opposite *limb.* Called *speedy cutting* in some texts circa 1900.
See: Page A-3.

knock knees: See: carpus valgus.

Kutrite: See: borium.

lame: Describes a *horse* who is suffering sufficient pain and/or mechanical defect to interfere with normal movement and weight bearing in one or more *limbs.* Limping.

lamella (plural lamellae): **See:** lamina.

lamina (lam′i-nə) (plural laminae): The tissues which attach the *PIII* and *lateral cartilages* to the *hoof wall.* The inner laminae are attached to the bone and are called sensitive laminae. The outer laminae are attached to the wall and are called *horny* laminae. With magnification from the *solar* viewpoint, the horny and sensitive laminae can be seen to be folded together or *interdigitated*. The unique structure of the laminae give the PIII/hoof wall union several square feet of attachment surface while allowing the wall to grow down in relation to the bone.
a.k.a: lamella.
See: hoof anatomy, basic; Page A-5.

laminitis (lam-i-nī′tis)**:** An aspect of a systemic illness in the *horse* which may involve the malfunction of the *AVAs* in the *hooves* and extreme chemical imbalance in the laminar tissues. The blood flow through the hoof may be increased (hot hooves with pounding pulse are often observed), but is diverted away from the fine *capillaries* which supply the *laminae.* The combination of high temperature and capillary *ischemia* results in the death of laminar tissue and disintegration of the *basement membrane*, causing the horse pain. Laminitis can be initiated by binge feeding (especially massive carbohydrate intake), poisoning, retained afterbirth, hormonal imbalance, allergic reaction, reaction to drugs, and various other forms of stress on the animal.

Cooling the hooves may enable the laminae to withstand the ischemia until the episode has passed, and may arrest the inflammation of the *anterior* laminae. This can prevent the *PIII* from being pushed backwards in the *hoof capsule* by the laminar swelling, thus avoiding damage to the *chondrocoronal ligament apparatus* and resultant *sinking*. The traditional remedy of standing the *horse* in water just over belly deep has merit in that it cools the feet and allows buoyancy to relieve some of the load.

Laminitis can lead to *founder*. Physical stresses on the hooves should be minimized until the *acute* phase passes. Very deep bedding and stall rest, with the horse being allowed to lay down much of the time, is usually advisable.

Even if the animal pulls through the laminitis attack and regains vitality and appetite without progressing into apparent founder, it is best to keep to a grass hay diet with plenty of clean water for several days to aid in detoxification before building back up to regular feeding. The hooves will also need to be closely monitored over the following months.

See: autointoxication; Cushing's disease; hoof anatomy, basic; Pages A-2; A-5.

lateral: **(1)** The outer side, away from the centerline. Opposite of *medial*.
(2) On the same side of the *horse*; such as the *near* foreleg and the near hind.
(3) Towards or on the side of something.

lateral cartilages: *Cartilage* structures which extend, one from either side, rearward from the wings of the *PIII*. These form the internal support for the *posterior* part of the *hoof*.
a.k.a: collateral cartilages.

lateral gait: Both *off limbs* move in unison, as do both *near* limbs. A pace is a good example of a lateral *gait*.

leg: The *equine limb* from the knee or hock down.
See: Page A-3.

leg vise: A form of *vise* traditionally used in a *smithy*. The "leg" support anchored into the floor made a relatively lightweight vise extremely solid and durable. The spring design took the thread play out of clamping work.

leg vise

L.H.L.T: Low Heel, Long Toe: A condition in *equine* hooves in which the heels are excessively low due to *trimming*, wear, or *underrun* growth; and the toe is excessively long, often in the form of a *flare*. L.H.L.T. is known to contribute to *navicular disease* and *gait* defects such as *forging* and *overreaching*.

It must be remembered that the heel and toe are part of the same *hoof* when dealing with this condition. Simply raising the low heels with a *wedge*, or mounting *eggbar* shoes, without correcting the underlying hoof form will usually make matters worse by crushing the heels further.

L.H.L.T. can be thought of as the whole *solar* plane of the hoof slipping forward relative to the internal structures. The underrun heels collapse on landing, driving the plane forward, then leverage on the long toe pulls it forward during *breakover*. Both aspects must be managed simultaneously. The toe of the hoof must be dressed back, then breakover should be enhanced by beveling up the bare foot, or fitting a *set-back*, *rolled toe*, or *rockered toe* horseshoe. The underrun, crushed heels must be trimmed back to the widest point of the frog to eliminate the crushing leverage on landing and loading. If this results in a *broken back hoof-pastern axis*, a wedge can be used to restore alignment. A *heartbar* or *Thera-Flex* insert in heartbar configuration can be used to unload the heels to allow them to regenerate. **a.k.a:** L.T.L.H.

See also: balancing the horse's hoof; hoof anatomy, basic.

ligament: Strong fibrous tissues which connect bones to one another. (Except for *check ligaments*, which connect *tendon* to bone.) Ligaments are subject to sprains and tears.

limb: The entire *equine* appendage, from the scapula or hip down.
See: Page A-3.

lime, hydrated: Calcium hydroxide, a white powder which is generally safe to handle, as opposed to quick lime, which is dangerous. Hydrated lime is alkaline, and can be used to disinfect and counter urine acidity in stall floors, which may decrease *thrush* and other *hoof* infections. A thin layer of lime is usually applied to the bare stall floor before new bedding is added.
a.k.a.: garden lime.

line gaited: Describes a *horse* who *trots* with each hind *hoof* following directly in line with its *lateral* fore hoof.
See also: passing gaited.

London pattern: A basic *anvil* design with a horn at one end, a heel at the other, and a flat face on the top. Most *blacksmith* and *farrier* anvils made in the last few centuries are derived from the London pattern, although double-horned and other anvil patterns are still seen occasionally.
See: Page A-7.

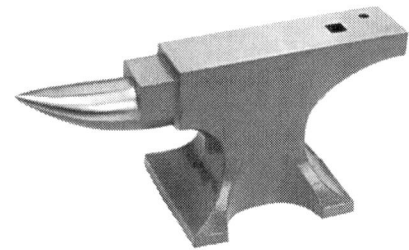

London pattern anvil

lope: A slow, relaxed *canter*. The term is used primarily by *western*-style riders and in western pleasure show classes. Although this is specifically cautioned against in the *AQHA* rule book, it is not uncommon to see western pleasure *horses* moving in an odd four-beat manner when they are supposed to be loping. *Walking* in the back and sort of hopping in the front to mimic the loping stride while moving forward as slowly as possible.

luxate [from Greek *loxos*, slanting]: To put out of joint or dislocate.

malnutrition: Significantly inappropriate diet. This is not limited to underfeeding, but also includes overfeeding and excessive or insufficient amounts of individual nutrients in the diet.

mare: A female *horse*, usually four years or older.

Mark Fisher: First American *anvils* in 1843. Cast *steel* faces welded to a cast *iron* bodies, rather than forged anvils.

shoe prepared for a **masselotte clip**

masselotte clip: A *clip* which is drawn without a source hole or divot in the *horseshoe*. This is done by *upsetting* the *bar stock* in the area where the clip will be placed, then *forging* the extra mass into an outward projection as the shoe is turned. This projection is then formed into a clip. This approach allows for a relatively wide, high, thick clip to be made without creating a weak spot in the shoe.
a.k.a: massolette.
See also: horseshoe, forging.

master: (1) Traditionally, a tradesman who is proprietor of his own business. Especially if that business employs others.
(2) A practitioner whose level of knowledge, skill, and experience is far beyond what is required for ordinary competence.
(3) A trainer of *apprentices.*
See also: RMF.

McClellan saddle

McClellan saddle: A medium weight saddle with a leather or rawhide covered rigid, wooden frame and the seat open between the bars. Introduced into American military service by General George McClellan in the mid 19th Century and used by US cavalry well into the 20th Century. The saddle provides better weight distribution than *English* saddles, and is lighter than many *western* style stock saddles. The design, often somewhat modified, has become popular with endurance trail riders.

medial: Toward the center-line of the animal. The inner half of the *limb*.
See also: lateral.

mediolateral balance: Describes the distribution of loading over the *medial* and *lateral* halves of the *hoof*.

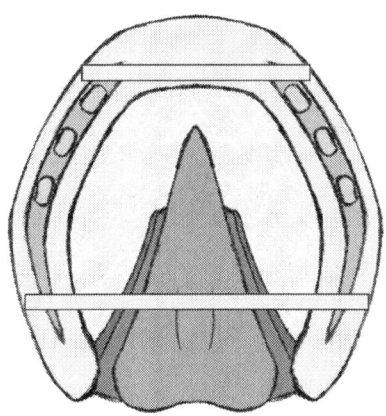

Memphis bar shoe

Memphis bar shoe: A *horseshoe* with bars welded across the ground facing surface. There are usually two bars, one just forward of the heels, the other set back from the toe. The toe bar may be set somewhat diagonally across the shoe to force off-center *breakover* to correct *gait* defects. This shoe creates a two-stage landing and strongly directed breakover. Once popular on harness track horses, still occasionally used on *gaited horses*.

mesaxonic: Species with an enlarged third *digit* which bears a large portion of the load for each *limb*. *Equines* are the most extreme mesaxonic species, having lost all but the third digit on each limb.

molly: A female *mule*. Normally sterile due to being a *hybrid*.

Monday morning disease: Describes *azoturia* in working *horses* who, although generally fit for their jobs, experience problems when returning to regular use after a day or two of inactivity. Can usually be prevented by cutting back or eliminating corn and sweetfeed during the horse's days off, and turning him out for free exercise.

morphology: The study of biological structures without consideration for their function.

mule: A *hybrid* produced by breeding a *jackass* to a *mare*. Mules tend to inherit size and tractable nature from the *horse*, while inheriting toughness, strength, and sureness of foot from the *ass*. Mules are considerably stronger for their size than horses, but not as fast on good footing. Mules can be more difficult to handle than horses, and have a reputation for being stubborn. Mule trainers argue that the difficulty in handling mules stems from their superior intelligence.

mule

The physical form of mules splits the difference between horse and ass, with some mules being more horse-like, while other individuals more closely resemble the ass. Their *hooves* are usually upright with large frogs. Their ears are usually much longer than the horse's. Mules may nicker and whinny like horses, bray like asses, or combine the horse and ass vocalizations. Mules range in size from miniature to *draft*, and are used under saddle and in harness. Because they are hybrids of two different species, mules are normally born sterile. There have, however, been reports of rare fertile females.

see also: horse mule, molly, hinny.

muled heels: Paired *extended heels* on a *horseshoe*.

mule foot: A narrow *hoof* with straight quarters and a large frog.

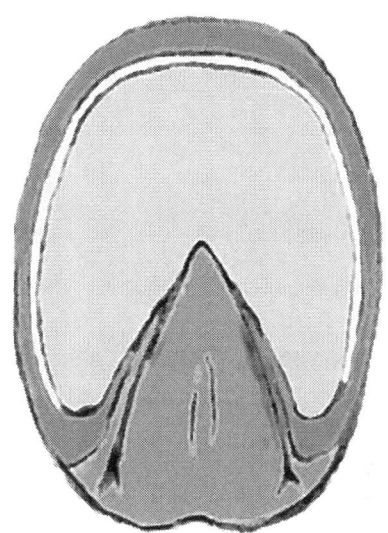

mule foot

Mustad: Sweden-based horseshoe *nail* manufacturer since 1885. Mustad currently owns *Capewell* and Cooper horseshoe nail companies, as well as a division which produces glue-on *horseshoes* and polyurethane-clad *aluminum* horseshoes. Mustad also produces *hoof* treatment chemicals and horseshoe *calks*.

mustang: A *feral horse*. American mustangs are originally descended from domestic horses brought to the New World by Europeans starting at the end of the Fifteenth Century. Escaped domestic horses have added new blood to the mustang gene pool over the centuries. Natural selection has favored mustangs who are hardy, short, stout, and *sound*, with solid *hooves* and thick *walls*. Captured mustangs can be trained and used like any other horses. They tend to be easy keepers (needing less feed than average). The average mustang may be able to withstand more *barefoot* use than the average domestic horse, but some mustangs do need *horseshoes* for heavy or frequent work.

nail hole pitch:
See: pitch, nail hole.

nail, horseshoe: Soft *steel* nails specially designed for attaching *horseshoes* to *hooves*. They are generally made with a four-sided, tapered shaft; the tip beveled on the inside, and a head shaped to seat into a horseshoe. A pattern or trademark is stamped into the inside face of the head to make it possible to distinguish the inside from the outside at a glance. Carpenter or masonry nails are not suitable substitutes for horseshoe nails.
a.k.a: horse nails.

horseshoe nail

Napoleon shoe:
See: backwards shoe.

Natural Balance Shoeing: A means of applying the principles of Gene Ovnicek *RMF's Natural Balance Trim* to *horses* who require *horseshoes*. The *hoof* is *trimmed* flat, with the heels trimmed back to the widest point of the frog, or as nearly so as is safely possible. A horseshoe such as the NBS, World Race Plate, or one specially *forged* or modified by the *farrier* is then applied. The shoe must have a very bold, *rolled toe*. The shoe is fit and placed to provide full coverage to the heels and to put breakover 1" to 1.5" (respective to the hoof size) in front of the frog tip without any attempt to match the outer perimeter of the shoe to the toe of the hoof. The hoof *wall* is not *dubbed* back to match the front of the shoe, but is allowed to hang over, with the toe being slightly

beveled up in front of the shoe to reduce chipping and breakage.
See: Page A-2; set-back horseshoe.

Natural Balance Trim: A *hoof trimming* approach for *horses* being left *barefoot*, developed and promoted by Gene Ovnicek, *RMF*, which is based on his studies of BLM captured *feral* horses (*mustangs*) in 1986 and 1987. This technique involves minimal trimming of the sole and frog. After locating the true tip of the frog, where it attaches to the sole, the ideal place for *breakover* is set at 1" to 1.5" (respective to *hoof* size) in front of the frog tip. Setting the breakover is done by beveling the toe up at 15° to 20° as though a mild *rockered toe horseshoe* was going to be applied. The heels of the hoof are trimmed back to the widest part of the frog, if safely possible. The quarters are trimmed slightly lower than the bearing plane of the *wall* and beveled upwards. *Flares* and trash wall are dressed away as in conventional trimming techniques. This trimming approach is supposed to produce a noticeable improvement in hoof shape, quality, and frog condition within two months. As with all trimming and shoeing techniques, a solid knowledge of hoof anatomy is needed for safe implementation. Some individuals have created problems by attempting to apply the Natural Balance Trim without a basic understanding of the need to respect the sensitive tissues within the *hoof capsule*.
See also: four point trim; Page A-2.

navicular disease [from Latin *navicula*, little ship]: Heel *lameness* resulting from navicular bursitis, *DDF* tendinitis, coffin joint injury, degeneration of the *distal* sesamoid, damage to the small connective *ligaments*, and other maladies are all commonly described as navicular disease. Fortunately, most of these benefit from similar management approaches.

Navicular lameness is usually identified by *bilateral* soreness of the forefeet, especially at the *trot* on hard surfaces, often indicated by unusually high and rigid head carriage. The hooves may land distinctly toe-first, and the *horse* may develop the habit of resting a fore *hoof* by standing with the toe pointed. *Radiography* tends to be inconclusive. *Posterior digital nerve blocks* are often useful in isolating the lameness.

Sore *suspensory ligaments* are sometimes mistaken for navicular lameness, which can be a problem, as different management is indicated.

Management of navicular problems generally involves reducing stress on the *DDF tendon* (which pulleys under the navicular bone and its *bursa*) and moving the load-bearing back under the *limb*. Although initially counter-intuitive, the heels often need to be trimmed to move the loading points of the *buttresses* back to the rearmost fourth of the frog, preferably to the widest point of the frog, as *underrun heels* transfer the impact forces of hoof-fall directly up at the navicular area, even if the shoe extends well-back.

Trimming for navicular problems also needs to address any toe *flares*, and, if the *horse* is to be left *barefoot*, something akin to a *four point* or *Natural Balance trim* may be employed to reduce *breakover* stress being transferred through the DDF.

Shoeing for navicular typically involves raising the *hoof angle*, extending posterior support, or both.

Raising the hoof angle is often done with *wedge shoes* or *wedge pads* between the *horseshoe* and hoof. *Blocked heels* may also be used. The *Tennessee Navicular Horseshoe* is essentially a shoe with very long blocked heels. In any event, excessive raising of the heels, especially if they are underrun, can result in the heels being crushed. So the overall *hoof-pastern axis* should not be made more than slightly broken-forward.

Extending posterior support is usually done with a *bar shoe*, most commonly an *eggbar*. It is important to trim-back underrun heels before applying an eggbar, as the leverage of the rearward-extending shoe will have a nutcracker-like effect if the hoof's heels meet the shoe at a shallow angle. If trimming back the heels results in a lower than desired hoof angle, wedge pads can be used in conjunction with the eggbar. *Aluminum* wedge-eggbars can be used for the same effect, and are generally preferred over *steel* wedge-eggbars due the the heel weight effect of the latter.

Most navicular cases also benefit from shoes designed to ease breakover, such as *rolled toe, rockered toe, set-back,* or *half-round* shoes. *Backwards shoes* (with new nail holes punched appropriately) function as an open-toed eggbar and can be useful on navicular problem horses.

Posterior digital *neurectomy* is sometimes employed to restore severe navicular cases to *serviceable soundness*. This does not solve the underlying mechanical problems, so *therapeutic farriery* should be continued.

a.k.a: navicular syndrome.
See: Hoof, anatomy, basic; Page A-5.

near: The side of the *horse* that faces west when the animal is walking north. The horse's left side. Horses are most often led, saddled, and mounted from the near side. Opposite of *off*.

necropsy: A post-mortem examination.

necrosis (ne-krō'sĭs, nē-krō'sĭs)**:** Death of animal tissues.

negative palmar angle: A newly popular, somewhat imprecise term describing the *solar* plane of the *PIII* being closer to the ground towards the heels than it is at the toe when the *horse* is standing flat. This is the opposite of what is usually seen in healthy hooves, where the PIII is slightly tipped downward at the toe.

While p*almar* implies the fore *limb*, this condition is observed in hind hooves as well. Angles are created by two aspects intersecting, in this case the solar margin plane of the PIII and solar plane of the *hoof*. If the PIII is level, or tipped-down at the toe, these planes will have no palmar (or *plantar*) intersection at all. Thus "negative" is meaningless due to the impossibility of a "positive" palmar angle.

Negative palmar angle is essentially a radiographic measurement related to crushed, *underrun heels*, low *hoof angle*, and/or a *broken back hoof-pastern axis*, conditions which are easily identifiable via external observation.

See also: balancing the horse's hoof; hoof anatomy, basic; L.H.L.T.; Page A-5.

nerve block: Veterinary procedure in which a nerve or nerve group is temporarily neutralized chemically. This is most often used as a diagnostic tool to pinpoint the source of a *lame horse's* pain, or to test whether a surgical *neurectomy* is likely to be effective.

nerving: See: neurectomy.

neurectomy: Removal of a section of a nerve to eliminate or reduce sensation in part of an animal's body. This procedure is often performed to alleviate pain within the horse's *hoof*. After such a neurectomy, the *horse* may not be considered entirely *sound* because the mechanical cause of the problem still exists.

Nicholson: Brand of rasps from 1864 to the present.

nippers: Cutting tool used to remove excess *horn* when *trimming hooves*. Largely supplanted the *toeing knife* and *butteris* in the 20th Century.
a.k.a: pincers.

hoof **nippers**

Norman: One of the five basic *hoof* shapes named in the *eagle eye* approach suggested by farrier Scott Simpson. The Norman pattern is considered the most normal fore *hoof* shape, and is generally round with the widest part of the foot located midway between the toe and heels.

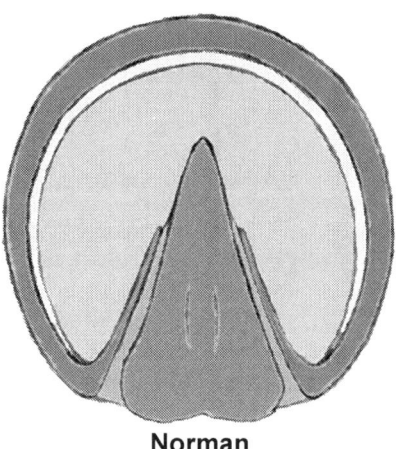
Norman

NPA: See: negative palmar angle.

NSAIDs: Non Steroidal Anti-Inflammatory Drugs. Used to relieve pain, swelling, and fever. Aspirin and *bute* are NSAIDs.

Obel lameness grades: A system of rating degrees of *lameness* resulting from *laminitis* developed by Niles Obel circa 1948. Obel Grade I features frequent shifting of weight between the feet, no discernible lameness at the *walk*, and *bilateral* lameness at the *trot*. Obel Grade II *horses* do not resist having a foreleg lifted, nor are they reluctant to walk, but they do show lameness at the walk. Obel Grade III horses do resist having a foreleg lifted, and are reluctant to walk. Obel Grade IV horses will walk only if forced.

occlusion: Blocking of an opening or passage within an animal's body.

OCD: See: osteochondrosis dissecans.

off: The *horse's* right side. The side of the horse that faces east when the animal is walking north. Opposite of *near*.

offset knee: See: bench knee.

onychomycosis (on-ē-kō'mī-kō-sis): Means a fungal disease of the nail or claw. Denotes the decay of the inner *hoof wall* and the *white line* as a result of infection by highly adaptable microorganisms.
a.k.a: white line disease; onycholysis.

open-toed eggbar:
See: backwards shoe.

orthopedic: Having to do with the skeleton and the muscles, *tendons*, and *ligaments* which hold it together and produce animation.

osselets: Arthritis of the fetlock joint, characterized by hard swelling.
See: Page A-3.

ossification (os'ə-fi-kā'shən): The hardening of soft tissues, such as *ligament* or *cartilage*, into bone. This is often a part of the natural aging process.

osteo- or **oste-:** Greek prefix meaning bone.

osteochondrosis dissecans: A developmental disease in which *cartilage* at the ends of long bones breaks down or fails to *ossify* correctly. Portions of the cartilage or bone may form loose flaps or detach. This may cause reduced range of movement and *lameness* when joints in the *limbs* are affected. The stifles and hocks are most commonly afflicted. *Horses* who grow and gain weight quickly, especially those who get uneven exercise (lots of inactivity, occasional hard work or play), are subject to this affliction. Management usually involves rest with only low-impact exercise to allow damaged cartilage to heal, and restricted feed intake. Some cases may be treated surgically.
a.k.a: osteochondritis; OCD.
See: DOD; Pages A-3; A-4.

osteolysis: Degeneration of bone.

out of: Refers to the *horse's* maternal parentage. For example: "Discovery is out of Ariadne" means that Ariadne is Discovery's *dam* (mother).

overreaching: A fault in *gait* which causes the toe of a hind *hoof* to strike the back of the *lateral* fore *leg* or the heel of its hoof or *horseshoe*. Similar, but not identical, to *forging*.

P III: Third phalanx. The most *distal* bone in each *equine limb*. It is situated completely within the *hoof*, and resembles the hoof in basic shape.
a.k.a: coffin bone; distal phalange; pedal bone; os pedis. See: Pages A-4; A-5.

P III rotation:
See: True P III rotation.

pace: A true *lateral*, two-beat *gait*, with the fore and hind *hooves* on each side of the *horse* moving in unison. The pace is uncomfortable to ride and undesirable in saddle horses. It is used mostly in harness race horses, who can be trained to pace at speeds akin to a moderate *gallop*.

pad: A sheet of leather, plastic, or rubber placed between the *horseshoe* and the *hoof* before the shoe is nailed-on. The pad is held in place by the horseshoe *nails* and sometimes also riveted or glued to the horseshoe. It serves to absorb shock, protect the sole and frog from injury, hold medication in-place, and/or to keep detritus out of the foot. Some pads are designed to apply pressure/support to the frog.

See also: rim pad; hospital plate. Page A-2.

paddling: See: winging-out.

pair: Two *horseshoes* or *hooves*. Unless otherwise specified, a pair means either both fores or both hinds.

palmar [Latin *palmaris*]: The palm side. This refers to the back side of the *horse's* fore *leg*.
a.k.a: volar.

palmar process: The rearmost portion of either side of a *PIII*. This is where the *lateral cartilages* attach to the bone.
See: Page A-5.

palpate: To examine by touch.

paso corto: The intermediate gait of pleasure and performance Paso Fino horses. A broken *lateral*, four-beat *gait* similar in pattern to the *rack*, but more even and efficient. Similar in forward speed to the *jog* or *trot*, the corto may be used to cover long distances without tiring the animal. This gait is remarkably smooth to ride.

paso fino: The signature show *gait* of Paso Fino horses. A highly collected, even, broken four-beat *lateral* gait performed with extremely fast foot action, yet very slow forward movement of the horse. Show Pasos may move forward at less than *walking* speed, with their feet being a veritable blur. The horses are often ridden across a sounding board to confirm that they are properly in gait by listening to the four-beat rhythm of the footfalls.

paso largo: The fastest forward motion *gait* of performance and pleasure Paso Fino horses. Essentially an extended *paso corto*, with the same, even four beat rhythm. This gait covers ground at speeds akin to most horses' *canter*. Almost as smooth to ride as the corto.

paso llano: The intermediate *gait* of Peruvian Paso horses. Similar in speed and footfall to the *paso corto*, but done with a flourish, called *termino*. This is a very smooth and efficient gait.
See also: Sobreandando.

passing gaited: Describes a *horse* who *trots* with his hind feet tracking wider than his front feet. Not a *gait* as such.

patho- or **path-** [Greek *pathos*]: Prefix denoting disease or suffering.

pathogenesis: Origin of suffering. The generation and development of a disease.

pathological: See: therapeutic.

pathology: Scientific study of the development and nature of disease.

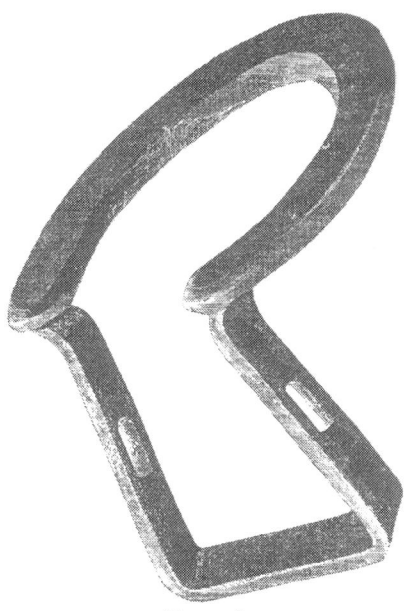
patten shoe

patten shoe:(1) A form of *bar shoe* that acts as an extreme wedge shoe. a.k.a: rest shoe.
(2) Original name for what is now called a *stifle shoe*.

pea coal: Hard, clean *coal* in small chunks. Ideal for use in a coal *forge*.

pedal osteitis: Severe and/or repeated *bruising* of the sole resulting in the inflammation of the *P III*.

pelvic limb: A hind *limb*.

penetrating crack: Any kind of *hoof* crack which exposes sensitive tissue, bleeds, and/or causes *lameness*.
a.k.a: deep crack.

peri- [Greek]: Prefix meaning around or enclosing.

periarticular: Situated around a joint.

perichondrium: The membranes which cover *cartilages*.

periople: The thin, tough, protective covering of the *coronary band*. The periople normally extends less than one inch down the *hoof wall*.
See: Page A-2.

periosteum: The fibrous membranes which cover the bones.

periostitis: See: exostosis.

peritendinitis:
See: bowed tendon.

Peter Wright: Brand of forged *anvils* from 1700 to 1930.

pH: A chemical scale from 0-14 used for measuring solutions with 7 as a base rating for a neutral solution, increasing with higher alkalinity, and decreasing with higher acidity.

phalange: See: phalanx.

phalangeal imbalance: A condition due to excessive heel growth. The *P III* and *hoof* are parallel, but not in line with the pastern. This condition can occur with *club foot*.
See: Page: A-5.

phalangeal lever: A theoretical line from the fetlock joint to the *breakover* point at the toe of the *hoof* or *horseshoe*. The shorter and more upright this line can be made without compromising the internal structures of the foot, the more efficiently the *horse* will be able to move. *Trimming* the hoof short and upright, dressing back toe *flares*, and setting the point of breakover back via a *rolled toe, rockered toe, squared toe,* or *set-back horseshoe* are effective means of shortening the phalangeal lever. While a short phalangeal lever tends to reduce stress on the hoof and *leg*, such efficient movement is not considered desirable for some kinds of *gaited horses* or heavy pulling *draft horses*.

phalanx: Any of the major bones in an *equine digit*. The plural "phalanxes" is used only for the military (non-anatomic) meaning of this word. The plural *phalanges* is used in anatomy.
See: Pages A-4, A-5.

Phoenix: Brand of *keg shoes* from 1882 through 1962.

physiology (fiz-ē-ol′ə-gē): The study of how the body functions.

pigeon toed: See: toed-in.

pitch, nail hole: The practice of punching *nail* holes in *horseshoes* at an angle only slightly more upright than the corresponding *hoof wall*. This means that toe nail holes are typically punched to around 60°, heel nail holes are punched nearly perpendicular, and the holes between are pitched at intermediate angles. This is most often done with *handmade* horseshoes. *Keg shoes* usually accommodate the differences in the hoof wall by graduating the nail placement from *coarse* at the toe to *fine* at the heels, and have all holes punched perpendicular.

plain horseshoe:(1) A *keg shoe* with no *calks* or special features. Usually *creased* just through the *nail* holes.
(2) A *handmade* shoe without any special features, calks, *fullering*, or creasing.

plantar [from Latin *planta*, the sole of the human foot]: The back side of the *horse's* hind *leg*.

plantar cushion: The sensitive, rubbery structure situated above the frog within the *hoof*. Because the word *"plantar"* implies the hind foot, and the cushions are common to all four hooves, they are sometimes referred to as *digital cushions*.
See: Page A-5.

plater: A *horseshoer* who specializes in shoeing race *horses*.

Platers Union: See: IUJH.

plexus [Latin]: A network of nerves or blood vessels.

pony: A short *horse*, usually under 14-2 *hands* for show ring purposes. There are several popular breeds of pony which are used in harness, to carry small riders (most often children), and shown in-hand. Pony breeds tend to be somewhat stronger for their size than other horses. They also tend to be tougher, physically and psychologically, and longer-lived than horses. Most ponies are very easy keepers, and overfeeding resulting in *founder* is a common problem for them.

popped ankle: See: windpuff.

popped knee: Any of several forms of inflammation of the *carpus*. May be a bursitis, a herniated joint capsule, or a distended *tendon* sheath.
a.k.a: big knee; capped knee; hygroma.

popped sesamoid: Inflammation of a proximal sesamoid bone or a

sesamoidian *ligament*. May result from uneven stress on the fetlock, or from direct injury such as may be caused by *interference*.
a.k.a: sesamoiditis.
See: Pages A-3; A-4.

Poseidon: God of the sea and of *horses* in classical Greek mythology. Said to have invented the horse while attempting to impress a goddess. Analogous to the Roman god Neptune.

posterior: Towards or on the back of something. Opposite of *anterior*.

post-mortem:(1) After death. (2) An autopsy.

prick: See: quick.

pritchel

pritchel: A hammer-driven punch with a rectangular, tapered shaft designed to form, clear, or re-size *nail* holes in *horseshoes*.

pritchel hole: The small, round hole found in the heel area of most *anvils*. This hole allows punches to be driven all the way through through metal without hitting the hard anvil face. The corner of the *hardie hole* is sometimes used for this purpose, as its larger size makes it an easier

target. But the smaller pritchel hole allows for more support beneath the stock being punched, and therefore tends to minimize distortion.
See: Page A-7.

profession: A calling considered superior to a lay trade or handicraft. Professions characteristically require years of study and practical training to achieve sufficient competence to practice and have formal credentials available to identify qualified practitioners. Clients are subject to substantial risk due to malpractice of any profession. Each profession has its own distinct traditions and vocabulary. There is a considerable initial investment in business start-up involved in any profession, as well as the potential to earn an above average income.

prolapsed sole:
See: dropped sole.

prophet's thumb: A birth-mark in the form of an indention in the *horse's* flesh, usually in the neck, as though the animal were made of clay and the sculptor had pressed his thumb into the spot. Legend has it that Mohammed miraculously marked his favorite *mares* this way, and mark has been passed down through their descendants. Superstition holds that the prophet's thumb is the mark of a good and/or fast horse. The indention appears to be caused by pressure on the area while the *foal* is developing in the *dam's* uterus.

proximal: In reference to *limbs*, proximal means close to the torso, or comparatively closer to the torso. Opposite of *distal*.

Pseudallescheria boydii: Microorganism implicated in some cases of *onychomycosis*.

pullers: Tool used to remove *horseshoes* after the *clinches* have been sheared or rasped off. Similar in general design to *nippers*, but with thicker jaws and no fine cutting edges.
a.k.a: pull-offs.

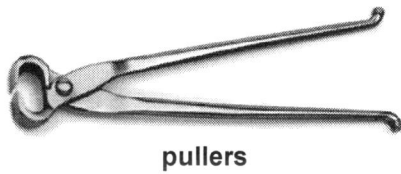
pullers

pus pocket: See: abscess.

Putnam: Brand of *horseshoe* nails from 1859 to around 1920. First successful machine made horseshoe *nails*.

pyramidal disease: Severe inflammation of the *P III* at the extensor process where the main digital extensor *tendon* is attached. *Dorsal* swelling above the *coronary band* and deformed *hoof* wall growth may occur.
a.k.a: buttress foot; extensor process disease.
See: Pages A-2; A-3; A-5.

quadrilateral: Involving all four *limbs*.

quarter crack:(1) Any *sandcrack* in the quarters of the *hoof wall*. May be *superficial* or *penetrating*; *basal* or *coronary*.
(2) This term has been used to specifically denote a coronary sandcrack in the quarter.

queens plate: Swedged aluminum racing *horseshoe* with no (or a very low) *toe grab*. Mandated on some turf tracks.

quench: To rapidly cool a piece of metal by plunging it into a liquid, usually to *harden* it. The speed at which the metal is cooled can have an effect on just how hard it gets. The cooling speed can be manipulated by quenching in water (fastest), brine (slightly slower), and oil (slower yet). Very high carbon *steels* may crack if cooled too quickly.

quick [From Anglo-Saxon *cwic*, alive or living]:**(1)** *(noun)* Any of the sensitive structures within the *hoof capsule*.
(2) *(verb)* To cut, or drive a *nail*, into sensitive structures.
a.k.a: prick; hot nail.

quittor [From Old French *quitture*, discharge]: *Necrosis* of the *lateral cartilages* due to infection. Characterized by severe *lameness* and puss discharge.

rack: A fast four-beat *gait* used primarily by five-gaited Saddlebreds. This is a broken *lateral* gait in which the high-stepping action of each front foot delays its landing until just after that of the hind foot on the same side. Sometimes called a 'single-foot', as there are moments within each stride where a forefoot is the only foot on the ground. This is strictly a show gait, and will exhaust even a fit horse rather quickly. The term 'rack' is often employed incorrectly to describe all manner of odd *trot* and *pace* gait variants in grade *horses*.

radiograph: An *"X-Ray"*. Image produced by photographing artificially generated radiation which passes through visually opaque matter. Only dense objects, such as bone, are normally visible on radiographs, although soft tissue images can be produced through special techniques.

Ralph: One of the five basic *hoof* shapes named in the *eagle-eye* approach suggested by *farrier* Scott Simpson. The Ralph pattern is generally asymmetric, with the widest part of the foot located in the rear third and one buttress farther back than the other.

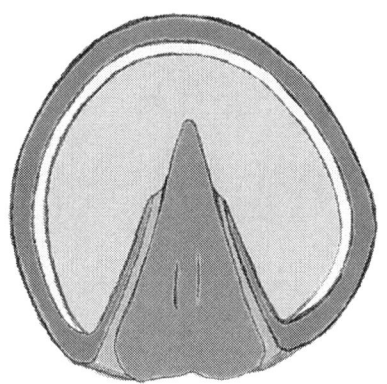
Ralph

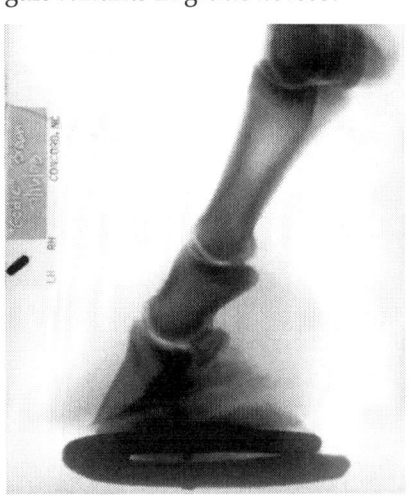
radiograph

rasp: The *farrier's* rasp is a large file designed for *hoof trimming* and *horseshoeing* applications. Modern rasps usually feature an *annealed* tang to accommodate a handle, very aggressive cutting teeth on one side, and finer smoothing teeth on the other. Farriers typically use a new rasp for trimming hooves until it becomes dull, then retire it to *clinching* and finishing duty, and finally use it to round and safe horseshoes.

rasp

registered: One who has met the necessary requirements and been included in a registry (list). The *Guild of Professional Farriers* uses the term registered to distinguish from *certified*, which is used by various horseshoeing *associations* and schools.
See also: RJF; RMF.

relieved: Describes a *horseshoe* that is beveled or depressed on the inner half of the *web* on the hoof-facing surface, except for the heels. This is done to prevent the shoe from applying pressure on the sole of the *hoof*.

resection: An operation involving the removal of part of an organ or structure.

reset: To remove a *horseshoe*, *trim* the *hoof*, then reapply the same horseshoe.
a.k.a: shift.

retained sole: The sole of a *hoof* which does not *exfoliate* normally. This can be a beneficial trait, as the retained sole provides extra protection for the hoof's internal structures.
a.k.a: false sole.

retrograde venous therapy: A veterinary procedure which involves placing a tourniquet above the fetlock, then injecting a substance into a *vein*, forcing it to flow backwards through the circulatory bed into the *arteries*. Infusing plasma from a healthy horse in this way has been suggested as a possible treatment for acute *laminitis*.

reverse shoe:
See: backwards shoe.

rhabdomyolysis, exertional:
See: azoturia.

rim pad: A *pad* placed between the *horseshoe* and the *hoof* which does not cover the entire bottom of the foot but is instead open to expose the frog and most of the sole. Such a pad can be used to absorb shock and protect the perimeter of the sole.
See: Page A-2.

rim shoe: A full-*swedged horseshoe* with a deep groove in the ground surface running from one heel all the way around to the other. Rim shoes are a popular means to provide traction without creating injurious torque stresses like those caused by *calks*.

See: Page A-9.

rim shoe

ringbone: *Exostosis* in or around the coffin or pastern joints, or on the pastern bones.

High ringbone is in or near the pastern joint and is usually palpable.

Low ringbone is in or near the coffin joint, and often is not directly visible.

Articular ringbone actually involves a joint.

Periarticular ringbone is located around, but not within a joint.

Exostosis on the pastern bones, between the joints, is called false ringbone or non-articular ringbone.
See: Pages A-4; A-5.

RJF: Registered Journeyman Farrier. The minimum membership credential of the *Guild of Professional Farriers* which denotes a fully competent *professional* farrier. To be eligible to apply for the RJF, a *farrier* must have at least four years' practical experience and be a full-time practicing farrier. The written RJF exam includes dual-aspect questions designed to test the applicant's real understanding of farrier science rather than his ability to memorize answers. The forgework phase of the RJF exam requires the applicant to demonstrate a combination of skills that would allow him to fabricate any functional *horseshoe* that may be required in practice. There are no restrictions on what equipment may be used to fabricate/modify the shoes. The live shoeing phase requires the applicant to shoe a horse all 'round with *handmade* shoes of the type and style suitable to the animal's use and condition (as determined in writing by a previous evaluation). The RJF exams are designed to evaluate practical ability to serve the public and are not based on contest standards. Time guidelines are flexible and fairly generous. *Journeyman*-level certifications from the *AFA*, *WCF*, and *IUJH* may be accepted in lieu of taking the RJF exams if the applicant meets the other RJF requirements.

RMF: Registered Master Farrier. The highest credential issued by the *Guild of Professional Farriers* which denotes a highly advanced *farrier* qualified to train *apprentices*. To become an RMF, the applicant must first prove practical competence as a farrier by achieving the *RJF*. He must also have a minimum of eight years' full-time experience as a practicing farrier. He may then submit to the Guild a proposal for an original project or thesis designed to demonstrate sophisticated understanding of applied *farriery* and the ability to clearly express that insight to others. If approved, the applicant may complete the project and submit it. The project is then evaluated by a panel of farriers who are not allowed to know whose work they are evaluating. There is no grandfather program for achieving the RMF. All farriers holding the RMF earned it through the process detailed here. The RMF should not be confused with any "master" certifications offered by schools or associations.

road founder: General breakdown of the *hoof* as a result of external stresses and/or age. Road founder often resembles *founder* proper, with failure of the *laminae* and loss of *horn* vitality, but usually has no *acute* onset via *laminitis*.

road puff: See: wind puff.

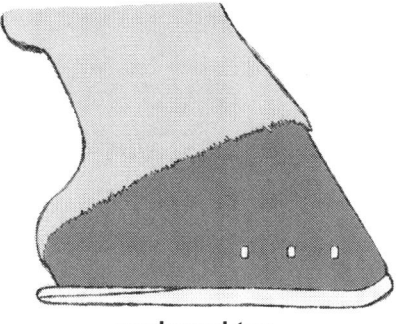
rockered toe

rockered toe: A *horseshoe* that has been bent upward toward the *hoof* at the toe. This eases and directs *breakover*. Hooves must be specially prepared to receive rockered toe shoes.

Roentgen rays: See: x-rays.

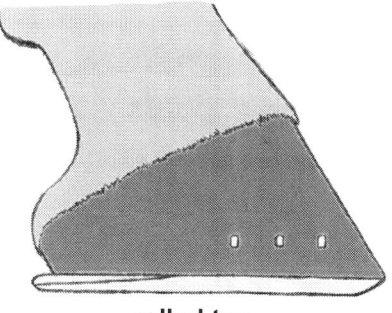
rolled toe

rolled toe: A *horseshoe* that has been rounded or beveled on the outer edge of the ground surface at the toe. This eases *breakover*.

The *hoof* side of the shoe is left flat, so the hoof needs no special preparation.

Rompun [® Haver Lockhart]: Popular trade name of xylazine, a drug used for *chemical restraint*, best administered *IV*. Somewhat supplanted by the newer *Dormosedan* for *horseshoeing* situations.

rope walking: A *gait* defect which results in the *horse's* tracks being left in a single line, as if the animal had been walking on a tightrope. Horses that ropewalk are likely to *interfere*.
a.k.a: cat walking.

rotation: See: true P III rotation; capsular rotation; founder.

R.S.S. : Registered Shoeing Smith. Previous title for English *farriers* at the level now called *D.W.C.F.*

run: The fastest natural *gait* common to most *horses*. It is similar to the *gallop* in that the hind *limbs* work together to drive the horse forward, and generally looks and feels like a fast gallop to observers and riders. But the non-lead fore foot, which would move in unison with its diagonal hind at the gallop, delays its timing a bit to assist the lead foot in holding the horse up while both hind feet are in flight. This causes the run to be a four-beat gait, as opposed to the three-beat gallop. Some fit horses can run well in excess of fifty miles per hour for short distances, and can maintain a rate of around forty miles per hour for well over a mile.

run down: Failure of the *suspensory ligaments* of the *horse's* hind *limbs*.

running walk: The signature *gait* of the Tennessee Walking Horse. This is a very fast *walk* with exaggerated, high-stepping action in the fore feet, and the hind feet reaching far up under the *horse's* body with every step. Because of the long, flowing stride, this is a smooth riding gait even at what would be *trotting* speed for most other horses. When done well this extremely flashy gait is called the *big lick*.

run-under heels:
See: underrun heels.

saber-legged:
See: sickle hocked.

safed: Describes a *horseshoe* which has the outer edge of the ground surface of the *medial* branch beveled. This is done to decrease the chance of it pulling another shoe or causing injury should the *horse interfere*.

sagittal (saj′i-təl) [from Latin *sagitta*, an arrow]: A sagittal plane divides the left side from the right. *Hoof* anatomy models are often cut into sagittal section. See also: transversal.

saline (sā′lēn): Containing a salt.

sandcrack: A *hoof* crack parallel to the *horn* tubules. May be *superficial* or *penetrating*, and can occur anywhere in the hoof *wall*.

scale: Flaky oxidation which forms when working *steel* heated in a *forge*.

scalping: Fault of *gait* which results in the toe of a fore *hoof* striking the *dorsal* surface of the *lateral* hind *hoof* or *leg*.

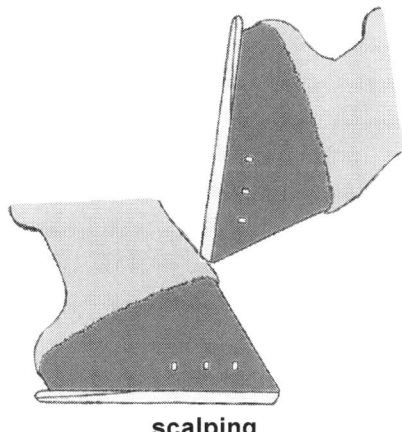

scalping

scientific process: Systematic use of *controlled experiments* to try to prove AND disprove a given *hypothesis*.

sclerosis (sklə-rō′s) [from Greek *skleros*, hard]: Hardening of soft tissues, especially nerves, due to disease.

scotched: Describes a *horseshoe* which has its outer edge sloped outward from the *hoof* surface down to the ground surface. This is usually done on *draft* horseshoes to give the horse a greater base of support and create the appearance of a larger hoof.

SDF: Superficial Digital Flexor Tendon. A *tendon* which runs down the back of the *leg*, splits below the fetlock, and attaches to the P I and P II. In the hind legs, the SDF acts primarily as a *ligament* of the *stay apparatus*. See: Pages A-3; A-5.

sealant: See: hoof sealant.

seating out: Sloping the inner part of the hoof-side of a *horseshoe's web* away from the *hoof*. This is done to prevent the shoe from putting pressure on the sole. See: relieved; Page A-2.

selenium: A nonmetallic element. Atomic number 34. Atomic weight 78.96. Selenium is a naturally occurring mineral nutrient which is deficient in nearly all American soils east of the Mississippi, and much of the rest of the country as well. Selenium deficiency in *horses* has been implicated in *suspensory ligament* soreness, poor *hoof* growth and quality, and dull haircoat. Henry Heymering, *RMF* suggests 4mg daily supplemental selenium for horses in selenium poor areas. Frogs discolored yellow are a sign of selenium deficiency.

sepsis (sep′sis): The presence of disease-causing organisms or their toxins in the blood or tissues.

sequestrum [From Latin *sequesto*, to sever.]: Portion of bone which has become detached in *necrosis*.

serviceably sound: Describes a *horse* who is capable of performing the work for which he is intended without becoming *lame*.

sesamoiditis (ses-i-moid′ī-tis): The inflammation or dislocation of the proximal sesamoid bone(s). May involve an actual fracture of a sesamoid bone. Sesamoiditis can be the result of direct injury, uneven weight bearing, or fatigue.
a.k.a: Popped sesamoid.

set: Four *horseshoes*.

set-back horseshoe: A *horseshoe* which has been intentionally placed farther back than in conventional application, so that the toe of the shoe does not fully cover the toe of the *hoof*. This is one way to shorten the *phalangeal lever* and reduce *breakover* stresses on the hoof and *leg*.

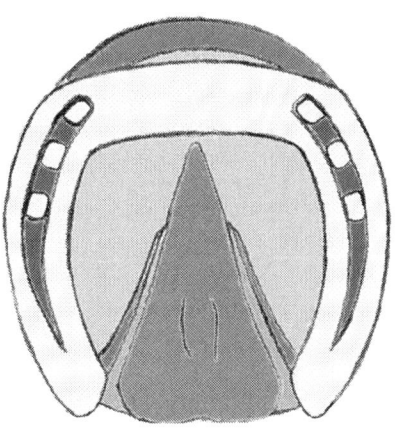

set-back horseshoe

set toe: European term for *rockered toe*.

sheared heels: Failure of internal structures which normally bind the heels together. Allows the heels to flex apart more than normal, and can cause *lameness*. This term was sometimes used in the past to denote a *jammed heel*.

shift: To "shift the shoes" is an archaic term for a *reset*.

shod: Describes *horses* or horse's *hooves* to which *horseshoes* have been applied.

shoeing stand: See: hoof stand.

sickle hocked: A conformation fault in which the *horse* stands with his hind *limbs* bent more than normal at the hock, placing the *hooves* farther forward than ideal. Extreme sickle hocks can be considered an *unsoundness*.
a.k.a: saber-legged.

sidebone: The *ossification* of one or both *lateral cartilages* within the horse's *hoof*. This sometimes causes *lameness*, but may be considered a normal part of the aging process in some *horses*.

side clips: Quarter *clips*. Particularly those placed near the middle of the quarter, on the sides of the *hoof*.
See: Page A-2.

Simonds: Brand of rasps and other *farrier* products from 1832 to the present.

sinker: A grave case of *founder* in which the entire bone column fails to be suspended within the *hoof capsule* and descends toward the sole. This can happen only when the *chondrocoronal ligament apparatus* fails to hold the *distal* end of the short pastern bone in-place within the hoof as it does during conventional, *rotation* founder.

Sir F. Fitzwygram's shoe: A *horseshoe* with a bold, full-*web rolled toe*, documented in late 19th Century texts. Notable for having some similarity to shoes used in approaches considered 'cutting-edge' a century later.

Sir F. Fitzwygram's shoe

sire: Paternal parent. Father.

sliding plate: A *horseshoe* designed to provide very little traction. Usually a wide *webbed* shoe with no *fullering*, *creasing*, or *calks* of any kind, *extended heels*, and a *rolled toe*. These are used on the hind *hooves* of reining *horses* to enable longer sliding stops. A milder form of sliding plate may be used on ranch and working cowhorses in training to make it easier for them to learn to stop hard on the hind end.

smith [From Anglo-Saxon *smitan*, to strike]: One who forms metal by hammering. Usually refers to a *blacksmith*. Smith, like Cooper, Thatcher, Tinker, and other occupational designations, has become a common surname over the centuries.

smithy: (1) The building or shop in which a *blacksmith* or *farrier* works and keeps his tools.
(2) Incorrectly used as a synonym for the blacksmith or *horseshoer*, which is a bit like calling an auto mechanic a "garage".

snowball hammer: A combination *hoof pick* and hammer often carried aboard coaches. Used to break up and remove packed snow and ice from the *horse's hooves*.

snow pad: Any of several *pads* designed to prevent the build-up of packed snow and ice in the bottom of a *shod horse's hoof*. Full snow pads usually have a hemispherical bulge in the middle, protruding away from the sole. Snow *rim pads* feature a compressible tube which runs just inside the *web* of the *horseshoe* and acts as a sort of spring to pop the snow out of the foot each time it is raised. Both versions can be employed for warm weather uses. The full pad can house a larger amount of medicated packing than a conventional pad, while the rim pad can provide good protection to the *solar* margin while allowing low-pressure stimulation.
aka: snowball pad.

full **snow pad** with shoe

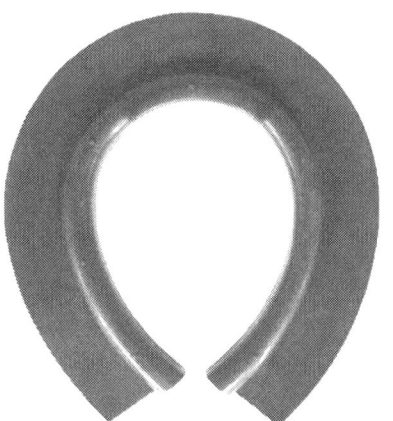

rim type **snow pad**

sobreandando: The fastest forward motion *gait* of Peruvian Paso horses. A broken *lateral*, four-beat gait like the *paso llano*, but faster and more extended. As the horse increases speed, this gait may become less even, with a discernible pause between the beats two and three of each four-beat. Similar in speed to the *lope* or *canter*.

solar: The bottom aspect of the *horse's hoof*.
See: Page A-2.

sound: Describes a *horse* who is not *lame*, and has no conditions or defects likely to lead to lameness in the future.

spavin [From Old French *espavent*]: Any swelling or abnormal growth in or on the hock. A "bog spavin" is a soft swelling on the *medial* and/or *dorsal* surface of the hock. A "blood spavin" is an enlarged vein, and a harmless *blemish*. A "bone spavin" is an *exostosis* on any of the tarsal bones. Large bone spavins are called "jack spavins". "Blind" or "occult spavins" are exostosises not visible on the exterior of the hock.
See: Pages A-3; A-4.

speedy cutting: (1) A gait fault which results in the *interference* of *lateral limbs* at the *canter* or *gallop*.
(2) High *scalping* by trotters.
(3) Used to denote knee hitting in some texts circa 1900.

Spike: One of the five basic *hoof* shapes named in the *eagle eye* approach suggested by *farrier* Scott Simpson. The Spike pattern is generally square, with straight quarters and sharply turned in heels. The widest point of the foot is midway between the toe and heels.

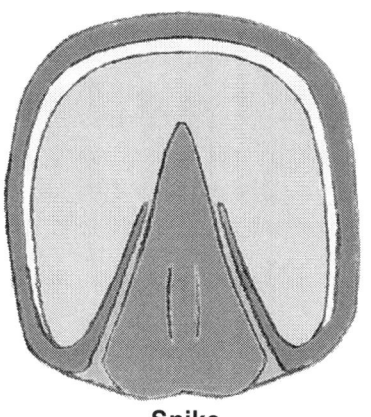

Spike

splint: *Exostosis* on the *ligament* which attaches a *splint bone* to the *cannon* bone, forming a bump on the *leg*. Splints are usually caused by *trauma* or heavy stress on the legs of a young *horse*. *Lameness* may be evident during the "green" phase, but when *ossification* is complete, the splint is considered a *blemish*.
See: Page A-4.

splint bone: Either of the two long, slender bones which run along the back of each *cannon* bone. The splint bones are attached to the cannon bone by *ligaments* which eventually *ossify* and fuse the bones

together. The inner splint bone is the second metacarpal in the fore *limbs* and the second metatarsal in the hinds. The outer splint bone is the fourth metacarpal in the fores and the fourth metatarsal in the hinds.
See: Page A-4.

square toe: A *horseshoe* shaped so that the toe of the shoe does not follow the curve of the *hoof* but is instead made square, and usually fit with the toe of the hoof extending out over the shoe. Square toed shoes are usually used on hind hooves to center and speed up *breakover*, and/or to prevent damage to the foreleg and its shoe should the *horse overreach*.

squaring horn: A small, rectangular projection, usually found on the side of a *farrier's anvil* near the base of the main horn, which can be used to easily produce a *square toe horseshoe*. Can also double as a *clip horn*.
See: A-7.

St. Croix Forge: Manufacturer of *steel horseshoes* from 1982 to the present. Expanded to produce *aluminum* horseshoes and *farrier* hand tools in the 1990s.

stabbing: Toe-first landing of a hind foot which causes it to stab into soft turf.

stallion: An entire male *horse*, usually four years or older.

stalljack: A miniature *anvil* with a built-on stand. Used by *platers* to shape light *horseshoes* without setting down the *hoof*.

Standard: Brand of *horseshoes* from 1890 until around 1940.

stay apparatus: The configuration of anatomical structures which allow the *horse* to remain in the standing position with extremely little muscular effort.

steel: An *alloy* of *iron* and carbon. The carbon in steel, usually between 0.2 and 2.0% allows it to be *hardened* and *tempered*. Modern steels often contain additional elements for other qualities as well.

sticker: A light, sharp form of *heel calk* often used on the *lateral* side of hind race *horseshoes*.

stifled: A stifled *horse* suffers from recurring, temporary immobilization of the hock due to the locking of the patella. This condition can be corrected through surgery.
See: Pages A-2; A-3.

stifle shoe: A *horseshoe* designed to prevent the *horse* from bearing full weight on the *shod* foot. In older texts, the stifle shoe is called a *patten shoe*.

stocks: A heavy framework which holds a *horse* in position for *horseshoeing* or *trimming*. These are most often used for shoeing *draft horses*, whose great size and strength can make shoeing them a physically difficult proposition even when they are relatively cooperative. Although it may be unwise to rely upon any rigid restraint to control a vigorously resisting horse, some seem to take comfort in the surrounding security provided by the framework and the support provided by the belly band commonly employed with stocks, and are therefore *shod* much more safely in stocks than without.

strawberry: See: bruise.

striker

striker: In blacksmithing and heavy shoe forging operations, the striker is a person who assists the *blacksmith* or *farrier* at the *anvil* by wielding a heavy hammer with two hands. The smith usually handles the tongs and uses blows with a light hammer to show the striker where and how he wants the heavy hammer to fall.

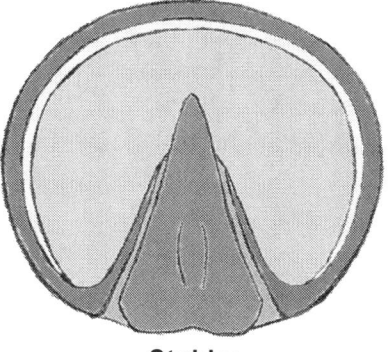
Stubby

Stubby: One of the five basic *hoof* shapes named in the *eagle eye* approach suggested by *farrier* Scott Simpson. The Stubby pattern is generally round, but wider than it is long. The widest part of the hoof will be about midway between the toe and heels.

stud: A form of *calk* attached by insertion into a hole punched or drilled into the *horseshoe*. Drive-in studs are affixed to and removed from the shoe while the shoe is off the *hoof*. Screw-in studs may be inserted or removed while the *horse* is wearing the shoe, so they can be changed by the rider as turf conditions dictate. The holes for screw-in studs are drilled and tapped after the shoe is shaped for the hoof, but before it is nailed-on. Shaping the shoe after the holes are drilled and tapped tends to deform the holes and cause studs to be difficult to insert, or to fall out in use.

stud: (1.) A *stallion* used for breeding.
(2.) A *horse* breeding farm.

suckling: A *foal* who has not yet been *weaned*.

sugardine: A thick liquid or paste used to draw-out infections. Made by saturating white table sugar with 7-10% povidone-iodine solution (such as Batadine). May be used under a bandage or *hospital plate* to help drain *abscesses*.

superficial crack: Any kind of *hoof* crack which does not expose sensitive tissues or cause *lameness*.
a.k.a: surface crack.

supracoronary depression: Indention of the tissue just above the *hoof*. Sometimes seen at the front of a severely *foundered* foot. Extends all the way around the foot in *sinkers*.
See: hoof anatomy, basic; Pages A-2; A-5.

surcingle: A strap which passes under the *horse's* torso. Usually part of a driving harness, or a means of holding a blanket, sheet, or turnout rug in-place. There are also training surcingles which are used to provide a point of attachment for reins, tie-downs, and driving lines. The term is rarely applied to straps of similar function on saddles.
See also: cinch, girth.

surface crack:
See: superficial crack.

suspensory ligament: Sometimes referred to as the interosseous muscle or *tendon*, this broad, complex *ligament* originates behind the knee or hock, runs down the back of the *leg*, *bifurcates* just above the *distal* ends of the *splint bones*, then splits again, with one fork on each side wrapping around to merge with the main extensor tendon in the front of the *digit*, while the others join the *proximal* sesamoids and sesamoidian ligaments. The overall function of the suspensory ligament is to support the fetlock, preventing the ergot from sinking to the ground. It is the primary shock absorber for the *limb*.

Page 140.

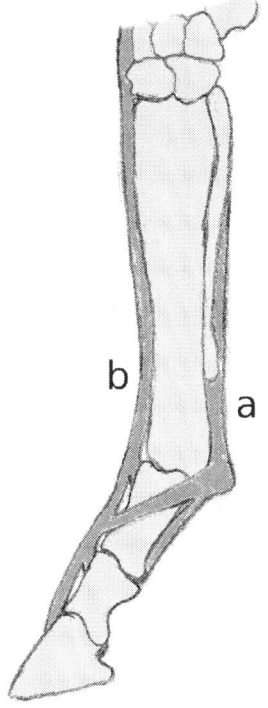

a = suspensory ligament
b = main extensor tendon

Suspensory ligament sprains and tears are a common injury in high performance *horses*. Mild sprains may also occur when *hoof balance* is radically altered, as when *trimming* severely overgrown hooves back to correct form, if the horse returns to vigorous activity before being allowed time to adjust. Severe suspensory failure is usually obvious, as the fetlock sinks toward the ground. This condition requires rest and veterinary treatment. The *farrier* may be called upon for support shoeing or to fabricate an appropriate brace.

More insidious is *chronic soreness of the suspensory ligament*, which may have no obvious cause, and does not result in the tell-tale sinking of the fetlock. This condition is sometimes mistaken for *navicular disease*, and responds positively to some shoeing approaches commonly employed for that malady, such as *eggbar horseshoes* with *rolled* or *rockered toes*. Raising the *hoof angle*, either by trimming, with *wedge shoes,* or *pads*, as is often done for navicular, usually has a negative effect on sore suspensory ligaments.

Sore suspensory ligaments are usually sensitive to *palpation*. *Selenium* deficiency has been implicated as a cause, and supplementation has been an effective remedy.

See: run down;
Page A-2; A-3; A-4; A-5.

swedge block: A molding tool which straps onto the *anvil* and/or fits into its *hardie hole*. Different swedge blocks can be

used to modify *bar stock* which can then be *forged* into *rim shoes*, polo plates, and other shoes with special cross-sections.
a.k.a: swage block.
See: Pages A-7; A-9.

swedged shoe: Any of a number of *horseshoe* styles which have the ground side molded into a traction modifying pattern. Most feature a deep groove which runs the whole way around the shoe.
a.k.a: full swedged shoe.
See Page A-9.

sweeney: Deterioration of the muscles in a *horse's* shoulder due to nerve damage.

swelled heel: The heel of a *horseshoe* which is folded up onto the hoof surface of the shoe. The hoof surface is then leveled. Swelled heels raise the heels of the *hoof* without creating as much traction as *blocked heels* or *heel calks*.

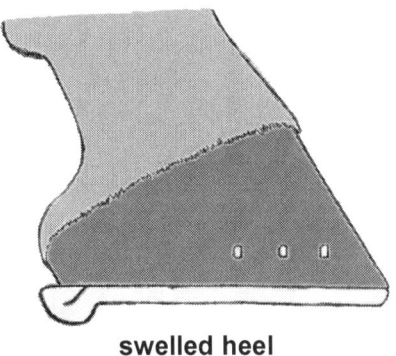
swelled heel

synovial (sin-ō'vē-əl) **fluid** [From Greek *syn*, with; and Latin *ovum*, egg]: A very slippery, oil-like substance which is produced by the body to lubricate the joints and *tendons*.

tack: A general term for the saddles, bridles, harness, and other equipment used to handle, ride, and drive *horses*.

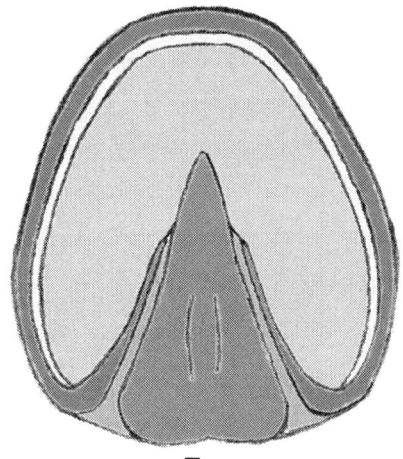
Tag

Tag: One of the five basic *hoof* shapes named in the *eagle eye* approach suggested by *farrier* Scott Simpson. The Tag pattern is most common in hind feet. It is somewhat pointed at the toe, straight through the quarters, and turns sharply at the heels. The Tag hoof is widest across its rear third.

tattoo: A permanent artificial marking created by injecting ink under the skin. Identification code tattoos are often found on the inside of *horses'* upper lips. Such tattoos are most common on, but not exclusive to, race track horses.

temper [French *tempérer*, from Latin *temperare*, to regulate.]: A level of hardness in given piece of *steel* anywhere between its *hardened* and *annealed* states. Tempering is done to achieve the ideal balance of hardness (the ability to resist bending and wear) and toughness (the ability to resist breaking or chipping when flexed or struck) for the tool being forged. Traditional *blacksmith* tempering is done by first hardening the steel, then slowly reheating it to a certain temperature to reduce the hardness and increase toughness. By polishing the metal before the tempering heat, the smith can judge the temperature by the changing color of oxidation which glazes over as heat increases. The effect of tempering is dependent upon the makeup of the steel *alloy*. Mild steel (such as *horseshoes*) will be nearly the same whether tempered to straw or blue. High carbon steels (such as rasps) have dramatically different properties when tempered to straw versus being tempered to blue.
See: graded temper.

tendinitis: See: bowed tendon.

tendon [from Latin *tendo*, to stretch]: Strong fibrous tissue which connects muscle to bone. Tendons function primarily to facilitate movement. Tendons slide within lubricated sheaths, are inelastic, and are subject to sprains and ruptures.

tendosynovitis:
See: bowed tendon.

tendovaginitis:
See: bowed tendon.

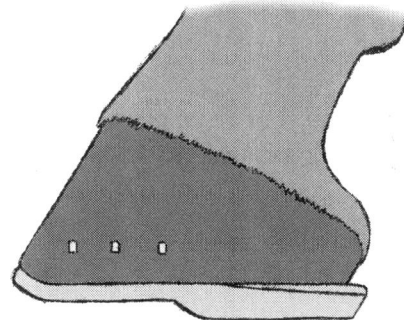

Tennessee navicular shoe

Tennessee navicular shoe: A *horseshoe* with *heel calks* or *blocked heels* which start at or just behind the widest part of the *hoof*. Originally made by *welding* the *posterior* halves of branches cut from one shoe onto the ground surface of the branches of an intact shoe. Factory-made shoes patterned on the Tennessee navicular shoe are

currently available, as well as a combination *eggbar* version.
See: navicular disease; Page A-8.

tenotomy: Surgical severing of a *tendon*.

termino: The outward swing of the fore *limbs* seen in Peruvian Paso horses as they *gait*. Considered a desirable trait in Peruvians, but much less so in Paso Fino horses.

dynamic frog support as opposed to the continuous frog pressure provided by rigid *heartbar*.
See: Pages A-2; A-9.

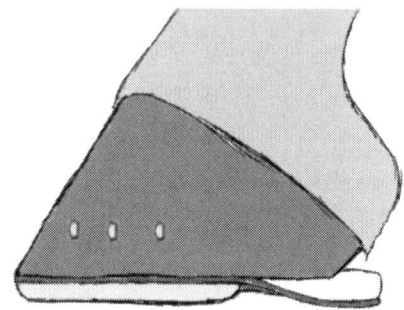

Lateral view of abbreviated shoe applied with **Thera-Flex** insert.

therapeutic: Describes *hoof* shoeing or *trimming* done in an attempt to relieve *lameness* or *unsoundness*.
a.k.a: pathological shoeing.
See: corrective and therapeutic farriery, basic principles.

thoracic limb: A fore *limb*.

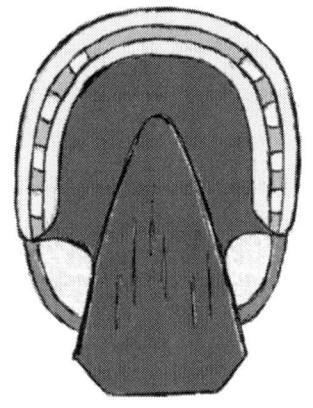

Solar view of **Thera-Flex** inert with abbreviated horseshoe.

Thera-Flex: Brand of *pads* with a thick, triangular, soft plastic wedge on the *hoof*-facing side. This wedge is designed to be custom-carved to transfer loading to the frog and/or the insides of the bars of the foot. This pad is often used with a 3/4 length *horseshoe* to allow the wedge to flex away from the frog when the foot is unloaded, thus creating

thoroughbred: Although commonly thought to be a synonym for "pure-bred" by people outside of the *horse* world, thoroughbreds are actually a specific breed of horse bred primarily for track speed at distances of around a mile. Thoroughbreds tend to be tall, long-bodied, lean, and high-spirited. The focus on breeding and training for optimum speed performance through a short racing career results in some thoroughbreds having *lameness* and other health issues as they age. But, with the help of skillful *farriers* and horsemen, many thoroughbreds have successful post-racing careers as riding horses. Thoroughbreds have been popular stock for out-breeding to add athleticism to other breeds including the American quarterhorse and various *warmbloods*. The thoroughbred breed itself was developed by crossing the faster European horses with imports from the Middle East, especially Arabians. All thoroughbreds are supposed to trace their direct paternal bloodlines back to one of three Arabian stallions who lived in the late 17th and early 18th Centuries.

thoroughpin: Soft swelling of the *tendon* sheath of the *DDF* just above the point of the hock. This swelling is often visible on both sides of the *limb*. Thoroughpin rarely results in *lameness*, but does indicate weakness in the hock, excessive stress, *trauma*, or a combination of these.
a.k.a: through-pin.
See: Page A-3.

through-pin:
See: thoroughpin.

thrush: Infection of the tissues of the frog by micro-organisms. This is seen as a foul smelling black crud or discharge in the commissures and frog. Advanced cases may invade sensitive tissues and cause *lameness*.
a.k.a: frush (archaic).
See: Page A-2.

toe angle: See: hoof angle.

toed in: The *horse's digit* appears to be twisted inward. This conformation fault usually causes the afflicted *limb* to *wing-out*. Horses who are toed in on both fore feet are called pigeon-toed.

toed out: The *horse's digit* appears to be twisted outward. This conformation fault usually causes the afflicted *limb* to *wing-in*. Toed out horses may be prone to *brushing*.

toe grab: A form of *toe calk* used on racing *horseshoes*. Toe grabs are curved with the toe of the shoe, and usually sharper than typical toe calks.

toeing knife

toeing knife: A mallet-driven blade used to *trim* the *hoof wall*. Toeing knives were listed as standard equipment for U.S. Cavalry shoers until after the War Between The States. Hoof nippers

have replaced the toeing knife in common use among *farriers* in the U.S. today.
See: Page A-6.

trailer: An extra long heel on a *horseshoe* which is usually turned 45° away from the center line of the hoof and the line of flight.

trailer

training plate: A very lightweight, usually *steel horseshoe* used on race *horses* between races. Training plates are also used on some young riding and show horses. Most training plates are *swedged*.

transversal: A transversal plane separates the front from the back.
See also: sagittal.

trauma (tro′mə): Injury caused by sudden shock or impact.

Trenton: Brand of forged *anvils* from 1898 until 1952.

trim: The removal of excess *horn* to restore proper form and *balance* to the *hoof*. This is done periodically for *barefoot horses*, and before the application of *horseshoes* on horses being *shod*.

trimming technique, basic: It is far easier to take away *horn* than to get it back, so cuts must always be made conservatively, with an eye toward preserving the integrity of the *hoof capsule*.

When a *horse* is to be left *barefoot*, the horn itself must protect the internal structures, and will dictate the traction and *breakover* characteristics of the foot. Greater length of *wall* and thickness of sole generally need to be preserved to accomplish this. The hoof knife should be used sparingly to remove only the loosest of sole horn, ragged frog material, and folded-over bars.

Using the frog as a reference, a center line dividing the hoof into *medial* and *lateral* halves can be envisioned. Another line, crossing perpendicular to the center line at the widest part of the frog, will cross the *buttresses* and indicate the points to which the heels should be trimmed back. Lines carried forward from those points (parallel to the center line) will cross the *anterior* wall. A line connecting these crossing points will indicate a desirable line of forward breakover, safely beyond the tip of the coffin bone and the most vulnerable part of the sole.

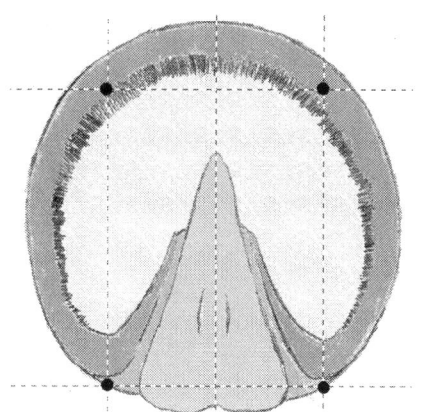

Untrimmed hoof with trim reference lines mapped.
Cuts are made <u>outside</u> the lines which intersect at the black dot points.

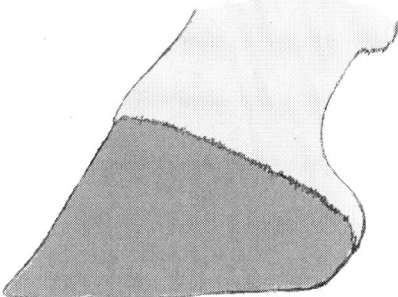

Hoof in need of trimming.

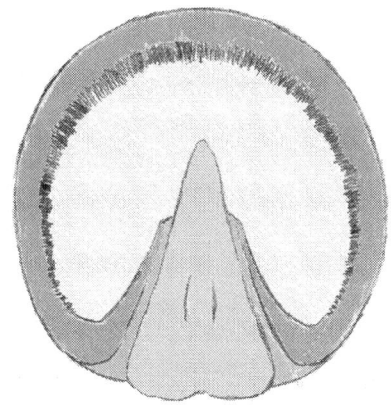

Untrimmed hoof.
Solar view.

Set the inner jaw of the *nippers* outside the line at one heel, and angle the reins slightly away from the center of the hoof. The amount of angle is based on how overgrown the hoof is, and the roughness of the terrain the horse will be working upon. If the hoof is very overgrown, and the horse will be working on turf, the nipper cut should be made with the reins pitched well-out. (Perhaps 15°.) If the foot is already fairly short, and the horse is going to work on rocky ground, the cut should be made almost level with the solar plane of the foot. In some cases, the nippers can be omitted altogether in favor of *rasp* work.

Repeat the process on the other side of the hoof. Then make a similar nipper cut across the front of the hoof, just forward of the breakover line. Since the toe of the hind foot is used to drive the horse forward at speed, the angle of the toe cuts in the hind hooves should be less pronounced than in fore hooves.

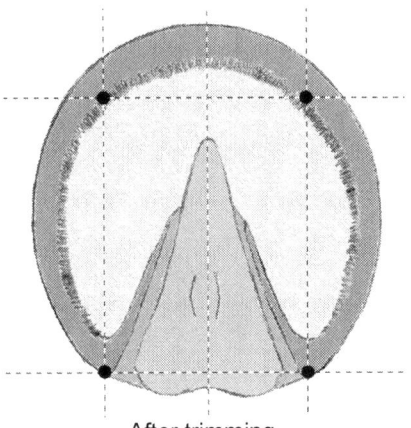

After trimming.
Note that the line across the widest part of the frog now crosses the buttresses instead of crossing behind them as in the untrimmed hoof.

A rasp is used to smooth and fine-tune the cuts. Then to round-off all sharp edges. There is no need to rasp the sole down, even if it appears slightly convex. The barefoot horse will be able to quickly wear away excess sole after the trim.

The final form of the hoof trimmed to be left barefoot will be beveled-up at the toe and on both sides. This reduces stress on the wall both when the horse is moving forward (breaking over the front of the hoof) and moving sideways (breaking over one side of the hoof). This helps prevent chipping and splitting, while minimizing stress on the foot and *limb*.

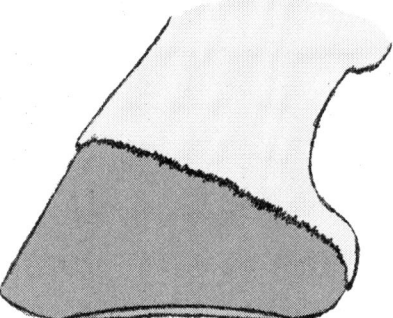

Trimmed to go barefoot.

When a horse is to be *shod*, the hoof will have the protection of the *horseshoe*, which will also dictate the traction and breakover characteristics of the foot. The horn that would be preserved for these purposes is essentially removed and replaced with *steel* (or other shoe material). The shorter hoof at the time of shoeing also compensates for the shod foot's inability to wear-down over the shoeing interval.

The hoof knife is used a little more aggressively, taking out more loose sole. But not so much as to leave the *corium* vulnerable. Trimming the tip of the frog to its junction with the sole can provide one reference for sole depth. Taking sole at the toe until it begins to yield under firm thumb pressure can provide another, although one would ideally stop a little before reaching that level.

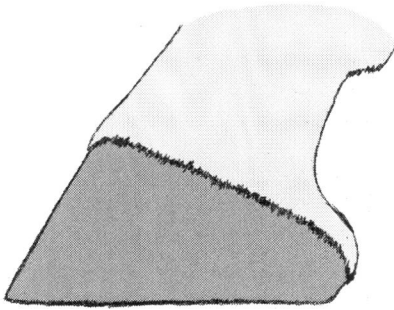

Flat trimmed to receive a horseshoe. This foot is actually almost identical to the barefoot trim, but with the "bumps" corresponding to the black dots in the diagrams trimmed down to about the depth of the bevels. This foot should still have sufficient mass to go barefoot under normal conditions. The barefoot trim is essentially the flat trim with a bit of extra horn at the "corners" added. Not a flat trim with bevel material subtracted!

The same lines and cuts can now be made as for a barefoot trim, except that the nipper reins are to be kept perpendicular to the *solar* plane, or tipped just slightly in, toward the frog. The goal being to make the bearing surface of the entire wall one flat plane, just beyond the level of the trimmed sole.

The rasp is used to smooth and level the bearing surface of the wall to accept the shoe. The fine side of the rasp should be used to slightly round-off the sharp outer edge of the wall.

If a horse which has recently been trimmed for shoeing needs to be left barefoot, the edge of the wall should be rounded with a rasp and left alone. One can not safely do a barefoot-style trim unless there is sufficient hoof mass to work with.

See also: balancing the horse's hoof; hoof anatomy, basic; Pages A-2; A-5; A-6.

trot [French *trotter*, ultimately from Latin *tolutare*, to trot]: The intermediate natural *gait* of most riding and harness *horses*. This two-beat gait is truly *diagonal*, with the *near* fore and *off* hind moving in unison, while the off fore moves in synch with the near hind. There is a moment after each diagonal pair of *hooves* leave the ground and before the opposite pair land when the horse is completely off the ground. Horses naturally trot at speeds comparable to a human jogging up to a fast human run. They can be trained to trot at human walking speed (called a *jog*), or to extend the trot up to speeds beyond which a horse would ordinarily transition to a *gallop*. For most riding horses, the trot is a good ground covering gait that does not quickly wind or exhaust the horse, although horses not accustomed to long-distance trotting may become leg weary.

trueness of gait: Describes the lack of *medial* or *lateral* deviation from the line of travel seen in a *horse's limbs*.

true P III rotation: The *hoof wall* is no longer parallel to the *P III* at the toe, P III is not in alignment with the pastern, and the sole is compromised by the tip of the P III. This happens in *foundered* horses.
See: Pages A-2; A-3; A-5.

tubules: See: hoof anatomy, basic.

turning a shoe: In general, the process of *forging* a *handmade horseshoe*. More specifically, the process of bending the *bar stock* into the shape of a horseshoe, exclusive of the *swedging, fullering,* stamping, punching, leveling, beveling, *boxing,* and other procedures involved in producing the shoe.
See: horseshoe, forging.

turning cams: Projections on a *farrier's anvil* which allow the branches of *horseshoes* to be bent inward more easily, especially when *cold shoeing*.

turning hole: A round hole in the heel of a *farrier's anvil* which facilitates the easy inward bending of *horseshoe* branches during *cold shoeing*. Farriers often used the *hardie hole* for this purpose on older anvil designs, but this left cut marks on the shoe. The turning hole was incorporated into some more recent designs to allow the same functionality without the cut marks.
See: keg shoe, fitting; A-7.

twitch: Any of several devices used to apply pressure to a *horse's* upper lip. This is used as a form of acupressure or distraction to calm and immobilize the animal. The use of a twitch produces widely varying results on individual horses. These range from semi-consciousness to rage. Twitches are sometimes applied to the horse's ear.

two finger radiograph: An expression describing the fact that the *dorsal hoof wall* is parallel to the dorsal aspect of the *PIII* from the *coronary band* down to an inch or so below, or about the width of two fingers. This allows a fairly accurate estimate of the position of the PIII within the hoof, no matter how distorted the lower wall may be.
See: Page A-2; A-5.

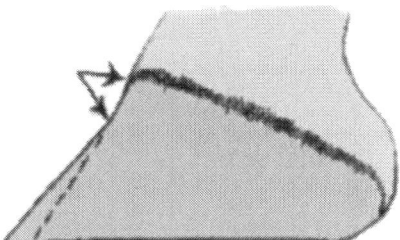

two finger radiograph
used to determine how much toe flare to dress back.

tying-up: See: azoturia.

underrun heels: From the *solar* viewpoint, a line connecting the heel *buttresses* should cross the rearmost 1/4th of the frog. If it crosses farther forward, the heels are underrun. This reduces the *posterior* support of the *hoof*. Although they may actually be quite long, such heels appear short when the *horse* is standing on the foot because their length runs more forward than down, and their height is compressed even further forward under a load. From the *lateral* viewpoint, underrun heels have a slope more than 5° shallower than the *toe angle*.
a.k.a: underslung heels; run-under heels.
See also: hoof anatomy, basic; balancing the horse's hoof; LHLT; navicular disease; eggbar;
Page A-2.

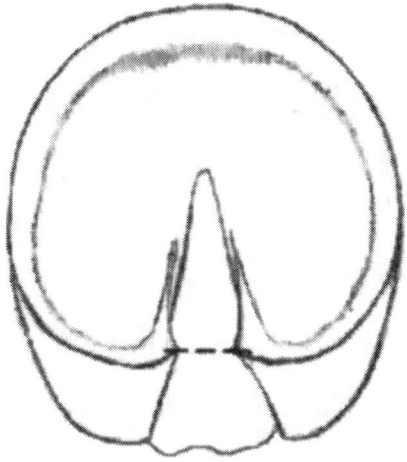

crushed, **underrun heels**

underslung heels:
See: underrun heels.

unguligrade: Describes a species which normally walks on its tiptoes, such as *horses* or deer.

unilateral: On one side only.

unsound: Describes a *horse* who suffers from a defect or condition which is likely to lead to lameness. An unsound horse might not be currently *lame*.

upset: To thicken metal stock by hammering it into itself. The middle of a length of *bar stock* can be upset by heating it in a *forge*, then setting one end of the bar on the face of an *anvil* while the other end is driven down with the hammer.

USEF: United States Equestrian Federation. National rule-making organization for equestrian spots. The USEF rule book is of particular interest to *farriers* who shoe *gaited horses*, as it includes technical regulations for allowable *horseshoeing*, weights, and *pads*.

This organization was known as the Association of American Horse Shows from 1917-1933, the American Horse Show Association from 1933-2001, and USA Equestrian from 2001-2003.

Current information and rules are online at http://www.usef.org/

vein (vān): Any of the relatively thin-walled vessels which carry blood from the tissues back to the the heart and lungs to be re-oxygenated.

Venice turpentine: A form of turpentine (resin/oil extract from pine sap) which is a thick syrup at room temperature and semi-solid in cool weather. It is traditionally used as a sole application to toughen the soles of sensitive *hooves*.

veterinarianitis: Expression coined by R.F. Redden, DVM to describe excessive use of the *hoof* knife by veterinarians.

vise: A heavy, mounted tool used to hold work pieces immobile. Modern *farriers* often use a spring-loaded, pedal-released vise built into their *anvil* stands designed specifically to hold *horseshoes*. *Smithies* usually included rugged *leg vises* and/or *calking vises*. Today's shops and shoeing rigs often settle for a heavy machinist's bench vise.

The value of a good vise is often underestimated by farriers. Finishing tools are dramatically more efficient when the shoe is held solidly in place.

vitamin A: A nutrient compound either $C_{20}H_{30}O$ or $C_{20}H_{28}O$ found in fish-liver oils, milk, some yellow and green vegetables, and egg yolks. Henry Heymering, *RMF* suggests 100,000 IU per day of vitamin A for an average sized *horse* to prevent *surface cracks* in new *hoof horn* and hoof infections. Scaly *periople* and chalky soles are signs of Vitamin A deficiency.

Vulcan: Brand of horseshoe *nails* from 1867 to 1936. First made with the cold rolled machine process.

Vulcan: Ancient Roman god of fire and *blacksmithing*, analogous to the Greek god *Hephaestus*. The word "volcano" is derived from his name.

walk [Anglo-Saxon *wealcan*, to rove, ultimately from Latin *volvo*, to roll]: The slow, broken *lateral* four-beat *gait* common to all *horses*. With most of his weight carried by the *limbs* on one side of his body, the horse raises the hind foot on the opposite side. While that foot is in still in flight, the lateral fore *hoof* is raised, leaving the ground just before the hind foot lands. Just as this fore foot is about to land, the diagonal hind foot leaves the ground. As this hind foot is in flight, its lateral fore hoof begins to be raised. There are at least two hoofs on the ground at all times at the walk. Horses tend to walk a little faster than humans, but they can easily walk slower or faster up to about human jogging speed.

wall: The outer, *horny* part of the *hoof* which is the primary weight bearing structure of the *equine* foot.
see: Pages A-2, A-5.

warmblood: While the obvious implication of the term would be a *horse* with both *hotblood* and *coldblood* heritage, this would include the vast majority of all horses in existence, rendering the designation essentially meaningless. The more specific application of the term refers to horses selectively bred for a type which combines the stature and power of coldbloods with the grace and athleticism of hotbloods. "Warmblood" often refers to horses produced by several European programs (not exactly breeds, as these registries may be based more on inspection than pedigree) which originally produced light *draft* and cavalry horses, but have out-bred to hotbloods to produce sporthorses in more recent decades.

w-bar shoe: An open-toed version of the *heartbar*. The open toe eliminates the possibility of shoe pressure on the *anterior* sole, and allows wear at the front of the *hoof*, which tends to grow forward in a *flare* in *chronic founder* cases. However, this shoe will not protect the anterior sole from ground injury as a full toe heartbar *horseshoe* does.

See: Pages A-2; A-5.

w-bar shoe

water line: Inner, unpigmented *hoof wall* which is sometimes mistaken for the *white line*.

W.C.F.: Worshipful Company of Farriers. An organization of *farriers* in England. Founded in 1356 as the "Marshalls of the City of London", it was chartered under its current name in 1674.

-**Address:** 19 Queen Street Chipperfield, Kings Langley Herts. WD4 9BT Great Britain.

wean: To transition a *foal* from drinking its *dam's* milk to complete dependence on a feed, hay, grass, and water diet. Foals normally start nibbling dry foods and drinking water on their own early in life, and are usually weaned between three and six months of age. Ideally, the foal should be completely separated from its dam at weaning, even to the point of getting the two out of earshot of one-another. This helps the *mare* to dry up and recover from supporting the foal, and allows the foal to become more oriented on humans as its primary care-givers. Once the mare has completely stopped lactating, and the foal is eating dry feeds well, they can be turned out together again.

weanling: A *foal* who has been *weaned*, but is not yet a *yearling*.

web: The width of the stock from which a *horseshoe* is made.

wedge pad: A *pad* which is tapered in thickness, usually placed between the *hoof* and *horseshoe* to raise the *hoof angle*.

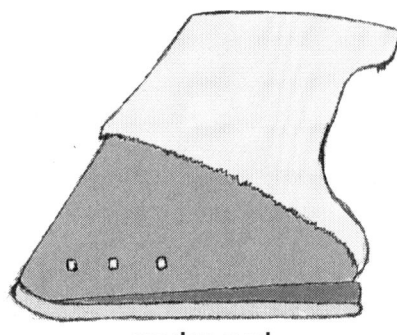

wedge pad

wedge shoe: A *horseshoe* which is graduated in thickness from a thin toe to thick heels. This has the effect of raising the *hoof angle*. A reverse wedge shoe raises the toe and lowers the hoof angle. *Lateral* wedge shoes alter the *mediolateral balance* of the foot.

welding, forge: The process of joining metal surfaces by heating them in a *forge* until they are slightly molten, then hammering them together on the *anvil*. Good forge welds are very strong, beadless, and may be impossible to detect with the naked eye.

forge welding

western: A broad classification of equitation and *tack* styles which evolved from those developed by American cowboys and their Mexican counterparts. Western saddles are relatively heavy, but provide a very secure and comfortable seat while distributing the rider's weight over a broad area of the *horse's* back. The most obvious feature of these saddles is the horn, which was originally developed as a place to affix a lasso when roping, but is often used as a hand hold. (This is considered very poor form in all but a few western disciplines, but can be an aid to beginners on their first rides.) Most western riding is done with the reins held in the left hand and the horse guided by "neck reining" with little or no contact (the reins are kept slack) when the horse is not being cued. This derives from the need for ranch horses to be easily controlled with one hand while the right hand is employed with the lasso or whip to manage cattle. Western riders typically ride with a long stirrup leather, so that standing it the stirrups raises them above the saddle seat only a couple of inches, and tend to sit more upright than *English* riders. In addition to being a popular choice for leisure riders across America and in several other countries, organized western disciplines range from "high fashion", sloth-speed Western Pleasure show classes to athletic performance competitions like reining and rodeo events.

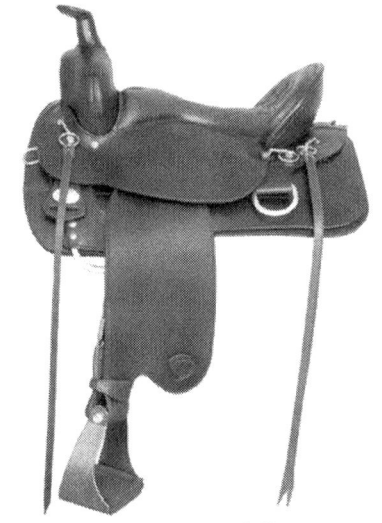
western saddle

white line: The border between the sole and the *hoof wall* as seen on the *solar* view of the hoof. Usually colored pale yellow, as opposed to the *water line* which is normally white. Deterioration of the white line and/or inner hoof wall is called white line disease, seedy toe, and *onychomycosis*.
See: Pages A-2; A-5.

Whitman: Brand of rubber *horseshoes* made from 1878 through 1911.

windpuff: A soft swelling which appears on either side of the fetlock area. Windpuffs are generally considered *blemishes*, but may indicate excessive strain which could lead to more serious trouble. "Articular windpuff" is the distention of the fetlock joint capsule. "Tendinous windpuff" involves the **DDF** sheath.
a.k.a: windgall; hygromata; road puff; popped ankle.

winging-in: A deviation in *gait* in which the *hoof* arcs inward (under the *horse*) in flight. Winging-in is often seen in horses with *toed-out* conformation, and may lead to *interference*.

winging-out: A deviation in *gait* in which the *hoof* arcs outward in flight. Winging-out is often seen in *horses* with *toed-in* conformation, and while it is more obvious to the untrained eye than *winging-in*, it is less likely to cause *interference*.
a.k.a: paddling.

wolf teeth: The first premolar teeth of a *horse*. Not to be mistaken for the more obvious canine teeth (tusks) which are usually seen in males and sometimes in females in the space between the corner incisors and the premolars. Wolf teeth are vestigial and only appear in the minority of horses. When present, they sometimes cause the horse discomfort when a bit is used. Such discomfort can lead to head-tossing, resistance in training, and even alterations of *gait* and carriage which may be mistaken for *lameness*. Extraction of the wolf teeth is a routine solution.

See also: Page A-11.

x-rays: Electromagnetic radiation with wave lengths between approximately 0.0000001 and 0.00000000001 centimeter. Because x-rays pass through soft tissue and are largely absorbed by bones, they are useful in *radiography*.

a.k.a: Roentgen rays.

yearling: A *horse* between one and two years old. Some breed and show organizations consider a horse to be a yearling on the first New Year's Day after its birth, even if the animal is well under twelve months of age. Older yearlings are sometimes called 'long yearlings'.

yeast infection: *White line* disease was thought to be an infection of Candida Albicans Yeast. More recent evidence suggests, however, that other fungi, such as Pseudallescheria Boydii are actually responsible.

zinc: A bluish-white metallic element. Atomic number 30. Atomic weight 65.37. Melting point 419.4°C. Blue-white in color. An important component in many *alloys*, solders, and metal coatings. As a dietary mineral, zinc appears essential to the proper functioning of the *basement membrane* between the *horny* and sensitive *laminae*.

zoonoses: Diseases communicable between man and other animals.

clxviii
. . .

APPENDIX of ILLUSTRATIONS:

A-1
Horseowner's Maintenance Kit.

A-2
External Hoof Anatomy.

A-3
External Anatomy of Equine Limbs.

A-4
Skeletal Anatomy of Equine Limbs.

A-5
Cross-Section of Equine Digit.

A-6
Basic Shoeing Box Tools.

A-7
Basic Anvil Tools.

A-8
Plain Keg Shoe Design.

A-9
Common Horseshoe Types.

A-10
Epiphyseal Plate Closure.

A-11
Aging the Horse by Teeth.

A-12
Shoe Size Chart.

clxx

Horseowner's Maintenance Kit.

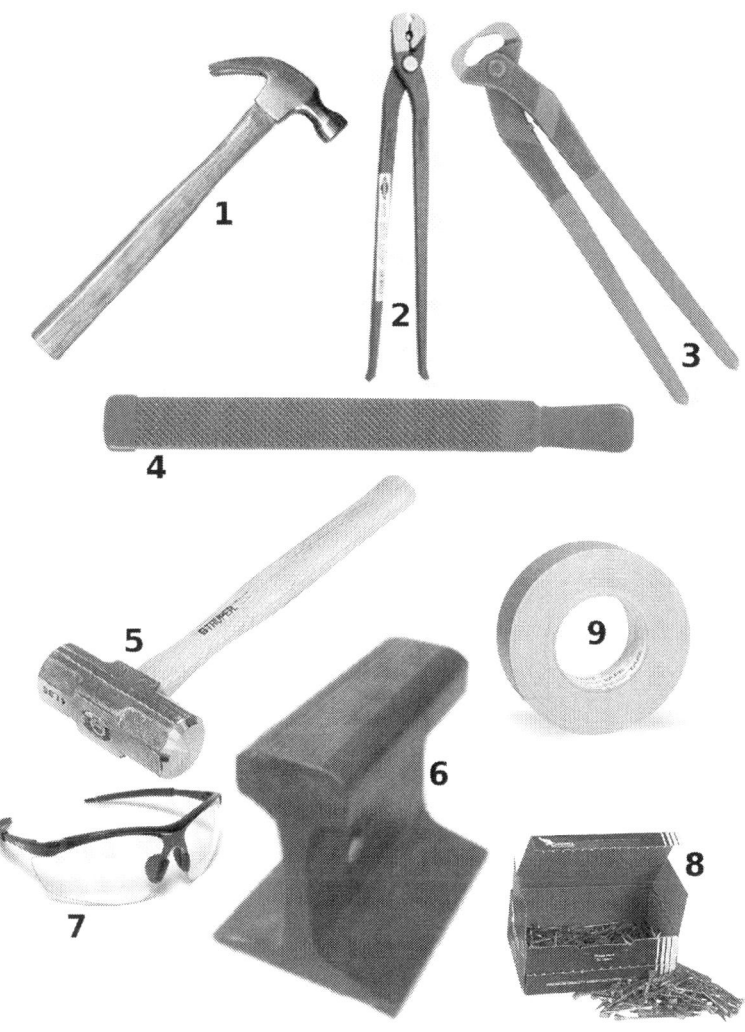

1. Light claw hammer for driving, bending/wringing-off nails
2. Crease nail puller (optional) for easier shoe removal.
3. End cutters to use as shoe pullers, nail cutters, and clinch block.
4. Rasp to file off old clinches, smooth new clinches, round-off hooves.
5. Heavy hammer for shoe leveling.
6. Railroad track "anvil". Machinist's vise may also substitute.
7. Safety glasses.   8. Supply of horseshoeing nails.
9. Duct tape for when all else fails.

External Hoof Anatomy.

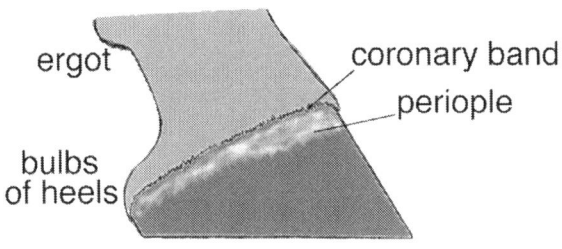

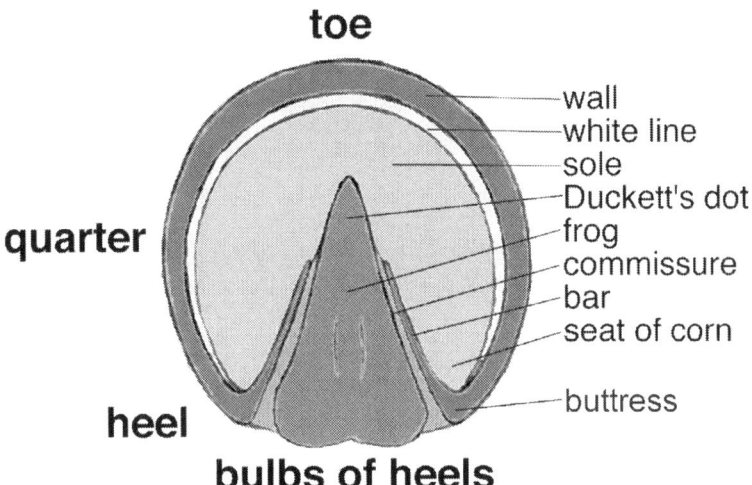

Anatomy of Equine Limbs.

forelimb

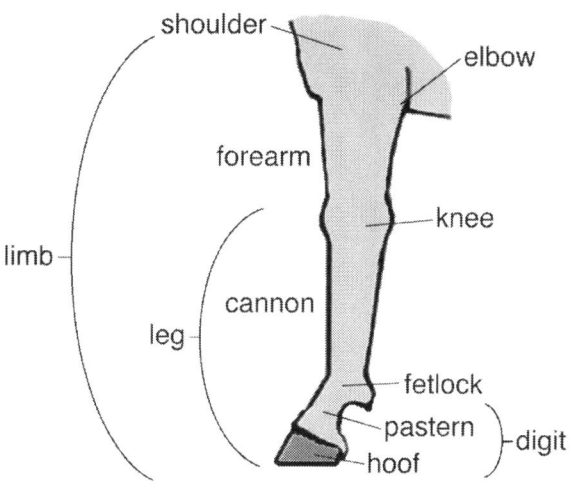

hind limb

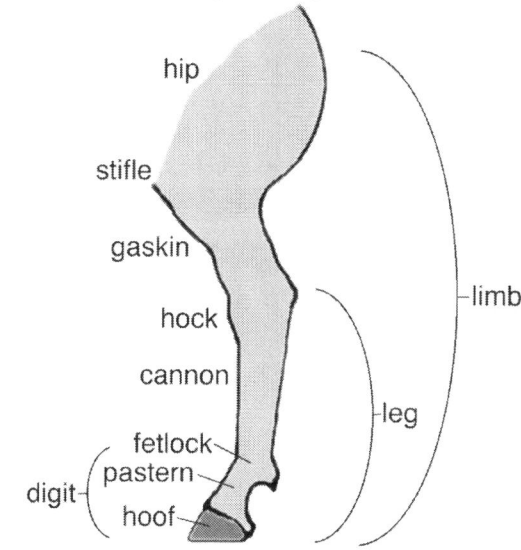

Skeletal Anatomy of Equine Limbs.

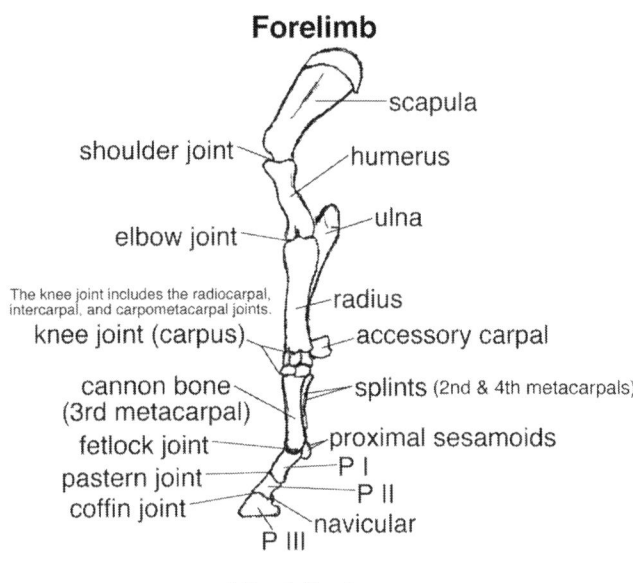

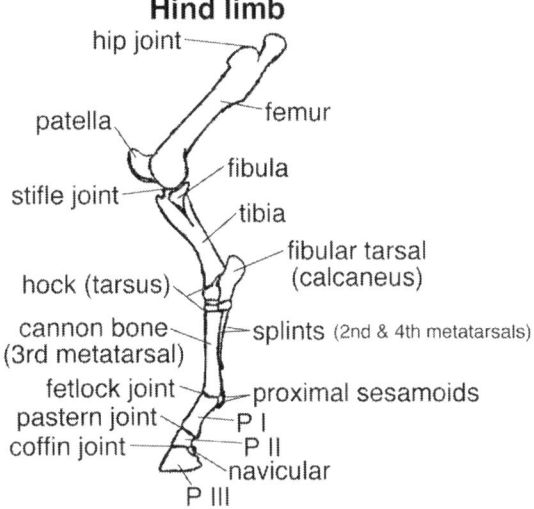

CROSS-SECTION OF EQUINE DIGIT.

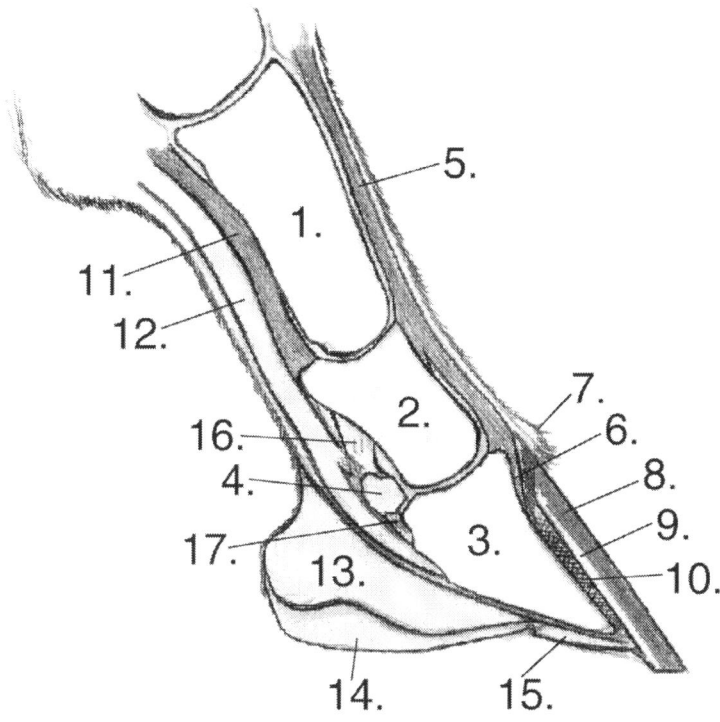

1. PI. (Long Pastern Bone, First Phalanx, Proximal Phalange)
2. PII. (Short Pastern, Os Coronae, Second Phalanx, Middle Phalange)
3. PIII. (Coffin Bone, Os Pedis, Pedal Bone, Third Phalanx, Distal Phalange)
4. Navicular Bone. (Distal Sesamoid)
5. Main Digital Extensor Tendon.
6. Extensor Process of PIII.
7. Coronary Band.
8. Outer, Pigmented Hoof Wall.
9. Inner, Unpigmented Hoof Wall.
10. Laminae.
11. Sesamoidian ligament.
12. DDF. Deep Digital Flexor Tendon.
13. Digital (Plantar) Cushion.
14. Frog.
15. Sole.
16. Suspensory Ligament of Navicular.
17. Distal Navicular Ligament.

Basic Shoeing Box Tools.

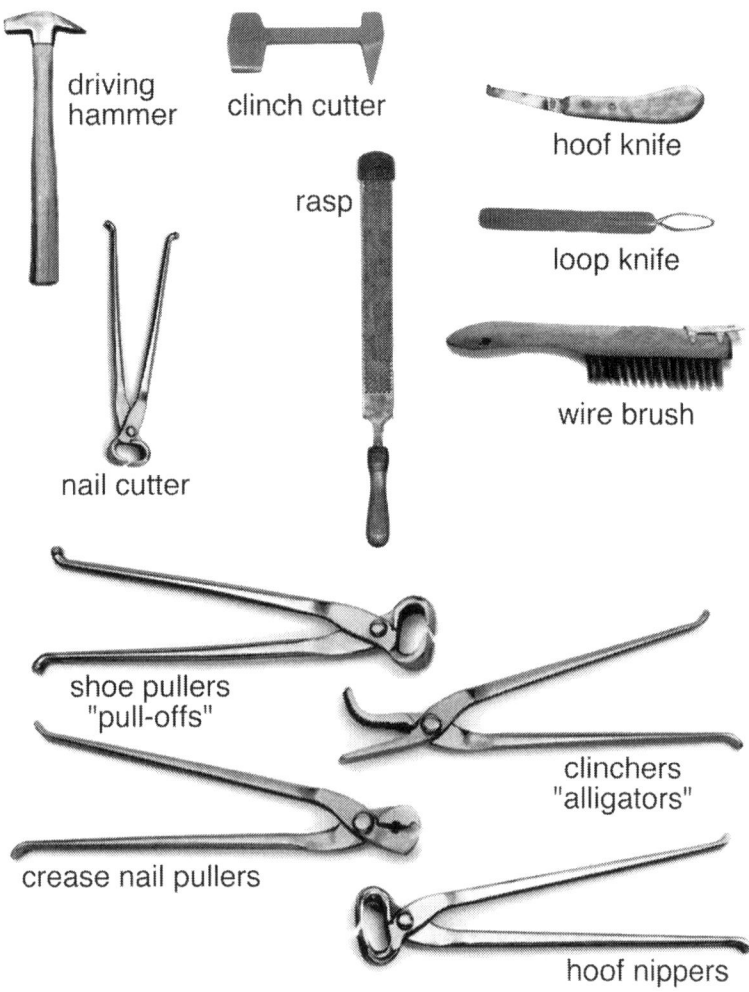

A-6

Basic Anvil Tools.

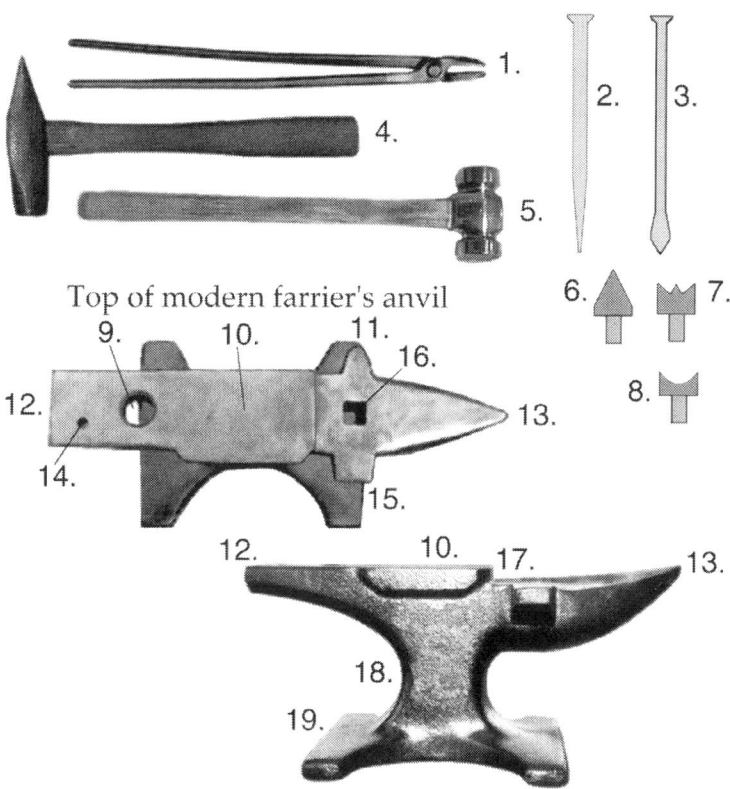

Top of modern farrier's anvil

1. Fire Tongs.
2. Pritchel.
3. Forepunch (Stamp).
4. Blacksmith's Cross-Peen.
5. Farrier's Rounding.
6. Hardie (Cut-Off).
7. Rim Swedge Block.
8. Half-Round Block.
9. Turning Hole.
10. Face.
11. Clip Horn.
12. Heel.
13. Horn.
14. Pritchel Hole.
15. Squaring Horn.
16. Hardie Hole.
17. Step.
18. Waist.
19. Foot.

PLAIN KEG SHOE DESIGN.
(Compromise pattern horseshoe.)

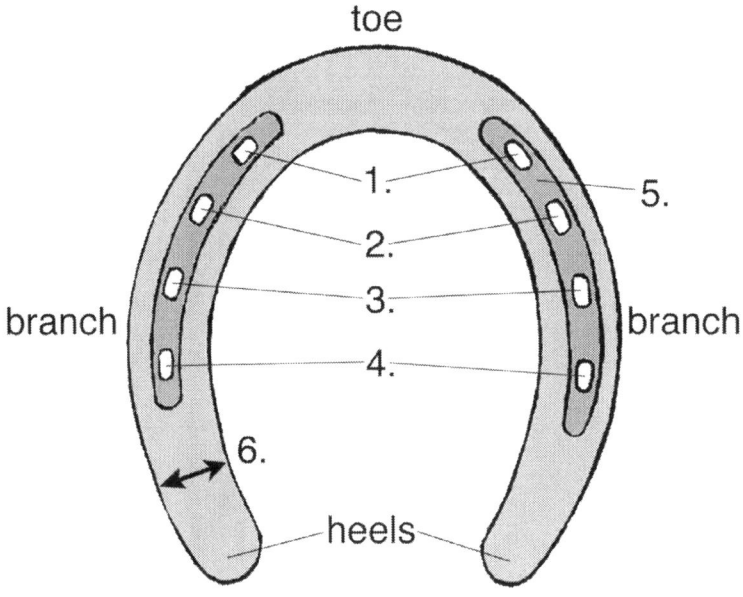

1. First (toe) nail holes.
2. Second (toe quarter) nail holes.
3. Third (heel quarter) nail holes.
4. Fourth (heel) nail holes.
5. Nail crease.
6. Web width.

Common Horseshoe Types.

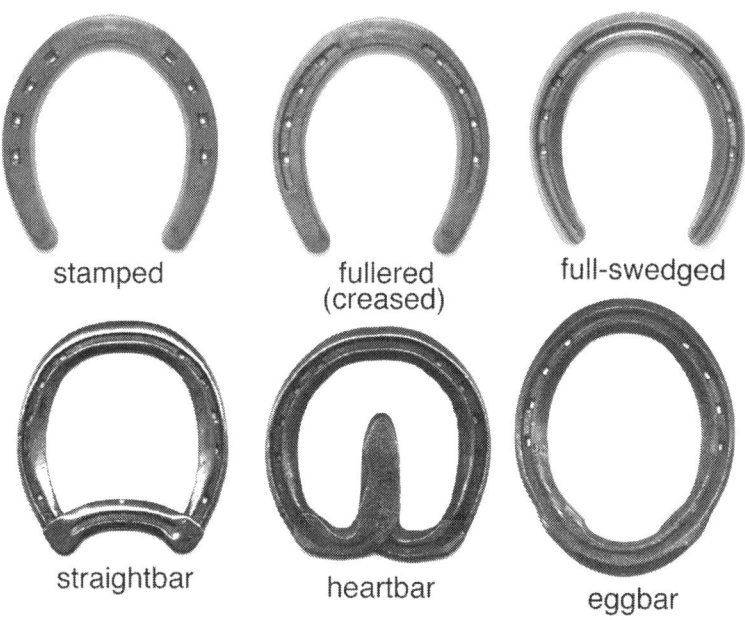

stamped   fullered (creased)   full-swedged

straightbar   heartbar   eggbar

Cross-sections of swedged horseshoes.

hoof-facing surface

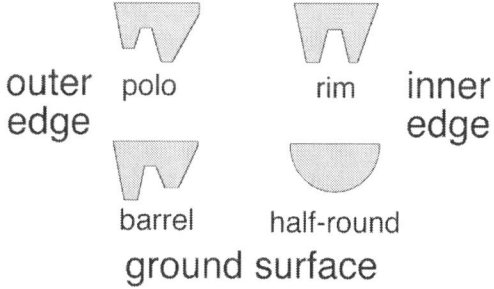

outer edge   polo   rim   inner edge

barrel   half-round

ground surface

Epiphyseal Plate Closure.

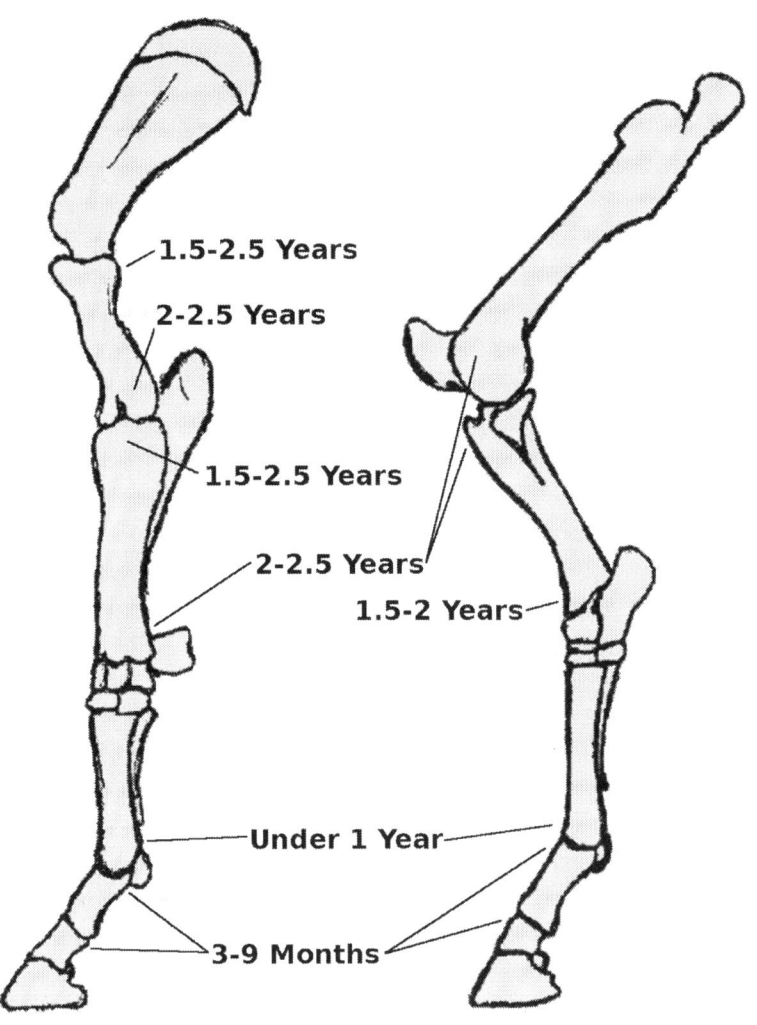

Approximate ages at which the epiphyseal cartilages (growth plates) ossify as the horse matures.

AGING THE HORSE BY TEETH.

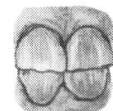
First deciduous incisors present shortly after birth.

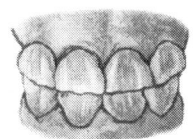
Intermediate deciduous incisors present after around five weeks.

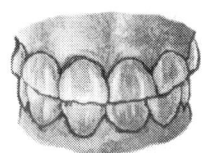
Corner deciduous incisors present after six to nine months.

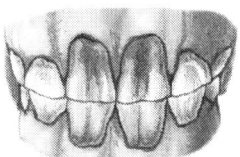
Front permanent teeth present after 2 1/2 years.

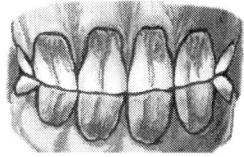
Intermediate permanent teeth present after 3 1/2 years. Lower canine teeth (not to be confused with wolf teeth) also appear in males and some females around this time.

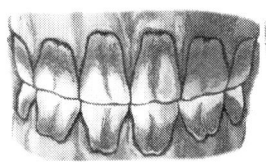
Corner permament teeth present after 4 1/2 years. Upper canine teeth (tusks) usually emerge in males.

Six years old. Front incisors worn flat.

Seven years old. Intermediate incisors worn flat.

Eight years old. All incisors worn flat.

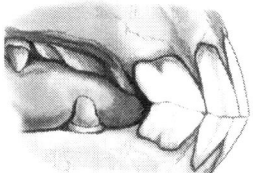
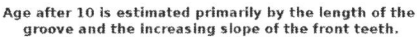
Ten years old. All permanent teeth present and in full wear. Galvayne's groove just appearing on corner incisors, will run the full length of the tooth by about 20. May disappear after 30.

Age after 10 is estimated primarily by the length of the groove and the increasing slope of the front teeth.

A-11

SHOE SIZE CHART.

These measurements are based on popular brand shoes. There is some variation between manufacturers. Others use an entirely different scale, especially with non-steel shoes.

"0" is usually pronounced "aught". "000" and "00" are "triple-aught" and "double-aught".

Size	Width	Length	
0 PONY	3 5/16"	3 3/4"	
1 PONY	3 7/16"	4 1/8"	
000	4 1/8"	4 3/8"	
00	4 3/8"	4 3/4"	
0	4 5/8"	5"	
1	4 7/8"	5 1/4"	
2	5 1/4"	5 5/8"	
3	5 1/2"	6"	
4	6 1/8"	6 5/8"	
5	6 1/2"	7 1/4"	
6 DRAFT	6 1/2"	9 1/2"	Heels uncut.
8 DRAFT	7 1/8"	9 7/8"	Heels uncut.

Historical Reference Appendix.

Farriery has a long and storied past, with an odd discontinuity due to the collapse of the horse industry through the middle third of the 20th Century.

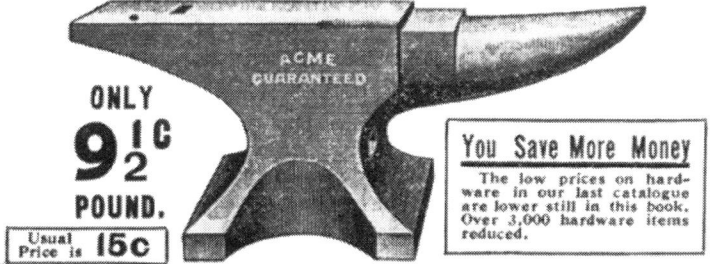

From the 1902 Sears-Roebuck catalog.

This section presents materials predating the First World War. Our predecessors were perhaps far less primitive than we might have imagined.

Indeed, it appears that much of what we have spent the last few decades doing was actually re-inventing the wheel.

Historical Reference.

BERKSHIRE COUNTY COUNCIL'S SCHOOL.

19th Century mobile shoeing rig.
A far cry from one man in a truck.

From 1898
A Handbook of Horseshoeing
Dollar & Wheatley

Historical Reference.

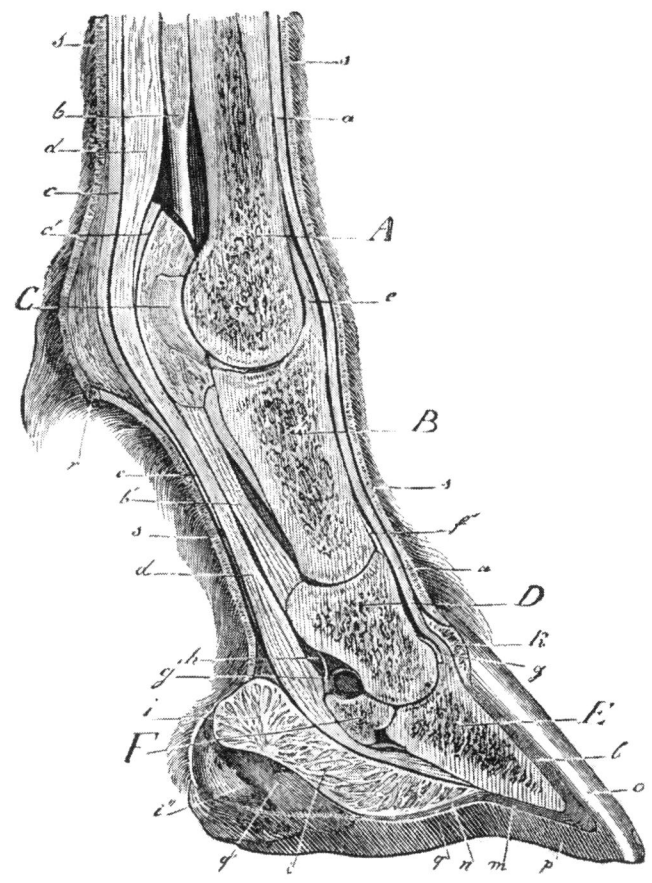

FIG. 10.—Perpendicular mesial section of right fore-foot (the position of the lower bones is shown rather too upright). *A*, lower end of great metacarpus; *B*, suffraginis or pastern bone; *C*, inner sesamoid bone (to render the bone visible, a portion of the intersesamoidean ligament has been removed); *D*, coronet bone; *E*, pedal bone; *F*, navicular bone; *a*, extensor pedis tendon; *b*, superior sesamoidean or suspensory ligament; *b'*, inferior sesamoidean ligament; *c*, flexor pedis perforatus tendon; *c'*, great sesamoid sheath; *d*, flexor pedis perforans tendon; *e*, capsular ligament of the fetlock joint; *f*, capsular ligament of pastern joint; *g* and *g'*, capsular ligament of coffin joint; *h*, bursa of flexor pedis perforans; *i*, plantar cushion; *i'*, portion of plantar cushion forming the bulbs of the heel; *k*, coronary band; *l*, sensitive wall; *m*, sensitive sole; *n*, sensitive frog; *o*, horny wall; *p*, horny sole; *q*, horny frog; *r*, ergot at base of fetlock; *s*, skin.

From 1898
A Handbook of Horseshoeing
Dollar & Wheatley

HISTORICAL REFERENCE.

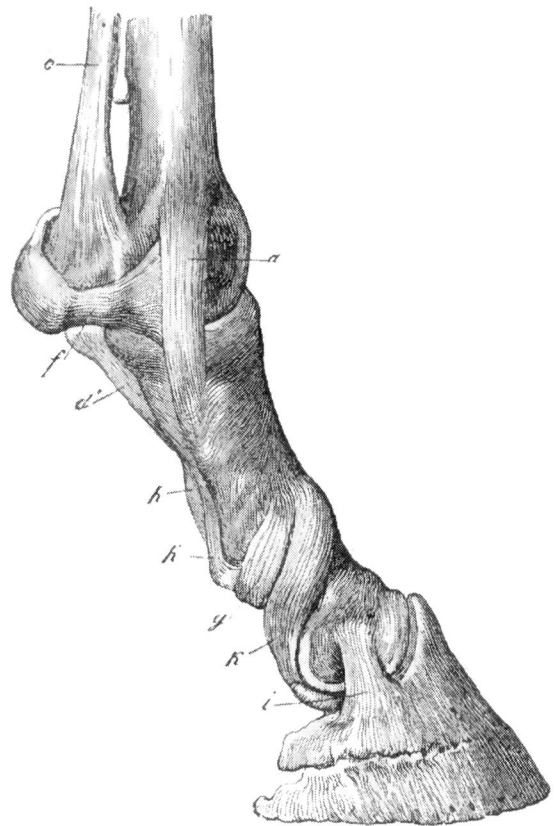

FIG. 21.

Fig. 21 shows the bones of the foot and their ligaments viewed from the side, figs. 22 and 23 viewed from behind. The letters indicate same parts in each figure. *a*, external lateral ligament of pastern joint ; *b*, intersesamoidean ligament ; *c*, superior sesamoidean ligament ; *d*, middle limb of inferior sesamoidean ligament ; *d'*, lateral limb of do.; *e*, cruciate ligament ; *f*, lateral sesamoidean ligament; *g*, outer lateral ligament of the pastern joint; *h* and *h'*, posterior corono-suffraginal ligaments ; *i*, outer lateral ligament of pedal joint; *k*, postero-lateral ligaments of navicular bone ; *l*, fibrous sheath of synovial membrane of coffin joint.

From 1898
A Handbook of Horseshoeing
Dollar & Wheatley

Historical Reference.

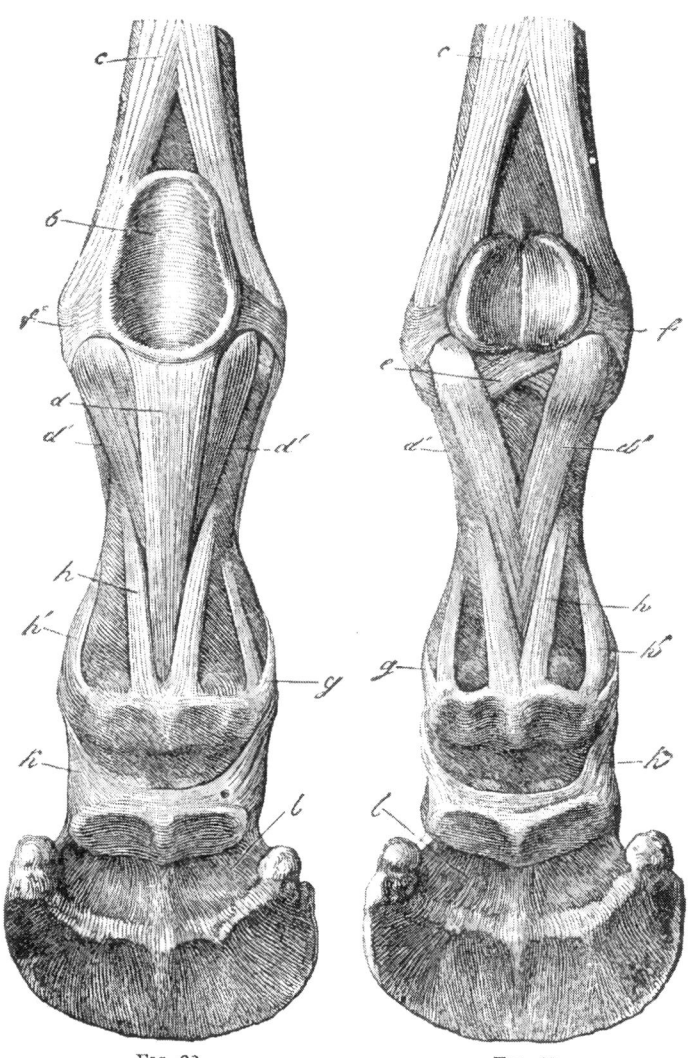

Fig. 22.   Fig. 23.

From 1898
A Handbook of Horseshoeing
Dollar & Wheatley

Historical Reference.

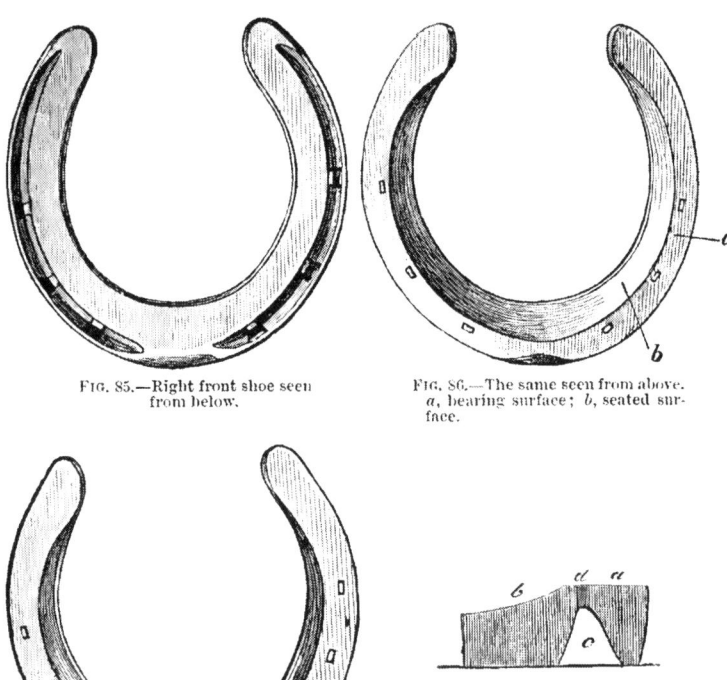

Fig. 85.—Right front shoe seen from below.

Fig. 86.—The same seen from above. *a*, bearing surface; *b*, seated surface.

Fig. 87.—Left hind shoe seen from above.

Fig. 88.—Transverse section of a fore shoe through one of the nail holes; natural size. *a*, bearing surface; *b*, seated surface; *c*, fullering; *d*, nail hole.

From 1898
A Handbook of Horseshoeing
Dollar & Wheatley

HISTORICAL REFERENCE.

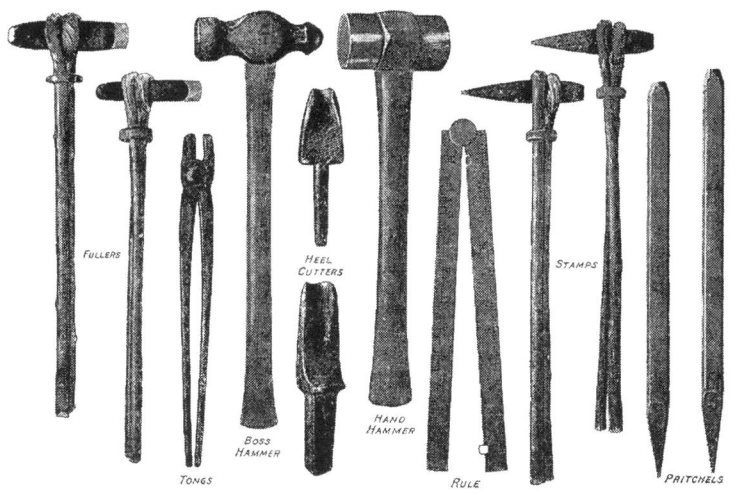

FIREMAN'S TOOLS.

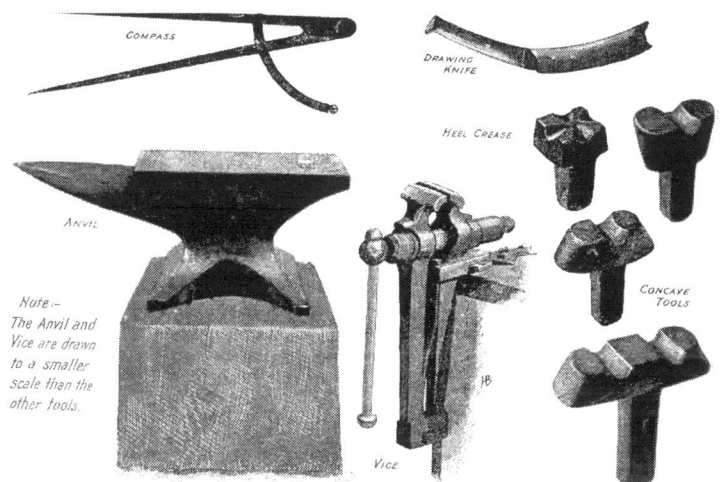

FIREMAN'S TOOLS

From 1898
A Handbook of Horseshoeing
Dollar & Wheatley

Historical Reference.

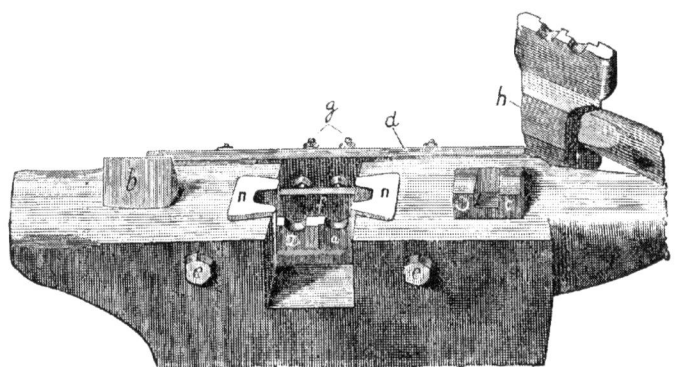

FIG. 114.—Anvil for making screws. *a*, mould for forming shank; *b*, cutter; *c*, mould for making sharp-headed screws; *d*, plate carrying set screws, *g*, and held in position by the two screws, *e*, *e*; *f*, die carrying the moulds, *a*, *a*. This can be set at any distance from the plate, *d*, by moving the set screws, *g*. The length of the shank is thus fixed; *h*, forging hammer.

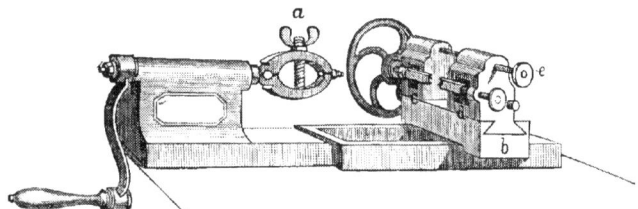

FIG. 116.—Screw-cutting machine. *a*, claws for grasping screw; *b*, slides for adjusting the cutting parts of die, *c* and *d*; *e*, set screw for determining the thickness of the finished shank.

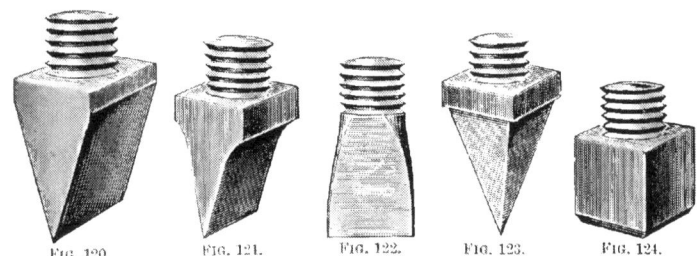

FIG. 120.   FIG. 121.   FIG. 122.   FIG. 123.   FIG. 124.

From 1898
A Handbook of Horseshoeing
Dollar & Wheatley

Historical Reference.

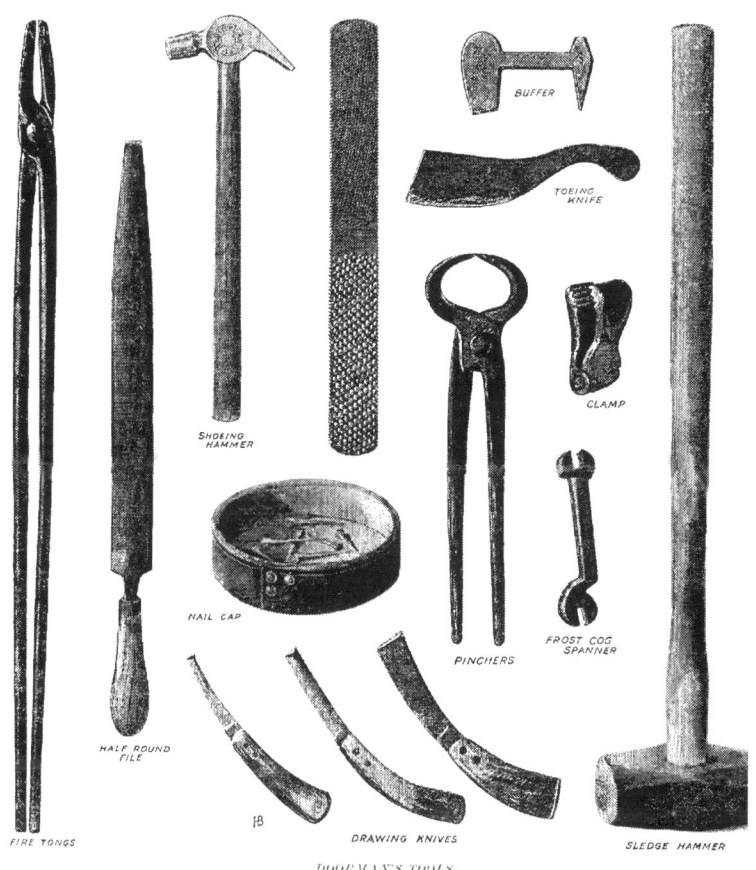

From 1898
A Handbook of Horseshoeing
Dollar & Wheatley

HISTORICAL REFERENCE.

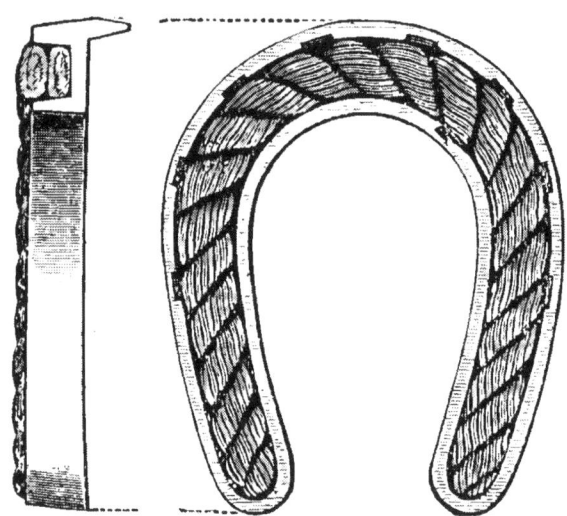

FIG. 264.

FIG. 337.—Fullered fore shoe (for harness horse), with frog plate.
Made from 1 × ½ inch iron.

From 1898
A Handbook of Horseshoeing
Dollar & Wheatley

Historical Reference.

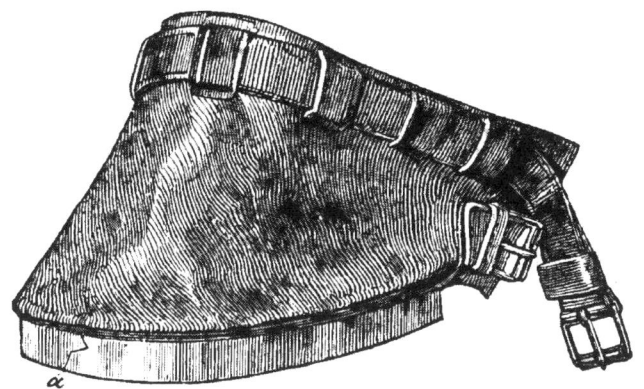

FIG. 215.—Temporary shoe with leather boot and straps. *a*, hinge.

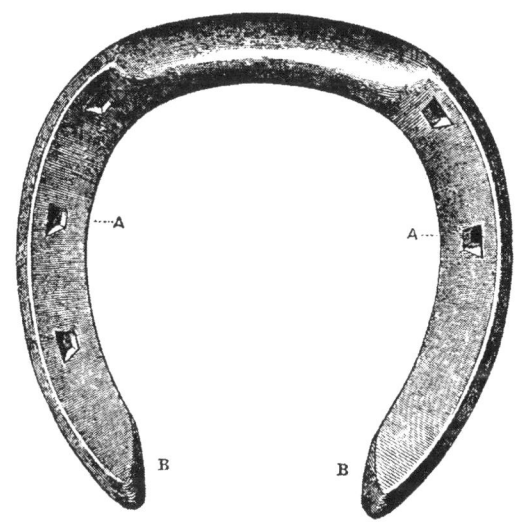

FIG. 261.—Sir F. Fitzwygram's shoe.

From 1898
A Handbook of Horseshoeing
Dollar & Wheatley

HISTORICAL REFERENCE.

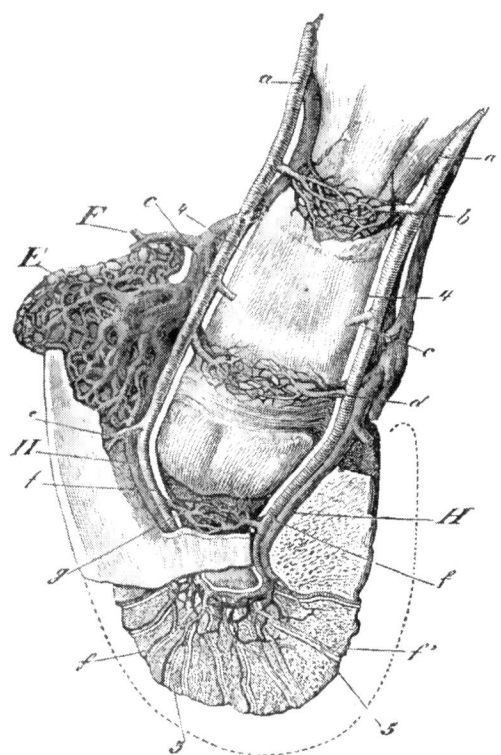

FIG. 33.—Right fore-foot, seen from below, behind, and somewhat from one side. The outer lateral cartilage is removed, together with sufficient of the pedal bone to render visible the vessels, etc., in its interior. The nerves accompanying arteries f are shown too thick; they should be less than half as broad as figured. a, digital artery; b, posterior suffraginal artery; c, artery of plantar cushion (cut through); d, posterior artery of coronary circle; f, plantar artery, which anastomoses with its fellow within the pedal bone, and gives off twigs f, which pass to the anterior surface of the pedal bone, just above its lower edge; g, twigs of plantar artery supplying coffin joint; E, deep lateral layer of coronary plexus, clothing inner surface of lateral cartilage; F, divided ends of superficial part of coronary plexus. From these arise the digital vein (not shown); H, plantar vein; 4, posterior branch of digital nerve accompanying vessels into pedal bone; 5, twigs of posterior branch passing towards sensitive laminæ.

From 1898
A Handbook of Horseshoeing
Dollar & Wheatley

Historical Reference.

Chapter III.

WORKING AND SHAPING IRON.

THE PLATE SHOE.

8. As a preliminary to instruction in shaping and preparing a shoe *for the foot*, it is best for beginners to learn the method of making and shaping a plate shoe, using an *old shoe* as a model.

The various parts of a shoe are commonly spoken of as follows: The toe is that portion between the first nail hole on one side and the first nail hole on the other side. The quarters are the portions in which the nail holes are punched. The heels are the remaining parts of the shoe. A side is one-half of a shoe, and includes one heel, one quarter, and one-half of the toe.

The plate shoe is made of ½ by ¼ inch steel which is much more easily worked than the heavier service shoe.

Take a bar of metal about 11 or 12 inches in length.[1]

9. To bend the bar, where the center of the toe will be.— Place the bar in the fire so that the center is directly over the draft. The coals of a properly-made fire should hold the bar about 6 inches above the twyer ball. When cherry red, remove from the fire, holding the nearest end with the tongs and lean

---

[1] The length of bar required to make a shoe *for a foot* will be found by measuring in a straight line on the sole of the foot from the edge of the wall at the center of the toe to the extremity of either bulb of the frog. A little more than twice this distance will be the length of the bar required to make the shoe.

From 1912
The Army Horseshoer
U.S. War Department

HISTORICAL REFERENCE.

22   THE ARMY HORSESHOER.

the other end on the edge of the anvil farthest from you. The bar is held on edge and at an angle of about 45° with the face of the anvil.

Strike lightly with the hammer at the center of the upper edge of the bar, and gradually bend the bar until it is right angled or L shaped.

From 1912
The Army Horseshoer
U.S. War Department

HISTORICAL REFERENCE.

THE ARMY HORSESHOER.

If, after bending, the L is not flat, but twisted, it must be leveled on the face of the anvil.

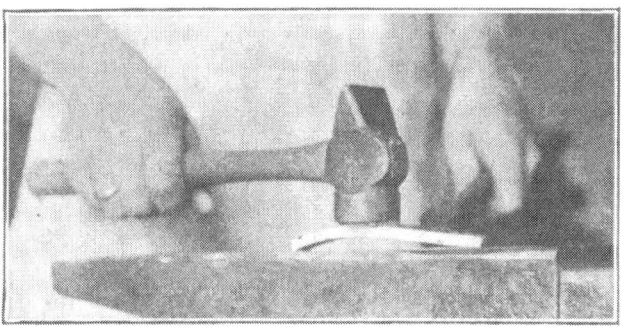

Remember to use only light blows on red metal. Heavy blows leave irregularities that are difficult or impossible to remove.

10. To shape one side.—Place one-half of the L in the fire and when heated seize the cold half with the tongs and hold

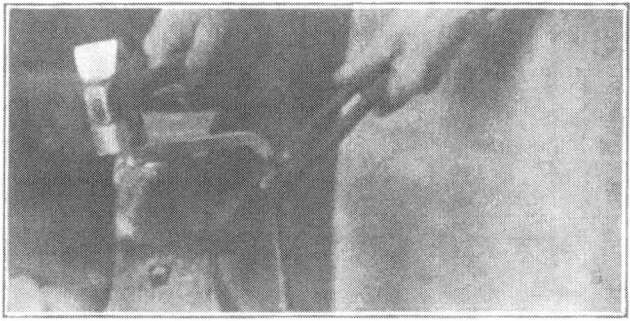

the heated side diagonally over the horn of the anvil, the left hand near the base and held low, the heated end projecting about an inch over the horn.

From 1912
The Army Horseshoer
U.S. War Department

24 THE ARMY HORSESHOER.

Begin striking at the end of the heated portion and, keeping the right hand steadily in position, shape the steel by gradually moving it beneath the hammer. Move the steel over the

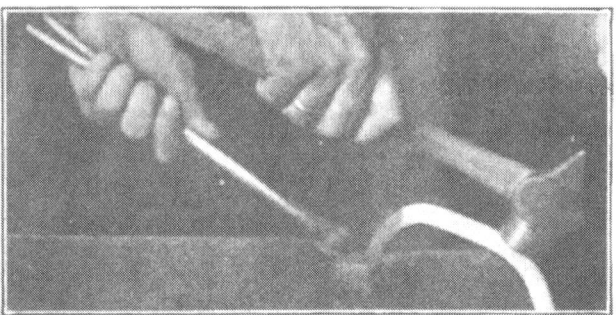

horn by raising the left hand and carrying it toward the point of the horn; that is, as the toe is approached, shift the work toward the point of the horn.

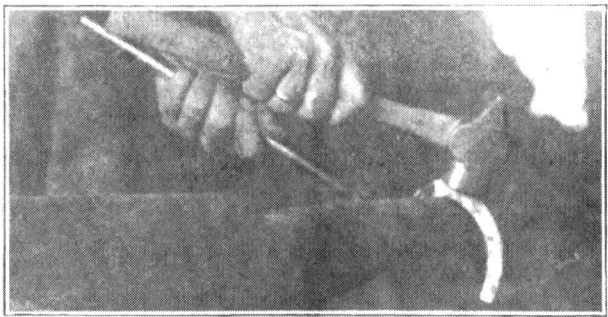

The horn of the anvil is so constructed that the diagonal curve across the center conforms to the shape of the heels and quarters of the average sized foot and the curve near the point is shaped like the toe. For a very large shoe begin near the base of the horn.

From 1912
The Army Horseshoer
U.S. War Department

HISTORICAL REFERENCE.

THE ARMY HORSESHOER.

To shape the opposite side, proceed in the same manner.

11. To center the toe.—After both sides have been turned, see if they are of equal length; that is, see if the toe is in the center. If not, then heat the toe, and grasping the longer side with the tongs, hold the shoe over the point of the horn so that it is correctly centered and strike just beyond the horn.

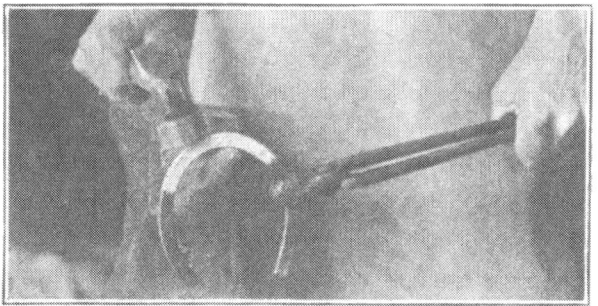

12. To draw out the heels.—Heat the heels to a white heat. Hold the shoe on the horn in the same position as for shaping and upon a diagonal that will insure close contact. The blows,

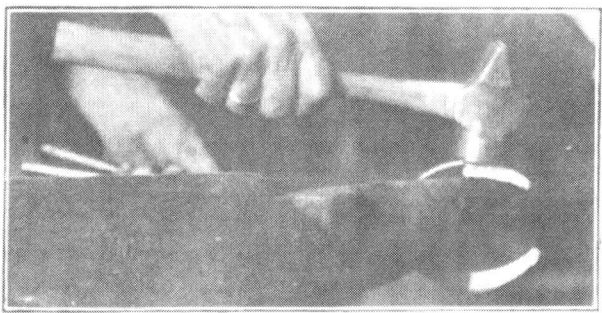

however, are struck on the part resting on the horn and the heel is brought toward the hammer by lowering the left hand.

From 1912
The Army Horseshoer
U.S. War Department

Historical Reference.

THE ARMY HORSESHOER.

In drawing out the heels the lower (or ground) surface of the shoe should be made slightly narrower than the upper (or bearing) surface.

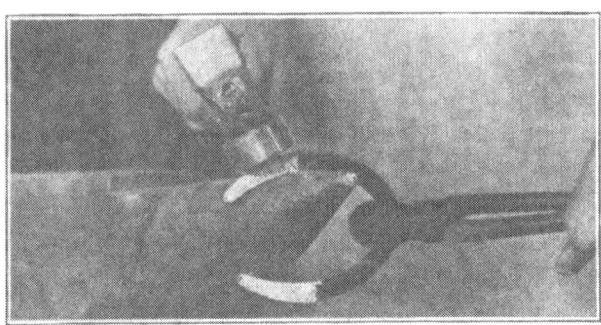

Notice that to draw out one heel the ground surface is on the left side when the heel rests on the horn.

To draw out the other heel the ground surface is on the right side, and the shoe is changed to the opposite diagonal of the horn.

In both cases strike on the edge of the ground surface, and as a result this surface will be the narrower.

For a left-handed man these positions will be reversed.

From 1912
The Army Horseshoer
U.S. War Department

Historical Reference.

THE ARMY HORSESHOER. 27

This drawing out narrows and at the same time thickens the heel. To restore it to its original thickness, work on the face of the anvil. Hold the ground surface down so as to preserve the bevel.

13. To cut off the heels.—Apply the shoe to the model and note how much must be cut from the heels. Care must be used,

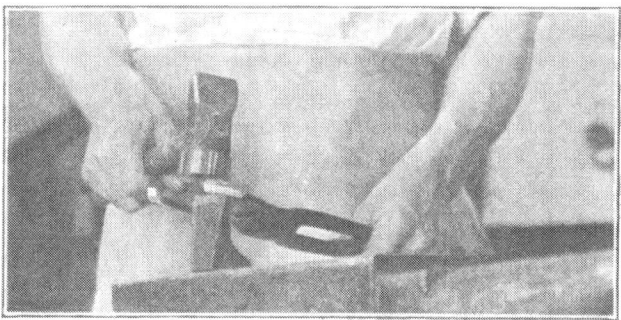

however, not to cut them too short. It is better to have them too long and to cut them off again if necessary.

After heating to a white heat, place the ground surface on the hardy so as to cut the heel off squarely, but hold the toe slightly lower so that the cut will also be beveled; that is, so

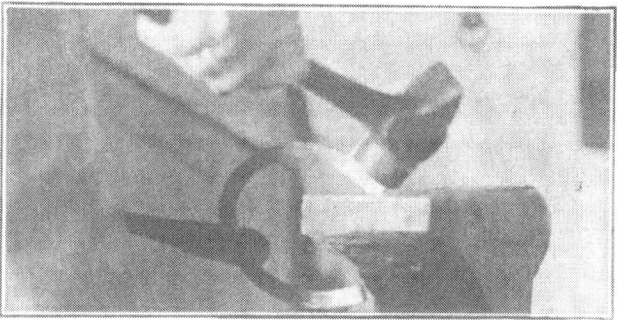

From 1912
The Army Horseshoer
U.S. War Department

THE ARMY HORSESHOER.

that the upper surface will be slightly longer than the ground surface. The cutting will widen the steel near the end.

To bring it back to the original width hold the inside edge on the heel of the anvil and strike on the outer edge.

This will also point the heel slightly and diminish the work of hot rasping (par. 14).

In fitting a plate shoe for a foot the nail holes should be punched *before* cutting off the heels so that if necessary the toe can be centered to correspond to the nail holes.

14. Hot rasping.—The heels are now finished by hot rasping. The shoe is placed in the vise with the ground surface toward you, and the heels are rounded, carefully preserving the

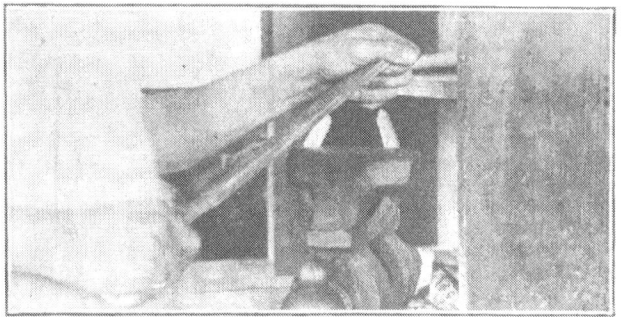

slight bevel (the upper surface being longer and wider than the ground surface).

Care must be used to leave no sharp edges on the heels that will cut the horse.

A pointed heel may cause a "shoe boil" (a bruise at the point of the elbow).

15. To punch out the nail holes.—Apply the shoe to the model; if the heels are of proper length and the shoe is an approximate fit, the nail holes are punched out.

The nail holes are started on the ground surface with the countersink because the point of this tool conforms to the shape of the head of the nail. The point should not be driven more than three-fourths through or the shoe will be bulged and ruined. The tool is held slanted outward to conform to the

From 1912
The Army Horseshoer
U.S. War Department

direction which the nail should follow and the hole is started a little outside of the center of the web.

Heat one side and first start the hole nearest the toe. Its proper position can be learned by examining a service shoe of the same size. The hole at the bend of the quarter is next started, and finally the hole midway between the two. The plate shoe, on account of its light weight, requires but six nails, three on each side.

Heat the other side and proceed as before.

The nail holes must not be placed too far back. A shoe nailed back of the turn of the quarter will impede the expansion of the hoof and eventually cause contraction of the heels.

If, in punching the nail holes, bulges appear near them on the edges of the bar or shoe, they must be removed by working over the horn. (Same position and means as for drawing heels.)

Examine the pritchel, and if it is not of the proper shape, point it before using. (*See* Tools, par. 1.)

Punch out the nail holes on the ground surface, holding the pritchel slanted outward; then punch out the holes on the upper surface, holding the pritchel slanted inward.

In pritcheling out a nail hole, to avoid blunting or breaking the point of the pritchel, that part of the shoe where the nail hole is to be, is held over the pritchel or hardy hole.

16. Fitting.—The shoe is now ready for its final trial and is applied to the model.

From 1912
The Army Horseshoer
U.S. War Department

HISTORICAL REFERENCE.

THE ARMY HORSESHOER.

If it does not exactly conform to the model, it will have at least one of the following faults, which must be corrected according to the explanation given in each case.

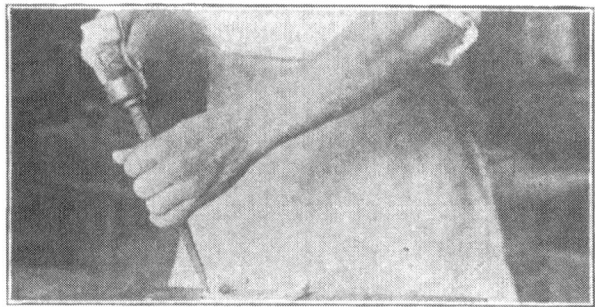

17. Not level.—To level the shoe, take it with the tongs near the toe on the far side and examine it by sighting over the upper surface. If it appears to be crooked, lay it on the face of the anvil in a position allowing the highest surface to be

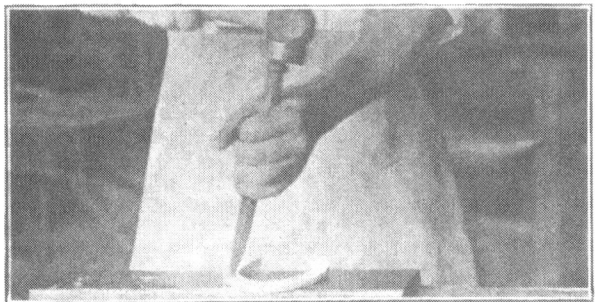

struck (par. 9). If, after remedying this defect, a similar one appears, it must be treated in the same manner. A crooked shoe will not stay on the foot and is apt to cause lameness.

When leveling the sevice shoe, if it be found necessary to strike on the ground surface of the shoe, let the blows fall over

From 1912
The Army Horseshoer
U.S. War Department

the crease in order to avoid spoiling the concave of the upper surface. Special care, however, must be used to strike a square blow. If the face of the hammer does not fall evenly, it will dent and close the crease.

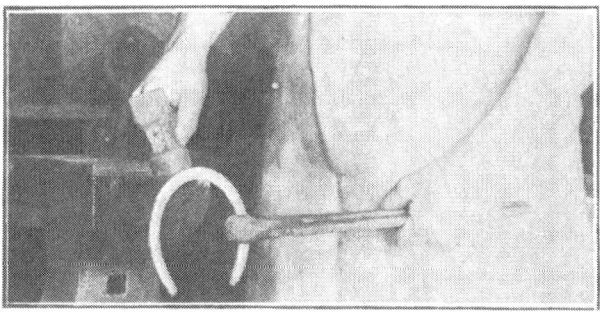

18. Too wide at the toe.—Heat the toe and hold it on the extreme point of the horn, the center of the shoe resting on the horn of the anvil. Strike lightly near the toe on the side farthest from you, then reverse the toe and strike as before.

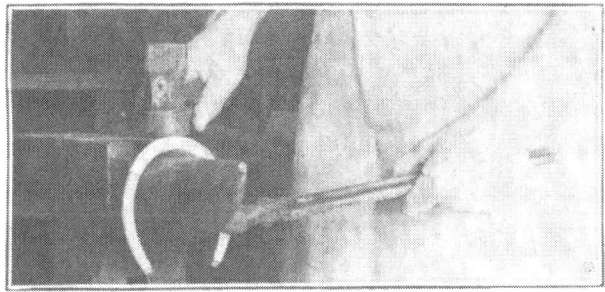

19. Too narrow at the toe.—Heat the toe and hold it on the horn of the anvil so that there will be a small space between the shoe and the horn. Strike lightly along the toe, not confining the blows to any one spot.

From 1912
The Army Horseshoer
U.S. War Department

THE ARMY HORSESHOER.

20. One heel and quarter too narrow.—To throw out a heel and quarter from a given point. Heat the quarter and, holding the heel on the horn, strike on the spot from which it is desired to spread or throw out the heel and quarter.

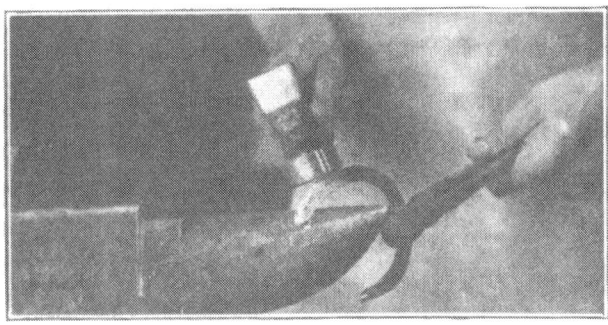

21. One heel and quarter too full.—(*a*) To throw in a heel and quarter from a given point. Heat the quarter and hold it over the point of the horn of the anvil so that the shoe

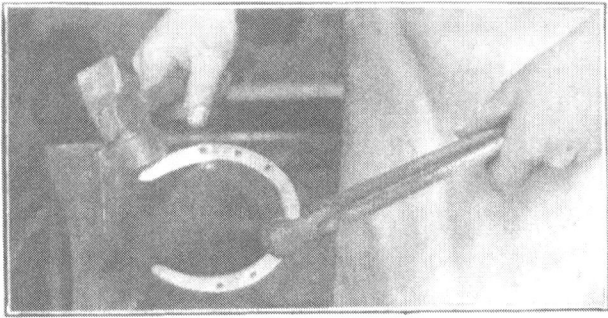

will rest upon the inside edge *at the point* from which the change is to be made. Strike near the heel on the part projecting over the horn.

From 1912
The Army Horseshoer
U.S. War Department

Historical Reference.

THE ARMY HORSESHOER.

(*b*) To throw in one side without changing its general shape. Heat the whole shoe and place the quarter that is correct in water until cool.

Close the shoe bodily (par. 24), which operation will affect the hot side only.

(*c*) If neither of these methods accomplishes the desired result the quarter must be reshaped over the diagonal of the horn.

22. A bulge in the quarter.—Heat the quarter and hold over the heel of the anvil. Strike directly over the bulge.

This will remove the bulge, but will also slightly straighten the quarter, which must later be reshaped.

23. A short straight place in a quarter.—Heat the quarter and hold the straight place on the point of the horn, as shown in paragraph 21, but strike alternate blows on each side of and close to the point to be rounded.

From 1912
The Army Horseshoer
U.S. War Department

THE ARMY HORSESHOER.

24. Both quarters too full (with the general shape correct).—Heat the whole shoe and, holding it on edge on the face of the anvil, strike down on the elevated quarter. This will narrow or close the shoe, but will not change its general shape.

25. Both quarters too narrow (with the general shape correct).—Heat the whole shoe and, holding one heel on the face of the anvil and one on the side, strike on the toe. This will open or spread the shoe without changing its general shape.

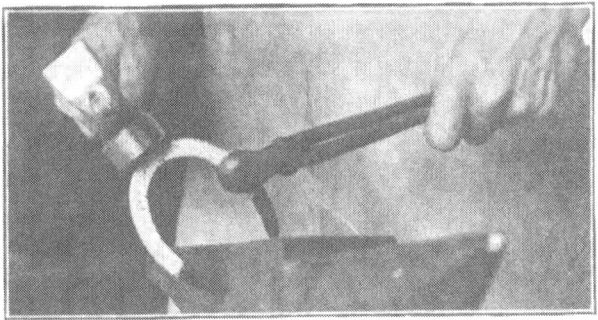

A perfect fit having been obtained the nail holes are repunched, if necessary, and the whole shoe neatly finished with the rasp.

From 1912
The Army Horseshoer
U.S. War Department

Historical Reference.

Chapter VIII.

SHOEING REFRACTORY HORSES.

102. Most horses that can be classed as refractory in shoeing have been brought to this condition by improper handling when green and unaccustomed to the sights and sounds of a shoeing shop.

When a young horse has been assigned to an organization, a common practice is to send him at once to the shop with instructions that he be shod by quiet means if possible, but by force if necessary.

No greater evil exists in the mounted service. It is as much our duty to gradually train a young horse to submit to shoeing as it is to patiently drill him to surrender to the bit and to work in the saddle or harness.

Summary methods not only ruin the horse's disposition, but subject the shoer to constant danger of injury.

103. Shoeing young horses.—The first step should be to teach the young animal that raising his feet will do him no harm, and this lesson should be given at the first grooming. The method of raising the fore foot and the hind foot, as explained in this manual, should be thoroughly understood by all enlisted men and be a part of the instruction of every recruit.

When the young horse surrenders his foot, lower it again quietly and pat him; later, use the brush on the soles of his feet; next tap the soles lightly with the currycomb; finally, take the shoer's position and go through the same steps. This complete instruction may be a matter of a day or of many days, depending upon the animal's disposition, but it should not be slighted nor hurried.

From 1912
The Army Horseshoer
U.S. War Department

Historical Reference.

THE ARMY HORSESHOER.

In the department of equitation at the Mounted Service School the following method is used with young horses that are disposed to kick when their hind legs are first handled. The horse is equipped with a cavesson, which is held by the animal's trainer. A surcingle is placed around the girth. The man that grooms the horse takes hold of the surcingle with the inside hand, in order to move with the horse and be secure against injury. With the outside hand he strokes the haunches and legs, gradually working downward. In the meantime the trainer pats the horse on the neck, but corrects him sharply with the cavesson whenever he displays temper. This method is almost invariably successful.

The second step is to let the young horse grow accustomed to the shop. While the horseshoer is at work on a *quiet horse* the young horse should be led into the shop and held by the man who has been grooming him and raising his feet.

The animal *should not be tied*, nor should he be held by any other man than the one he knows and trusts.

When the animal shows neither timidity nor excitement the shoer begins work on the feet. Frequently the removal of the surplus growth of horn is all that can be accomplished without excitement or resistance. At the first sign of either, work for that day should be abandoned and the horse removed from the shop.

The shock of the hammer is conveyed to the joints of the pastern bones, and the green horse, startled thereby, will struggle to free his foot. The shoer can usually handle a fore foot easily unassisted. If a good helper holds the hind leg in a comfortable position on his thigh and holds the hoof firmly with both hands, the shoer can work with more certainty, the shocks of nail driving will be taken up, to a great extent, in the helper's wrists and arms, and the horse will stand quietly.

Patient, quiet work will eventually succeed and thereafter each shoeing is more easily completed.

104. There are, however, certain highly nervous horses in nearly every organization that are refractory as a result of previous bad handling, and in the emergencies of active service there may be insufficient time to quietly prepare new mounts for shoeing as explained above.

From 1912
The Army Horseshoer
U.S. War Department

In these cases some form of restraint is required, but in each instance no more force should be employed than is absolutely necessary—*the gentlest method should be tried first.*

The cavesson, as a means of correction, will usually make a horse stand still and is to be preferred to the twitch. The latter, although effective, is a brutal instrument, and should never be used except upon an outlaw; moreover, after repeated use of the twitch the horse dreads any approach of the hands to his muzzle, and can be bridled only with the greatest difficulty. Severe use of the twitch will also permanently disfigure the animal's appearance.

105. If the cavesson is insufficient, the rigging described below should be used.

The cuff.—A strap of double thickness of leather, 18 inches long and 1½ inches wide, is sewed to a D ring 3 inches long and made of ⅜-inch round iron. A piece of thin leather 9 inches long and 3 inches wide is sewed on the inside of the strap next to the D ring; a buckle and keeper are sewed on the outside of the strap as shown.

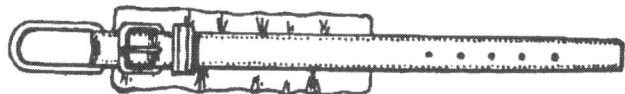

The surcingle.—Two 3-inch rings are sewed on the outside of the issue surcingle and are so placed that when the surcingle is adjusted the rings will hang down in the position of the quarterstrap rings of a saddle.

A **rope** ¾ inch in diameter and about 20 feet long; an eye splice should be made at one end.

This rigging can be easily made in any organization. For use in the field, the rope is replaced by a lariat. The cuff and surcingle together weigh only 2 pounds 5 ounces, and can readily be packed in a saddle bag.

TO RAISE A FORE FOOT.

106. Strap the cuff around the pastern, the ring above the heels. Pass an end of the rope through the ring and hand both ends over the horse's back to a helper.

From 1912
The Army Horseshoer
U.S. War Department

Historical Reference.

PLATE XVI.—RAISING FOOT OF REFRACTORY HORSE.

From 1912
The Army Horseshoer
U.S. War Department

Historical Reference.

THE ARMY HORSESHOER.

The horse's head, as usual, should be held by the man that grooms and trains the animal.

This man should stand on the side of the foot to be raised in order to avoid injury if the horse strikes.

The shoer gently but forcibly flexes the knee and raises the foot, while the helper takes in the slack of the doubled rope. If the horse is fractious, the helper passes both ends through the ring on his side. Grasping the rope close under the surcingle ring with the hand nearest the horse's head, and holding the ends securely against the hip in the other hand, the helper is secure against injury, can move with the horse and control the slack to the best advantage.

If a helper is not available, the shoer secures one end of the rope to the D ring (by the eye or by a knot), passes the other end through the surcingle ring on his own side and, after raising the foot, ties a half hitch.

TO RAISE A HIND FOOT.

107. Strap the cuff around the pastern, the ring above the heels. Draw the horse's tail to one side and make a loop in it; fasten one end of the rope in the loop by a "single sheet bend." Pass the other end through the D ring and draw it to the rear, where it is held by helpers. The horse is tied, but the head is held as usual. When the shoer raises the foot, the helpers draw in the slack of the rope and the foot is supported (by the animal himself) in a good position for work. If he kicks he can do no harm, as his foot must move along the rope. After one or two such efforts he will ordinarily stand quiet.

If helpers are not available, the end of the rope may be secured to a post or tree, but must be fastened in a manner to permit of prompt release in case of a protracted struggle, during which the horse might throw himself and be injured.

Mr. Churchill, instructor in shoeing, used this device for 14 years in civilian practice with unfailing success.

108. When it is found that a horse is so vicious that it is dangerous to shoe him unless he is rendered helpless, **two** courses are open. One is to put him in the stocks; the other is to throw him and tie him down.

The latter method is a *last resort*, to be used only when quieter methods have been tried and proved unsatisfactory.

From 1912
The Army Horseshoer
U.S. War Department

Historical Reference.

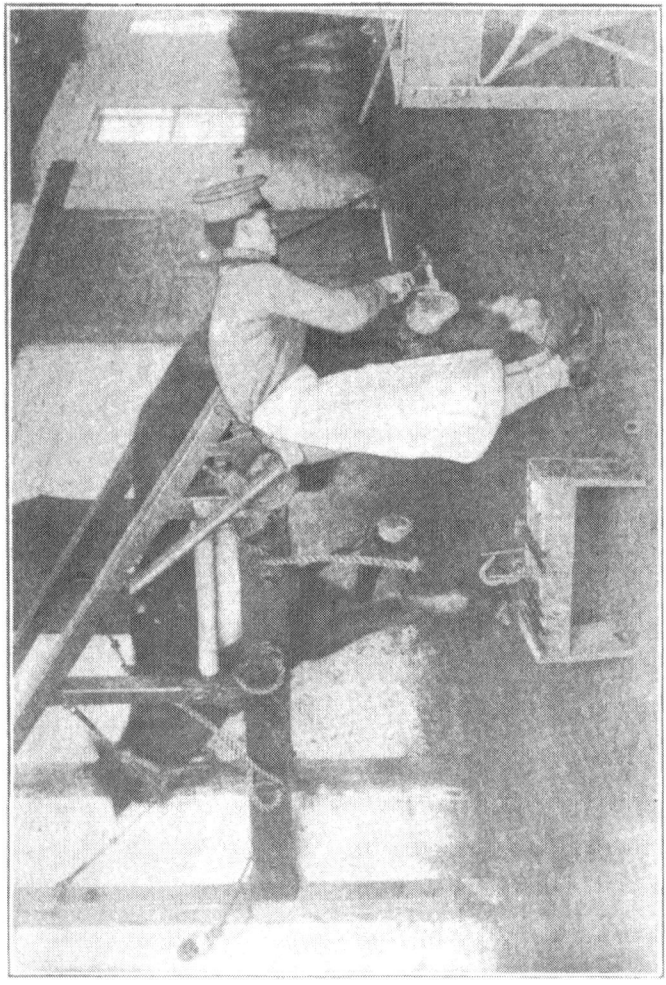

PLATE XVII.—HORSE IN STOCKS.

From 1912
The Army Horseshoer
U.S. War Department

Historical Reference.

104   **THE ARMY HORSESHOER.**

The harness used in the farriers' branch of this school to throw horses for minor operations has been found to answer the purpose and does not harm the horse. Throwing and "hog tying" a horse without other appliances than a rope should be

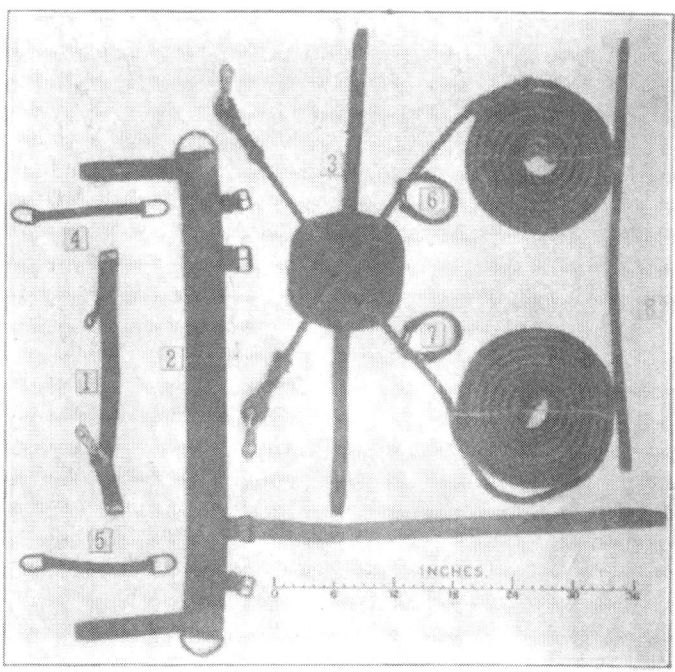

PLATE XVIII.—HARNESS FOR HORSE THROWING.

avoided, as this method usually burns the horse badly and has been known to result in permanent injury.

The throwing harness (Pl. XVIII) consists of:
1. Bellyband with snap hooks for front hobbles.
2. Breast strap with suspending neck strap.

Historical Reference.

PLATE XIX.—THROWING THE HORSE FOR SHOEING.

From 1912
The Army Horseshoer
U.S. War Department

Historical Reference.

THE ARMY HORSESHOER.

3. Saddle pad with crossed ropes, each 20 feet long.
4 and 5. Front hobbles.
6 and 7. Hind hobbles.
8. Check strap, used to connect the saddle pad with halter crown strap.

The harness is shown in detail in the illustration. The scale of inches will enable any good saddler to manufacture it accurately, and Plate XIX also shows clearly the manner in which it should be adjusted and used.

O

From 1912
The Army Horseshoer
U.S. War Department

Note: Virtually all of the content from *The Army Horseshoer* was duplicated in the 1917 *Manual For Army Horseshoers*. Other War Department publications, such as the 1914 *Manual for Farriers, Horseshoers, Saddlers, and Wagoners or Teamsters* cited *The Army Horseshoer* as the primary manual for horseshoeing.

Historical Reference.

From 1915
Trade journal and advertisement.
Note the beginning of the recombination of the blacksmith and farrier trades... Less than a decade later later, *American Blacksmith* would be absorbed by an automotive publication.

Historical Reference.

HORSE-SHOES

AND HORSE-SHOEING.

CHAPTER I.

THE VALUE OF THE HORSE AS A LIVING MACHINE DEPENDS TO A GREAT EXTENT UPON HIS FEET. THE CARE OF THEM BY ANCIENT PEOPLE. XENOPHON AND HIS ADVICE. THE NECESSITY FOR SOUND FEET. HISTORY OF THE ART OF SHOEING. THE HOOF IN A NATURAL STATE. EFFECTS OF DOMESTICATION AND CLIMATE. THE PERSIANS, ETHIOPIANS, ABYSSINIANS, TARTARS, MONGOLS, AND OTHER NATIONS. THE GREEKS. DIFFICULTY IN TRACING THE ORIGIN OF SHOEING. SCRIPTURAL TIMES. HOMER, AND 'BRAZEN-FOOTED.' TRYPHIODORUS. BRONZE SHOES, AND SHOELESS HOOFS. XENOPHON ON THE MANAGEMENT OF HORSES' FEET. ARISTOTLE. POLYDORE VERGIL. THE GREEK MARBLES. CLIMATE OF GREECE. EFFECTS OF MARCHING. TRANSLATORS' AND COMMENTATORS' MISTAKES. ARRIAN AND ARTEMIDORUS. THE COIN OF TARENTUM.

THE horse is justly considered, even in these days, when the application of steam power has to a certain extent limited some of his more important functions, one of the most tractable and serviceable living machines, viewing him as a motor, ever pressed into slavery by man, and consequently ranks high above all those crea-

Historical Reference.

tures which have submitted themselves to domestication and toil for the benefit of the human species.

The varied uses to which he has been subjected, since taken from a wild state, and the willing and cheerful manner with which he has undergone fatigue, and performed duties which are, one would think, quite foreign to his nature, have all been owing to his combined and unequalled qualities of strength, courage, speed, fidelity, and obedience, as well as docility; and though his great value depends essentially upon a just disposition of these, yet more especially is it as a living machine, capable of moving or producing motion, and communicating it to inert masses at all times and in nearly all situations, that he is to be prized.

Where, and at what period of the world's history, he was first brought into a state of servitude; whether at one or more points of the earth's surface man commenced to utilize his noble attributes, we know not. Certain it is, however, that some of the pre-historic races of the human family sought his aid; and the ancient Aryans, more than three thousand years ago, as we learn from the Riga-Veda, in their home towards the upper valley of the Indus, loved and bred the horse, harnessed him to their chariots with spoked-wheels, and made him assume the principal part in their greatest religious sacrifices.

The history of mankind abundantly testifies, that every possible use and application of this animal, whether in war, commerce, or pleasure, seems to have been anticipated by the most ancient peoples; proving the earliest sense and conviction of his immense importance to man. Those old-world nations which, long ages ago, most largely

From 1869
Horse-Shoes and Horse-Shoeing
Fleming

Historical Reference.

QUALITIES OF THE HORSE.

employed the horse, were the great centres of antique civilization; and it may safely be asserted, that, without him, the human race could not have reached its present state of refinement, or have been able to contend against the numerous obstacles to comfort and happiness which have surrounded it; indeed, it has been said, that next to the want of iron, the want of horses would have been, perhaps, one of the greatest physical barriers to the advancement of the arts of civilized life.

Doubtless, what might be termed the moral qualities of the horse, had largely conduced to make him so serviceable in all ages, but by far the largest share must be attributed to those of a physical kind. Strength, speed, endurance, and astonishing alacrity have endowed him with his most useful characteristics, and given him the pre-eminence over all other domesticated animals; and these qualities again depend upon a marvellous adaptation of the organs and textures of which he is composed to the most varied requirements.

Cuvier has somewhere said of the horse, that but for the space of bare gum between the incisor and molar teeth which affords space for the insertion and action of the bit, it would never have been subjected to the power of man. Far rather with truth may it be said, that but for the horse being endowed with a hoof which covers and protects the most beautiful and delicate of structures, and which being solid and a slow conductor of heat and cold, fits it for travelling in snow and ice during the winter of northern regions, and in the burning sands of tropical climates, he would scarcely have proved himself worth the trouble of domesticating. Means could have been

From 1869
Horse-Shoes and Horse-Shoeing
Fleming

Historical Reference.

employed to ride and drive him without a bit in his mouth, but no invention or device of man could have compensated for the absence of his solid, hoof-cased foot. From the earliest ages, the attention of horsemen and horse-loving nations has been directed to the conservation or perfectioning of those attributes which make this ever-willing slave so worthy of our admiration and gratitude; and those horses which had the best conformation, and proved themselves fleetest and hardiest, were ever selected as models for breeding and purchasing. And curiously enough, though it was not to be wondered at, nearly every one of the ancient writers, when speaking of the horse, centre their attention on his feet; no matter how beautifully formed the other *points* of his conformation may have been, if his feet were defective, all was bad. The excellent horseman and gallant soldier, Xenophon, to whose extant treatises on the horse we are indebted for so much of what we know of equestrian matters in the ancient world, tersely specifies how essential even in his day, when the uses of this animal were more limited, it was that he have good feet, or there was no profit in him. He says: 'In respect to the horse's body, then, we assert that we must first examine the feet; for as there would be no use in a house, though the upper parts were extremely beautiful, if the foundations were not laid as they ought to be, so there would be no profit in a war-horse, even if he had all his other parts excellent but was unsound in his feet; for then he would be unable to render any of his other good qualities effective.'[1]

And from the days of Xenophon to the present, when

[1] De Re Equestri.

From 1869
Horse-Shoes and Horse-Shoeing
Fleming

the uses of the horse have been so multiplied and so much more necessary for our business or pleasure, the truth of this advice has been daily receiving confirmation, until the aphorism 'No foot, no horse,' has become a painful reality in modern days, though it is but a re-echo of what was enunciated centuries beyond two thousand years ago.

For the manifestation of his strength and the due performance of his useful qualities, the horse must, therefore, rely upon the soundness of his feet, as in them are concentrated the efforts created elsewhere; and on them depend not only the sum total of these propulsive powers being properly expended, but also the solidity and just equilibrium of the whole animal fabric. So that it is wisely considered that the foot of the horse is one of the most, if not *the* most, important part of all the locomotory apparatus; and that all the splendid qualities possessed by the noble creature may be diminished in value or hopelessly lost, if through disease or accident, natural or acquired defects, or other causes, this organ fails to perform its allotted task.

Seeing, then, the great interest which attaches to this animal, in its being of all creatures most concerned with man in promoting a progressive and long-continued civilization, and to the means and appliances which the lord of the creation has from time to time brought to bear in increasing the utility (would I could say comfort and happiness!) of this devoted servant, I have entered on the present inquiry into the origin and early history of what is generally looked upon as a humble art; for the simple reason that it affords us a glimpse, or rather a faint idea, of an obscure occupation, a modest handicraft, in-

Historical Reference.

creasing a hundred-fold the value of the horse, and testifies to what an apparently insignificant operation very much of our immense progress in civilization has depended. I refer to the art of shoeing, by which, in arming that portion of the horse's hoof coming in contact with the ground, and sustaining the whole weight, while it receives the full force of the propelling power, would (in our northern climate, at least) under the strain of load-bearing or draught, soon be destroyed, and the animal rendered useless, injury is not only averted, but the utility and power of the horse are largely increased.

An art which has exerted some influence on the destinies of man, and lent its aid to the restless wave of human action, deserves some notice from those who care to note the sources and influences on which improvement and increased communication have relied; and if this be a modest one, it is at least endowed with all the more interest in consequence of its being so closely related to the conservation of the best qualities of the noblest quadruped on earth.

In a state of nature the hoof requires no protection. The solidity and toughness of its inferior border; the absence of artificial roads; nothing but the weight of the body to be supported; and the matter of which the horny case is composed never being subjected to any other influences than those which it is naturally adapted to resist, all tend to obviate any injurious amount of attrition in the roaming-at-will life of the feral horse. But in connection with climate, domestication alters, more or less, the conditions on which the horn depends for its integrity as an efficient protection to the highly sensitive

From 1869
Horse-Shoes and Horse-Shoeing
Fleming

Historical Reference.

UNSHOD HOOFS.

and vascular textures it encloses. In eastern countries, where the climate is dry and the earth elastic and soft, and where the equine species is usually wiry and firm in its organization, with dense inflexible hoofs, an armature of any kind is seldom, if ever, required. Not unfrequently, however, we learn that the care and attention of the people who so employ horses is bestowed on the quality and resistance of the hoof; and as this has an important bearing on our inquiry, we will notice a few of the authorities who mention the fact. Thevenot informs us that the Persians cared little for shoes for their horses;[1] the Ethiopians, in the time of Ludolphus, although they seldom rode, did not employ any defence for the hoofs, and when they had to travel over rough and stony ground, they dismounted and sat on the backs of mules, leading their horses in hand, so that these might tread lighter, and do their hoofs less damage. 'They do not defend their horses' hoofs with iron shoes; if they travel over rough and uneven ground, they lead them, and ride mules.'[2] The same authority asserts that the Tartars, who ride so much, never shod their steeds. 'In the winter time, when, on account of the frost, roads are rough and hard, they cover their horses' feet with the recently flayed hide of cattle, if nothing else is at hand.'[3]

A recent traveller in Abyssinia states that the horses

[1] Voyages, vol. ii. p. 113. Paris, 1684.

[2] *Joh. Ludolphus.* Hist. Æthiopic., vol. i. cap. 10. 'Ideo nec ungulas eorum soleis ferreis muniunt: si per aspera et salebrosa loca eundum fit, eos ducunt, ipsi mulis insidentes.'

[3] Ibid. in Commentario, p. 149. 'Tempore vero hyemis, viis ob gelu asperis et duris, *corio boum, etiam recenti,* si-aliud non suppetat, pedes equorum suorum involvunt.'

and mules of that country are not shod.[1] The wandering Mongols who roam between the Great Wall of China, the desert of Gobi, and the Russian frontier, with their flocks of sheep and droves of horses and cattle, do not employ shoes for their hardy but uncouth solipedes, according to the account of my friend and fellow-traveller, Mr Michie. Whenever a pony selected from a drove has become footsore from being ridden too long a time, the rider dismounts, a fresh steed is caught from the crowd, and the hoof-worn one is set at large again, to recover as it best may the loss it has sustained. So that a traveller often requires to change his invaluable steed when crossing these inhospitable wilds. But in this there does not appear to be any difficulty, as an exchange can be readily effected by paying a slight difference to the nomadic owner of a drove, who knows that by allowing the lame creatures to pasture quietly for a few weeks, they will soon have replaced the lost horn, and be as serviceable as ever.

It would appear, however, that horses are sometimes shod here, but they may only be Russian ones. Timkowski in travelling through this country, and when at a halting-place, writes: 'While the smith was *shoeing* our horses, a lama, who kept walking about, and seemed very attentive to what he was doing, suddenly mounted his horse and galloped away. It was afterwards discovered that this priest had stolen one of the smith's tools.'[2]

Marco Polo, in the 13th century, travelling in Badakshan, says: 'The country is extremely cold, but it breeds

[1] *Mansfield Parkyns.* Life in Abyssinia, vol. ii. See also *Baker*, Nile Tributaries in Abyssinia. Proc. Roy. Geo. Soc., 1866.

[2] Travels through Mongolia to China, vol. i. p. 188.

From 1869
Horse-Shoes and Horse-Shoeing
Fleming

Historical Reference.

ABSENCE OF SHOEING.

very good horses, which run with great speed over these wild tracts without being shod with iron.'[1]

The *Tanghans*, or Tibetan ponies Hooker saw in the Himalayas, are described as wonderfully strong and enduring. '*They are never shod*, and the hoof often cracks and they become pigeon-toed.'[2]

Horses are never shod in the Moluccas, or the Straits of Malacca. With regard to Java, Sir Stamford Raffles says: 'Horses are never shod in Java, nor are they secured in the stable as is usual in Europe and Western India. A separate enclosure is appropriated for each horse, within which the animal is allowed to move and turn at pleasure, being otherwise unconfined. These enclosures are erected at a short distance from each other, and with separate roofs. They are generally raised above the ground, and have a boarded floor.'[3] The same kind of floor is in use at Manilla.

Lichtenstein remarks of the Cape of Good Hope horses, that, owing to their being accustomed from their youth to seek their nourishment upon dry mountains, they are easily satisfied, and '*grow so hard in the hoofs* that there is no occasion to shoe them.'[4]

Anderssen, describing some of his journeys in South Africa, says: 'On an after-occasion, I remember to have performed upwards of ninety miles at a very great pace, only once or twice removing the saddle for a few minutes. And be it borne in mind that the animals were young, in-

[1] Narrative of the Travels of Marco Polo. London, 1849. p. 234.
[2] Himalayan Journals, vol. ii. p. 131.
[3] History of Java, vol. ii. p. 319.
[4] Travels in Southern Africa, vol. ii. p. 27. London, 1812.

differently broken in, *unshod*, and had never been stall-fed.'[1]

Dr Browne reports of the horses in Jamaica: 'They are generally small, but very sure-footed and hardy, which renders them extremely fit for those mountainous lands; and their hoofs are so hard that they seldom require shoes; but this is the effect of the heat of the country and dryness of the land.'[2]

Iron shoes are not used for horses in Japan, and Head, in his ride across the Pampas of South America, tells us that shoes are utterly unknown to all the South American country horses. 'But even when unshod, the wear of their boundless plains, on which scarcely a stone is seen, is so insignificant, that to keep the hoofs of a proper length, they have even to be shortened by the hammer and chisel.'[3] Another traveller in that region asserts that the mule of the Peruvian Sierras, with its massy and well-rounded hoof, needs no shoes on hard or soft ground, in summer or in winter.

Clark says of the north of Sweden: 'Neither the men nor their horses are shod, but go bare-footed. In some parts of Sweden, as at Naples, the hinder feet only of the horses are left unshodden; but here horses of a beautiful breed were put to our waggon, without a shoe to any of their feet, as wild and fleet as Barbs;' and again, when entering Finland from Sweden, he writes: 'The horses are, as usual, small, but beautifully formed, and very fleet. The peasants take them from the forests when they are

[1] Lake Ngami, p. 339.
[2] The Civil and Natural History of Jamaica, p. 487. London, 1756.
[3] A Ride Across the Pampas, p. 387.

From 1869
Horse-Shoes and Horse-Shoeing
Fleming

Historical Reference.

CUSTOMS OF DIFFERENT COUNTRIES.

wanted for travellers, and, with very little harness, fasten them to the carriage. In this state, *they are without shoes*, and seem perfectly wild; but it is surprising to observe how regularly and well they trot.'[1] Brooke, however, remarks, that 'so dangerous are the wolves in some parts of Sweden that the peasants, on turning their horses out, generally tip their feet with iron, by which means of defence they are frequently enabled to beat off their ferocious assailants.'[2]

It is well known that in many southern regions there is but little need for any attempt at shoeing. The littoral of Libya, and some parts of Arabia and Persia, furnish examples. In Tartary, whole tribes ride horses without shoes of iron, and in Senegal the French squadron of Spahis have no farriers, for the simple reason that they have no shod horses.[3] In the East Indies, among some races shoeing is far from general.

So we can easily understand, that in certain parts of the world, horses have been and can be made serviceable to a certain extent without employing an iron defence. If one may judge from the paintings of Ancient Egypt and the sculptures of Assyria, where we see the horse portrayed with great skill, and with that minute perception of his external form which seems to us even now very remarkable, no protection for the hoof was ever had recourse to, and no remains of anything bearing a resemblance to such an appliance have been found. And though these countries were acquainted with many arts,

[1] Travels in various countries of Scandinavia. London, 1838.
[2] Travels in Sweden, p. 19.
[3] *Megnin*. Ferrure du Cheval, p. 8.

From 1869
Horse-Shoes and Horse-Shoeing
Fleming

Historical Reference.

and had attained a comparatively advanced state of civilization, in which the horse played no insignificant part, yet in the absence of this craft, even with their favourable climate and soil, the use of this animal must have been but limited, compared to what it is in our own days. It is only when we reach the period in which the ancient Greeks begin to figure in history, that doubts and inquiries arise among modern investigators with regard to a real iron or other metal shoe being employed; and for nearly two hundred years, various writers have spared neither time nor patience in attempting to arrive at some definite conclusion as to whether or not the Greeks and Romans were cognisant of this art, or at what period it first became known.

With the spread of civilization, the demands upon the services of the horse became, doubtless, very much extended; and the diversity of climate, as well as of races, would lead one to suppose that greater wear and modifications, more or less wrought in the nature and consistency of the hoof, must at an early period have rendered some kind of defence absolutely necessary; and that this again would be mentioned in the writings of men who largely devoted their attention to the welfare of this animal. Nevertheless, the antiquity of shoeing, notwithstanding the well-directed labours of many learned men, is yet a subject admitting of considerable diversity of opinion, simply because of the absence of written documents, or records of a positive character, by which this art could be traced to its origin in any particular part of the world.[1] True, there

[1] Among the principal writers who have occupied themselves in this investigation may be mentioned the following:—

Historical Reference.

REASONS FOR TRACING THE ART.

would not probably be much gain in finally deciding as to which race of the human family, or to what age, the successful utilization of the horse by arming its hoofs with a hard rim of metal is due; and it would, perhaps, be more satisfactory and instructive to trace briefly the progress of the art from its earliest known introduction into the social economy of civilized nations, up to the present time, than attempt to seek its inventors in the perplexing obscurity surrounding this subject. But, as before noticed, the interest which attaches to all that pertains to the horse, and particularly to the management of its feet, by those people who were among the first to discover the beauties and merits of that noble animal, and to press its strength, fleetness, courage, and endurance

Raphael Fabretti. Syntagma de Columna Trajani.

A. Winckelmann. Description des Pierres Antiques Gravées, p. 169. Florence, 1760.

I. Pegge. Archæologia, 1776.

Beckman. History of Discoveries and Inventions, vol. ii. London, 1797.

Bourgelat. Essai Théorique et Pratique sur la Ferrure.

Huzard. Théâtre d'Agriculture, vol. i. p. 630. Paris, 1804.

Bracy Clark. An Essay on the Knowledge of the Ancients respecting the Art of Shoeing the Horse. London, 1831.

T. D. Fosbrooke. Encyclopædia of Antiquities. London, 1840. An anonymous writer in United Service Magazine, 1849.

C. H. Smith. The Naturalist's Library, vol. xii. p. 128.

H. Bouley. Dictionnaire Vétérinaire, vol. vi. *Art.* Ferrure.

H. S. Cuming. Journal Archæological Association, vol. vi. xiv.

F. Defays. Annales de Méd. Vétérinaire, p. 256. Brussels, 1867.

J. P. Megnin. De l'Origine de la Ferrure du Cheval. Paris, 1865.

La Maréchalerie Française. Paris, 1867.

Nickard. Mémoires de la Soc. Nationale des Antiquaires de France, 1866.

From 1869
Horse-Shoes and Horse-Shoeing
Fleming

Historical Reference.

into their service, is a great inducement to review, in as graphic a manner as possible, all that has been said in relation to the existence, non-existence, or *status* of this art among them. And in this inquiry the poet, painter, and sculptor have some interest, inasmuch as the correctness or incorrectness of their delineations, when this apparently trifling detail comes to be treated, will depend. This will be exemplified hereafter.

It is a remarkable circumstance that, considering the mighty influence the horse has been called on to exercise on the destiny of nations and the progress of civilization from the earliest times,—at one period an important adjunct to luxury, as well as a mainspring of utility; at another, an essential element in the arts of peace, and a still more potent one in that of war,—the first written indication of horse-shoeing (as we now understand the term) is only found in the annals of a comparatively recent period. The knowledge of being able to defend from undue wear and injury such an important organ as the horse's foot, and by such an efficacious, yet simple means, one would think indispensable to those who, in primitive times, so largely employed horses, and sought from them such important services. Such is not the case, however, if an entire omission of the fact in their writings or on their monuments be received as proof; and though several authors of some weight have in recent years asserted that the ancients were acquainted with this art, and have adduced evidence which appears to substantiate their opinion, yet a careful examination of the times and the meaning of the texts has, in nearly every case, tended to lead others to the opposite conclusion.

From 1869
Horse-Shoes and Horse-Shoeing
Fleming

Historical Reference.

ANCIENT HISTORY.

That shoeing was not known to Old Testament people, no one has yet, so far as I am aware, offered a doubt. Deborah [1] (B.C. 1296) sings, 'Then were the *horse-hoofs broken* by the means of their prancings, the prancings of their mighty ones ;' or, as it might perhaps more correctly be rendered, 'Then did the *horses' hoofs* smite the ground, and were broken from the haste of their riders.' Isaiah [2] (B.C. 760), in the grandly prophetic language in which he foreshadows the downfall of Jerusalem by the armies of Rome, mentions the hoofs of their horses and what was esteemed their best quality. He says, 'Whose arrows are sharp, and all their bows bent, *their horses' hoofs shall be counted like flint*, and their wheels like a whirlwind.' And Jeremiah [3] (B.C. 607), when foretelling the punishment of the Philistines, says: 'At the noise of the *stamping of the hoofs of his strong horses*, at the rushing of his chariots.'

It is in Homer (B.C. 1000) that we find some investigators contending for the first notice of a metallic foot-defence. Among these appear Fabretti, Bourgelat, Montfauçon, Cuming, and a few others. In reality, however, it was Eustathius, who lived in the 12th century, who, in his Commentaries on Homer, first speaks of that poet mentioning horses as shod. In the 'Iliad' (Book xi., lines 150-2) occurs the passage noted by Eustathius:

> πεζοὶ μὲν πεζοὺς ὄλεκον φεύγοντας ἀνάγκῃ
> ἱππεῖς δ' ἱππῆας—ὑπὸ δέ σφισιν ὦρτο κονίη
> ἐκ πεδίου, τὴν ὦρσαν ἐρίγδουποι πόδες ἵππων.

[1] Judges v. 22.   [2] Isaiah v 28.
[3] Jeremiah xlvii.

From 1869
Horse-Shoes and Horse-Shoeing
Fleming

And this striking picture has been thus translated by a recent and celebrated scholar:

> ' Foot on foot, and horse on horse:
> While from the plain thick clouds of dust arose
> Beneath the *armèd* hoofs of clatt'ring steeds.'

This it will be readily perceived is an error. The passage, literally rendered, ought to read something like the following: 'Foot on foot and horse on horse, they perished forcibly while flying; and under them the dust arose from the plain, and the loud-sounding (crushing or thundering) feet of the horses raised it.'

The word is ἐρίγδουποι. Another translator of the Iliad renders this passage:

> ' Horse trod by horse lay foaming on the plain,
> From the dry fields thick clouds of dust arise,
> Shade the black host, and intercept the skies;
> The *brass-hoof'd* steeds tumultuous plunge and bound,
> And the thick thunder beats the labouring ground.'

In another place (Book viii., lines 44-5) Bourgelat, Cuming, and others, found their opinion in favour of the Greeks having shod their horses at this early period, on the fact that Homer speaks of Jove's horses as

> ' The *brazen-footed* steeds
> Of swiftest flight, with manes of flowing gold.'

The translation of χαλχόποδ' ἵππω is correct, and is rendered so by Chapman, an old versifier:

> ' This said, his brasse-hou'd (brass-hoof'd) winged horse
> He did to chariot binde.'

The 'brass-hoof' was undoubtedly used by Homer in a metaphorical sense to denote firmness and solidity, not

From 1869
Horse-Shoes and Horse-Shoeing
Fleming

a hoof shod with brass; it was meant to convey an idea of the really good qualities of the horn in those days, and which, not being garnished with a defence of brass or bronze, was ever in danger of being destroyed when of a weak nature. Besides, brazen-footed and solid or strong-footed ($\chi\rho\alpha\tau\epsilon\rho\omega\nu\upsilon\xi$) appear to be synonymous terms; thus (in Book xxii., lines 192-3) he sings of the time

> 'When the *solid-footed* horses fly
> Around the course, contending for the prize.'

And again (Book xxiv., line 331), strong-hoofed mules are mentioned. The terms were used for many purposes, but never as an indication of shod hoofs. Homer made Achilles and Stentor brazen-voiced.[1] Bulls, fabular stags, and horses, had solid or metallic feet. Thus Pindar[2] (B.C. 520) tells us that Bellerophon was enjoined to sacrifice a *strong-footed* bull to the mighty encircler of the earth before subduing the winged horse Pegasus; and we find that the Grecian heroes who went in search of the golden fleece would all have been destroyed by the *brazen-footed* bulls, from whose nostrils flames issued, had not Medæa interposed and driven away these taurine monsters belonging to King Ætes.[3] Virgil[4] frequently mentions animals of various kinds with metal feet, and Ovid[5] also alludes to them oftener than once. And an older authority than

[1] Iliad, book v. 785.
[2] Olymp. xiii.
[3] Ibid. Olymp. iv.:

> 'His furious bulls, whose nostrils bright
> Flames of consuming fire diffused,
> Battering the ground with *brazen tread.*'

[4] Æneid, book vi. 803.
[5] Heroid. ep. xii. 93: Metamorphosis vii. 105: Apollonius, iii. 228.

Historical Reference.

either of these, and next to Homer himself, the prophet Micah (B.C. 710), exclaims: 'Arise and thresh, O daughter of Zion: for I will make thine horn iron, *and I will make thy hoofs brass:* and thou shalt beat in pieces many people.'[1]

So that really there is no foundation for supposing that the words quoted bear any reference whatever to shoeing. Homer is very minute in some of his descriptions of horses, chariots, armour, and equipment, but there is nothing particular in his poem to lead any one to suspect that the steeds of his warriors were shod. Had they been so, or had he been aware of the art, we can scarcely doubt but he would have introduced some notice of it; entering as he does into so many particulars about horses, which were, next to man, the chief figures in his word-pictures. For instance, he speaks of the method of securing horses; Neptune's team was stabled in a cave

'Twixt Tenedos and Imbro's rocky isle.'

After driving the brazen-footed steeds through the sea, skimming the waves of blue, Neptune takes them to his retreat, then

> 'Loosed from the chariot, and before them placed
> Ambrosial provender; *and round their feet
> Shackles of gold,* which none might break nor loose,
> That there they might await their lord's return.'[2]

As Homer's famous epic describes the misfortunes and the siege of Troy, occurring about twelve hundred years before our era, it is important that the words supposed to denote shoeing be properly understood.

[1] Chap. iv. 13.   [2] Iliad, xiii. 41-5.

From 1869
Horse-Shoes and Horse-Shoeing
Fleming

Historical Reference.

THE WOODEN HORSE OF TROY.

A passage from the Greek poet Tryphiodorus has often been quoted to support the argument in favour of Homer's brazen-footed horses being provided with shoes; and it has been asserted from this passage that shoes of a description similar to those now in use were known at the siege of Troy, because this poet, when speaking of the fabrication of the Trojan horse, mentions that the artist did not forget to put the metal or iron on the hoofs of that wooden machine, in order to make the resemblance more complete. It must be remembered, however, that Tryphiodorus flourished at some period between the third and sixth centuries of our era, when, as will be shown hereafter, this art was not unknown; and as the poem is of comparatively modern date, he may have introduced imaginary shoes to make his picture more complete, just as some of the modern translators of the *Iliad* have done, but without the slightest authority, to prove that these were in use at the time of the war between the Greeks and Trojans.

In his verses, however, I can find no proof of any such intention, nor any mention of an iron rim for the wooden horse's hoofs.

A literal translation of the original Greek is as follows: 'Then at length he finished the work, the hoofs *appearing* not without brass, and shone forth, being covered with tortoise-shell.' Dr Merrick,[1] who furnishes a Latin and English version, renders the passage thus:

> 'To deck each hoof and grace the artist's skill,
> The clouded tortoise yields her polished shell.'

There has been nothing more advanced, so far as I

[1] Tryphiodorus, by Merrick. Oxford, 1742.

From 1869
Horse-Shoes and Horse-Shoeing
Fleming

Historical Reference.

am aware, to prove that the ancient Greeks were cognizant of hoof defences, as we now employ them, except the finding of a horse's hoof (of stone?) in the ruins of the Parthenon. In alluding to this, Mr Syer Cuming, who appears to have taken some interest in the subject, asks, 'Does not Homer allude to shoes when he speaks of "brazen-footed horses?" (χαλκοποδες ιπποι). Mr Cureton informs me that he has seen horse-shoes of bronze.'[1]

And at a later period he writes, 'Since the publication of my paper a few facts have come to light, which tend to prove in an eminent degree the assertion therein advanced, namely, that the horses of the classic ages were shod in a similar way to those of our own day. At the time the paper was produced, we had little to countenance the idea that the early Greeks protected the feet of their steeds with metallic shoes, beyond the bare fact that some ancient horse-shoes of bronze were known to be in existence, and the poetical mention of "brazen-footed horses" in the Iliad (viii. 41, xiii. 23). Within these few years, however, Mr Charles Newton, while Vice-consul at Mytilene, found among the fragments of the Parthenon, a horse's hoof with holes all around the inside, clearly indicating where a metallic shoe had been fastened, and it is quite unlikely that any such defence should appear upon a statue if a similar article had not been in actual use at the time.'[2]

It must be confessed that the discovery of a horse's foot among the world-renowned ruins of the Parthenon, with what appeared to be holes *all round the inside* only,

[1] Journal of the Archæological Association, vol. vi.
[2] Ibid. vol. xvi.

From 1869
Horse-Shoes and Horse-Shoeing
Fleming

Historical Reference.

THE GREEK POETS.

is no indication whatever that a metallic shoe had ever been fastened to it. Had such an article been used, the ancient Greeks would have left us more indisputable proof than a few holes *only round the inside* of the hoof of one of their statues. The holes were doubtless made for some other purpose, and it is to be regretted that no description beyond this is to be found. This, however, will be referred to hereafter.

An allusion to hoofs of horses is frequently discovered in the Greek poets and writers of a later date than the days of Homer, but all negative the idea that they had any brass, bronze, or iron protection. Aristophanes (B.C. 427), for example, in his Comedy of the 'Knights,' makes the chorus address Neptune as the god 'who loves the *noise of the hoofs of horses* and their neighing.' Further reference to the noise made by the hoofs of horses will be furnished when we speak of the Romans.

The strongest evidence that shoeing was not practised among the Greeks of this period, is to be found in the great attention paid to the nature and durability of the hoofs by horsemen and others, and this testimony one would think perfectly convincing. Of these we may select Xenophon, the celebrated Athenian General, in whose eloquent writings enough will be found to satisfy the most incredulous in this respect. This celebrated cavalry officer appears to have carefully studied that animal's character and habits, and all the precepts he gives in his treatise on horsemanship are dictated with an amount of wisdom and humanity which has not, perhaps, been excelled since his day. The safety and comfort of that animal and his rider were ever before him, and his teach-

From 1869
Horse-Shoes and Horse-Shoeing
Fleming

Historical Reference.

ing was principally directed to make the horse particularly adapted for war, as the importance of cavalry was beginning to be perceived by the Greeks in their contests with that nation of horsemen, the Persians. He displays great judgment when specifying the proper form and disposition of parts which collectively make up the nearest approach to a perfect horse, and markedly shows to what a high degree in that distant age this kind of knowledge was cultivated; indeed, from his writing, we are led to infer, that in his time, and perhaps for long before, there were accomplished horse-breakers and public riding masters, as well as men who were excellent judges of horses' qualities.

Xenophon's instructions are well worthy of a place in every treatise on horses and horsemanship, and as his chief experience was no doubt derived while following the profession of arms, and during his command of the cavalry in conducting and covering the glorious retreat of the Ten Thousand Greeks from the interior of Persia, abundant opportunities must have presented themselves to justify him in afterwards urging on the attention of those who had the care of horses, the most scrupulous circumspection in the preservation of their hoofs; thus strongly indicating that shoes were not in use.

In advising as to the good 'points' to be sought for in a horse, he employs the clearest terms to express his meaning. 'A person,' he says, ' may form his opinion of the feet by first examining the hoofs; for *thick* (or strong) hoofs are much more conducive to firmness than *thin* ones; and it must not also escape his notice whether the hoofs are high or low, as well before as behind; for high

From 1869
Horse-Shoes and Horse-Shoeing
Fleming

Historical Reference.

XENOPHON'S INSTRUCTIONS.

hoofs (that is, concave or hollow-soled hoofs) raise what is called the frog (χελιδούα) far above the ground; and low ones tread equally on the strongest and weakest parts of the foot, like in-kneed men, or like cripples among men, who limp on parts which were never intended by nature to support them.[1] Simo[2] says that horses which have good feet may be known by the *sound;* and he says this with great justice, for a *hollow hoof* rings against the ground like a cymbal.' It is somewhat strange to find Markham, in the 17th century, laying stress on this sounding property of a good hoof: 'If a horse's hoofs be rugged, and as it were seamed one seam over another, and many seams; if they be dry, full and crusty, or crumbling, it is a sign of very old age: and on the contrary part, a smooth, moist, *hollow, and well-sounding hoof* is a sign of young years.'[3]

Xenophon continues: 'As attention must be paid to the horse's food and exercise, that his body may be vigorous, so must care be likewise taken of his feet. Damp and smooth stable-floors injure even naturally good hoofs; and to prevent them from being damp, they ought to be sloping; to prevent them from being smooth, they should

---

[1] Οἱ γὰρ παχεῖς πολὺ τῶν λεπτῶν διαφέρουσιν εἰς εὐποδίαν. ἔπειτα οὐδὲ τοῦτο δεῖ λανθάνειν, πότερον αἱ ὁπλαί εἰσιν ὑψηλαὶ ἢ ταπειναὶ, καὶ ἔμπροσθεν, καὶ ὄπισθεν, ἢ χαμηλαί. αἱ μὲν γὰρ ὑψηλαὶ πόῤῥω ἀπὸ τοῦ δαπέδου ἔχουσι τὸν χελίδονα καλουμένην, αἱ δὲ ταπειναὶ ὁμοίως βαίνουσι τῶ τε ἰσχυροτάτω, καὶ τῶ μαλακωτάτω τοῦ ποδὸς, ὥσπερ οἱ βλαισοὶ τῶν ἀνθρώπων.—ΠΕΡΙ ἹΠΠΙΚΗΣ, Ed. Leunc. p. 932.

[2] Simo, an Athenian, mentioned by Suidas and cited by Pollux, was, according to Pliny, the first who wrote on horsemanship. Some reference to him is made in a fragment of Hierocles, which is inserted in the *De Re Veterinariâ* of Simon Grynæus. Basil, 1537.

[3] The Perfect Horseman, p. 129. London, 1655.

have irregularly-shaped stones inserted in the ground (or be paved), and close to one another, similar to a horse's hoofs in size; for such stable floors give firmness to the feet of horses that stand on them.' In alluding to grooming a horse out of doors, he continues: 'The ground outside the stable may be put into excellent condition, and serve to strengthen the horse's feet, if a person throws down in it, here and there, four or five measures full of round stones, large enough to fill the two hands, and each about a pound (?) in weight; surrounding them with an iron rim, so that these may not be scattered; for as the horse stands on these, he will be in much the same condition as if he were to travel part of every day on a stony road.

Isaac Vossius observes on this passage, that Xenophon speaks of iron shoes περὶ ἱππιχῆς, where he directs the hoofs of horses to be protected with iron περιχηδῶσαι σιδήρου. This is the iron hoop to bind the stones. He also says that in an old manuscript of the Greek Hippiatrics in his possession, which was illustrated with paintings, the *marks* and *traces* of the nails that pierced their hoofs were plainly seen. No reliance can be placed on this author's statements, unfortunately, for marks on a hoof in an old drawing are no great proofs of shoeing; and besides, the strange construction he puts on Xenophon's words, furnishes another instance of how little he could be received as an authority on such a subject. He was remarkable for believing the strangest inconsistencies, and almost anything but the truth; which caused Charles II. to say of him, 'This learned divine is a strange man; he believes everything but the Bible.'

From 1869
Horse-Shoes and Horse-Shoeing
Fleming

Historical Reference.

GREEK AND ARAB EXPRESSIONS.

The Greek warrior adds: 'A horse must also move his hoofs when he is rubbed down, or when he is annoyed with flies, as much as when he is walking; and the stones which are thus spread about strengthen the FROGS of the feet.' In another book he[1] repeats the suggestion as to the improvement of the feet by this kind of pavement, and adds, 'He that makes trial of this suggestion will give credit to others which I shall offer, and will see the feet of his horse become firm.' The word Στρογγύλους, here employed to denote firmness, has evidently the same signification as the Latin word *teres:* that is, something smooth, round, and of a proper shape, indicative of strength, soundness, and durability.

It is curious to note a similar expression in use at the present day among the Arabs of the Sahara. 'The hoof round and hard. The hoof should resemble the cup of a slave. They walk on hoofs hard as the moss-covered stones of a stagnant pool. The frogs hard and dry. The frogs concealed beneath the hoofs are seen when he lifts his feet, and resemble date-stones in hardness.'[2]

Furthermore, Xenophon says: 'Those horses whose feet are hardened with exercise, will be as superior on rough ground to those which are not habituated to it, as persons who are sound in their limbs to those who are lame.' In the same work, when treating of the duties pertaining to a commander of cavalry, he dwells on the necessity of attending to the horses' feet: 'You must pay attention to their feet, so that they (the horses) may be in a condition to be ridden even on rough ground, knowing

[1] Hipparchicus, p. 611.
[2] *Dumas:* The Horses of the Sahara.

From 1869
Horse-Shoes and Horse-Shoeing
Fleming

that when they suffer from being ridden they become useless.' He also, in the treatise on horsemanship, speaks of the water used to wash the horses' legs as doing harm to the hoofs by, I suppose, softening them, as the spirit of his teaching was to keep them hard and dry. He makes no mention whatever of any defence for the horses' feet; though he notices the fashion of defending the legs of soldiers by *embattai* or leggings (ἐμβάται), and in passing them under the feet, he says, they might also serve as shoes. These may have been used in cases of emergency for horses, but nothing is said on this point. He specifies horse-armour and its value: 'Since, then, if the horse is disabled, the rider will be in extreme peril, it is necessary to arm the horse also with defences for his head, his breast, and his shoulders. But of all parts of the horse we must take most care to protect his belly, for it is at once a most vital and a most defenceless part; but it is possible to protect it by something connected with the housings. It is necessary, too, that that which covers the horse's back should be put together in such a way that the rider may have a firmer seat (than if he sat on the horse's bare back), and that the back of the horse may not be galled. As to other parts, also, both horse and horseman should be armed with the same precaution (so that the armour may not chafe).'[1]

In a treatise on hunting, ascribed to this author, in speaking of the horse, it is remarked: 'Before the task is accomplished, he falls, the hoofs worn off.'[2] And in another work[3] he incidentally relates that certain people of

[1] Hipparchicus, c. xii.   [2] *Sturz*, Lex. Xenoph. Cynegeticon.
[3] De Cyri Min. Expedit., p. 228.

Historical Reference.

ARISTOTLE AND CAMEL'S FEET.

Asia (Armenians?) whom he saw, were in the habit of tying sandals, or rather, drawing socks over the feet of their horses when the snow lay very thick on the ground, to prevent their sinking too deeply. 'The horses in this country were smaller than those of Persia, but far more spirited. The chief instructed the men to tie little bags (Κυρ Αναβ) round the feet of the horses, and other cattle, when they drove them through the snow, for without such bags they sank up to their bellies.'

This is the only mention made of a garniture for the feet of horses by the renowned author and soldier, and I am not aware of any recent writer mentioning this contrivance in the uplands of Armenia. It may be remarked, however, that in Kamschatka the dogs employed to draw sledges or catch seals wear socks provided with small holes to allow the claws to protrude. These may to some extent not only protect the feet from injury, but also help to guard against sinking in the snow. Arctic travellers have likewise availed themselves of these appliances for their dogs.[1]

The only Greek writer before the Christian era, after Xenophon, who alludes to a defence for the feet of animals is Aristotle (B.C. 340). In describing the camel's foot, he writes: 'The foot is fleshy underneath, like that of a bear; wherefore, when camels are used in war, and become footsore, their drivers put them on leather shoes (ΥΠΟΔΕ-ΟΥΣΙ Καρβατιναις).'[2] They were probably most frequently

[1] *See* Beiträge zur Phys. Oekonomie der Russischen Länder. Berlin, 1786. Captain Cook's Last Voyage, and the later Voyages of Arctic Explorers.

[2] Hist. Animal. lib. ii. p. 850.

From 1869
Horse-Shoes and Horse-Shoeing
Fleming

made of raw hide or coarse cloth (as Ludolphus tells us the Tartars used cow-hide for their horses' feet), passing round the feet and up the legs, like a laced boot. They will be noticed hereafter as *solea*.

Polydore Vergil (A.D. 1550), in his 'De Inventoribus Rerum,' informs us that the Thessalians were reported to have been the first who protected their horses' hoofs with shoes of iron. 'Hos quoque (Peletronios, qui Thessaliæ populi sunt) primos equorum ungulas munire ferreis soleis cœpisse ferunt.'[1] This author, whose Latin was generally more elegant than his descriptions were faithful, does not give his authorities for this statement, which is unsupported by any proof of its correctness. In all likelihood, as Mr Pegge observes,[2] he has misled himself by referring to Virgil, where that poet asserts that

> 'The Pelian Lapithæ
> Invented bits, and mounted on the back;
> Broke horses to the ring, and made them spring
> Under the arm'd, and proudly pace the round.'[3]

Vergil made a mistake, or allowed himself to be deceived, when he described these primitive people of North Greece as the inventors of horse-shoes.

If we turn from the Greek writers who lived previous to our era, to the wonderful productions of the Greek sculptors, those divine works of art—those graceful chisellings portraying groups of men and horses, which are

[1] Lib. ii. cap. 12. [2] Archæologia, 1776.
[3] Georgics, iii. 115:

'Frena Pelethronii Lapithæ gyrosque dedere
Impositi dorso, atque equitem docuere sub armis
Insultare solo, et gressus glomerare superbos.'

Historical Reference.

GREEK SCULPTURE.

> 'Not yet dead,
> But in old marbles ever beautiful,'

we will find our suspicions as to the inaccuracy of those who assert that this people provided an armour for their horses' feet, more than confirmed.

It must be remembered that the Greeks were the first true interpreters of nature. To this their physical organization, their climate, but, perhaps, most of all their religion, concurred to develop those principles of beauty that induce man to select from nature the forms and combinations which give the highest and most endurable pleasure.

The creations of these people, who, according to Pindar,

> 'Strew'd o'er their walls, their public ways,
> The sculptured life, the breathing stone,'[1]

now that two thousand years have passed away, yet, and will ever, command the admiration of refined taste, speaking, as they do, to our imagination and understanding, while carrying with them the greatest beauty of proportion, the utmost simplicity and truth in design, and blending a harmony with a purity and regard for nature such as has never been surpassed. We recognize in their sculptures of horses that intense and astonishing expression of life, which none but the greatest artists are capable of bestowing on their imitations of nature, when teeming with vitality and action. Theocritus, two thousand years ago, was enraptured with these chisellings:

> 'How true they stand, and move, and quite appear
> Alive, not wrought! What clever things men are!'[2]

[1] Olympic Ode, VII. [2] Idyll xv. 83.

From 1869
Horse-Shoes and Horse-Shoeing
Fleming

Such a people must have loved the bold, dauntless courage of the horse, and while seeking to do its unmatchable powers justice in their poetry and adoration in their religion, they have testified to all posterity, by the unerring delineations of their chisels, the beauty and the grandeur of his form and disposition. We have an example of this in the Panathenaic frieze, where the horses are not only of exquisite beauty, but full of life and fire. No two out of the hundred and ten which are introduced are in the same attitude, and each is characterized by a different expression. Flaxman ever spoke of these horses with enthusiasm, and we cannot wonder at it. 'The horses in the frieze in the Elgin collection,' he said, 'appear to live and move, to roll their eyes, to gallop, prance, and curvet; the veins of their faces and legs seem distended with circulation; in them are distinguished the hardness and decision of bony forms, from the elasticity of tendons and the softness of flesh. The beholder is concerned with the deer-like lightness and elegance of their make, and although the relief is not above an inch from the background, and they are so much smaller than nature, we can scarcely suffer reason to persuade us they are not alive.'[1]

The horses of Thessaly are there depicted as they exist at the present day, even to the characteristic large heads and thick necks.[2]

To say that they are exactly portrayed in every anatomical detail, is to declare nothing but the simple truth, and is sufficient for our object. And yet the very

[1] Lectures on Science, vol. iv. p. 104.
[2] *Dodwell*. Travels, vol. i. p. 339.

Historical Reference.

EXACTNESS OF THE GREEK SCULPTORS.

closest scrutiny of the horses' feet in these marbles with a practised—might I add a professional—eye, leads to the unhesitating conclusion that they are exact copies of nature in every respect, but nature never adorned or protected by an iron or bronze furniture. So true do they appear to real life, that we can almost fancy the animals in their spirited movements have chipped their hoofs at the sides (or quarters); and they are of a shape and perfectness which one seldom sees in hoofs that have been shod for any length of time.

These unrivalled relics of antiquity offer additional proofs that metal shoes were not in use. The ancient Greeks were very careful in representing the different costumes worn by the riders of these horses, even to the fashion of their foot covers. Not only this, but they had their marble statues adorned with metals in many instances, which again were not unfrequently gilt. ' For the fragments show that the weapons, the reins of the horses, and other accessories, were in metal, probably gilt.'[1] The horses appeared to have had bits in their mouths, and the holes yet remain at the commissures of the lips wherein they have been fixed; but no evidence is to be found that any metal was attached to the hoofs. In a bas-relief of Castor and Pollux in the Townley gallery of the British Museum, instead of metal bridles for the two horses, red paint appears to have been used. No paint, however, is to be discovered on the feet of any horses to indicate that shoes were worn.

In the Temple collection (case 56) in the British

[1] Description of the Collections of Ancient Marbles in the British Museum. Part IV. page 26. London, 1830.

From 1869
Horse-Shoes and Horse-Shoeing
Fleming

Historical Reference.

Museum, among bronze fragments of a statue and sacrificial implements, is a very perfect hind foot and pastern of a horse, from Magna Græcia. This is unshod, and from the shape and general appearance of the hoof, there can be no doubt that the original of this model had never been submitted to this badge of servile subjection, as old Gwillin has been pleased to designate the modern horse-shoe. And among all the relics to be found in this and other museums, nothing can be discerned that the most lively imagination would transform into a horse-shoe, as employed by the ancient Greeks. Weapons there are without number, articles belonging to religious and domestic requirements, armour and spurs for riders, armour and bits for horses, and in the British Museum are also two excellent specimens of muzzles for horses. Xenophon informs us that, in his day, the groom put on the muzzle (κημὸς) when the horse was led from his stable to be groomed or exercised; indeed on every occasion when he had no bridle on his head or bit in his mouth, to prevent his doing any mischief to other horses or to men. While it prevented the horse from biting it did not interfere with his breathing.[1]

A civilized nation which prized the horse so highly, and so largely employed it in war and in the public diversions, could not but display its wisdom in providing everything for its comfort and well-being; but it appears that the Greeks did not understand extending its utility by preventing undue wear of the hoofs and consequent lameness. All the paintings on vases and elsewhere represent the horse with nude feet.

[1] Xenophon, Hipp., chap. v. 3. Pollux, i. 202.

From 1869
Horse-Shoes and Horse-Shoeing
Fleming

Historical Reference.

CLIMATE OF GREECE.

The climate of Greece, it must not be forgotten, is dry, and favourable to the hardness and durability of horses' hoofs; so that solipedes brought from the north or west, where their journeys would be of a limited character without shoes, may there acquire sufficient strength and cohesiveness in the horny box covering the inferior extremity of the limbs, as to perform a certain amount of labour with no defence.

Paul Louis Courier,[1] who translated Xenophon's treatise on horsemanship, was so pleased with his method of managing the feet of horses, that during the very brief campaign in Calabria in 1807, while with the army corps to which he belonged, he rode horses without shoes, and, as he believed, with advantage. In a note he adds: 'The ancients did not shoe their horses; this is evidenced in all the writings and monuments they have left us, and we cannot be astonished that the people who, in so many different countries, do not know the use of shoes, should not yet have introduced them. The Tonguses, as well as the majority of the Tartars—the best and the most indefatigable horsemen in the world—scarcely work at all in iron; and for that reason it is impossible for them to shoe their steeds. The Dutch at the Cape of Good Hope have little horses which are never shod, according to Sparmann. And M. Thunberg has made the same remark in the island of Java. Another traveller assures us, that at Mogador, and the west coast of Africa, all the horses journey without shoes, and Niebuhr says the same for those of Yemen. Pallas has seen the horses of the Kalmucks, which have small and extremely hard hoofs,

[1] Traite de Xenophon sur l'Equitation. Panthéon Littéraire.

From 1869
Horse-Shoes and Horse-Shoeing
Fleming

ridden without any shoes, and the Cossacks' on the banks of the Jaïk, he adds, are never shod.'

Of the evil effects of prolonged marches, and consequent excessive wear of the undefended hoofs in the Greek armies, we find casual mention now and again in the early historians. Diodorus Siculus (B.C. 44) in one of his volumes, when describing the victories of Alexander, states that 'the hoofs of the horses, through ceaseless journeying, had been worn away, and the matériel of war was used up.'[1]

And Cinnamus speaks in the same strain of the war in Attalia. 'He ordered them to await the rest of the army in Attalia, and to look after the horses, for a disease to which they are liable had attacked their hoofs, and had done serious hurt.'[2]

In the account which Appian gives of the victory achieved by Lucullus over Mithridates, King of Pontus, at the siege of Cyzicum (B.C. 73), we find that Mithridates sent part of his cavalry back to Bithynia, such as were useless, feeble from want of forage, and footsore or lame in consequence of their hoofs being worn out (καὶ χαλευόντας ἐξ ὑποτριβῆς).[3]

This description has been differently given by H. Stephanus (edit. Stephanus, 1592, p. 221), and this has

---

[1] Diod. Siculus, lib. xvii. cap. 94, p. 233. Edit. Weissilingii. 'Equorum ungulæ propter itinera nunquam remissa detritæ et armorum pleraque absumptæ erant.'

[2] Edit. Tollii Traject. ad Rhenum, 1825. Lib. iv. p. 194. 'Cæteras copias manere in Attalia et equos curare jussit, nam malam cui est obnoxium equinum genus plantes pedum acciderat, graviterque effecerat.'

[3] De Bello Mithrid. p. 371. Edit. Tollii.

given rise to a serious mistake. His translation is as follows: 'Equos vero tum inutiles et infirmos ob inediam, claudicantesque solearum inopia, detritis ungulis, aversis ab hoste itineribus, misit in Bithyniam.' No such words as *solearum inopia* occur in the original text; they are an interpolation by the learned translator without the faintest authority, and have led several writers of note to believe that horse-shoes were then in use: whereas the contrary may be inferred, for the horses, it is explicitly mentioned, were lame by the attrition of their hoofs; which implies that horses were not shod. Montfauçon was led astray by this addition to the original account. He writes: 'There are *certain and undoubted proofs* that the ancients shod their horses; thus much Homer and Appian say;'[1] and Fosbrooke[2] remarks that 'an *iron horse-shoe* is mentioned by Appian; so that the conclusion from Xenophon's recommendation for hardening the hoof, that the ancients did not shoe beasts of burden, is too rash.'

Subsequent to the Christian era, we find Arrian[3] (A.D. 200) comparing the human body to a pack-ass—ὀνάριον ἐπισεαγμένον, and speaking of a kind of shoe for that animal: 'Ὅταν ἐχεῖνο ὀνάριον ᾖ, τἄλλα γίνεται χαλινάρια τοῦ ὀναρίου, σχημάτια, ὑποδηματια, κριθαί, χόρτος. Some translators have rendered ὑποδηματια as 'ferreæ calces;' but Didot, in his new Collection of Classical Greek authors, translates it as *sparteæ calces:* 'Si asselus est corpus, cetera freni erunt aselli, clitellæ, sparteæ calces, hordeum, fœnum.'

Artemidorus, in his Interpretation of Dreams, about

[1] Antiquité Expliquée, vol. iv. p. 50.
[2] Ency. of Antiquities. London, 1840.
[3] Commentar. in Epictetum, lib. iii.

the same period as Arrian, also speaks of a horse shod with a sock or shoe, ὑπόδημα, which was probably made of spartea, like the above.

I find on a silver coin of Tarentum,[1] now in the British Museum, and struck, it is surmised, about B.C. 300, a curious representation of a horse and two men, which might, at the first glance, be supposed to be connected with our subject (fig. 1).

fig. 1.

The horse is beautifully delineated, and admirably represents the breed then famous in this part of Magna Græcia. A groom or boy, nude as the horse attendants are generally represented on ancient Greek vases and sculpture, is seated on the horse's back, and strokes his

[1] Tarentum, the modern Taranto, an ancient town of Italy, in the kingdom of Naples, is built on a small island, in the Gulf of Taranto, near Brindisi. It was founded B.C. 700, as a Greek colony, by Lacedæmonian Parthenii, the descendants of a people noted for their love of horses and excellent horsemanship. This city was one of the most flourishing and powerful of Magna Græcia, and was distinguished for its luxury and splendour, as well as for its encouragement of the fine arts. For a long time it resisted the Romans, but at last submitted to them, B.C. 272. The above drawing is twice the size of the coin.

From 1869
Horse-Shoes and Horse-Shoeing
Fleming

Historical Reference.

TARENTUM COIN.

mane as if to soothe him, while another individual, also nude, holds up one of the fore feet, as if to apply a shoe. The attitude is very striking, and it would be interesting to discover why such a group should be represented on a coinage.

It may be observed, however, that there is no instrument in the hands of the dismounted figure whereby to fasten on the shoe, if such be his vocation, and that his attitude is not a very convenient one. This is, nevertheless, the posture assumed on the continent of Europe, and generally all over the East, by the workman who arms the hoofs, but then there is another person to hold up the limb. In this example he may be only trying on a shoe; though the figure on the horse's back would not add to the facility with which this operation might otherwise be performed. I may mention that I have seen and heard of troop horses which, though otherwise tractable, would scarcely allow themselves to be shod unless a man were seated on their backs, stroking their ears and necks in the manner shown on the Greek coin; and Cæsar Fiaschi,[1] in the fifteenth century, recommends for horses that will not be shod quietly, that 'mots plaisants' be used, and 'faire mettre un cavalier sur le dos.' It has been suggested that a stone is being removed from the sole; but without shoes it is almost, if not quite, impossible that a stone could lodge in the foot. Might he not be fastening on a temporary shoe or sock?

Beyond the illustration this affords, we have no evidence of shoeing among the Greeks; and, after all, this may be only an allegorical representation, or a reference to some mythological subject.

[1] Maréchalerie. 3rd French edit., cap. 29. Paris, 1563.

From 1869
Horse-Shoes and Horse-Shoeing
Fleming

cclvi
. . .

Selected Resources: Books.

Gregory's Textbook of Farriery
(2011) by Chris Gregory
Heartland Horseshoeing School. heartlandhorseshoeing.com
327 SW 1st Lane, Lamar, MO 64759

An in-depth, fully illustrated, new textbook from a well respected and highly credentialed farrier school instructor.

Principles of Horseshoeing (P3)
(2004) by Dr. Doug Butler and Jacob Butler.
Doug Butler Enterprises, Inc. www.dougbutler.com
P. O. Box 1390 LaPorte, CO 80535
 now
495 Table Road Crawford, NE 69339

This is the second major update of the textbook (the original was published in 1974) used by almost all students of farriery in America today. Detailed, profusely illustrated, and thoroughly researched.

The companion softcover **Farrier Science Study Guide & Workbook** *(1991) contains many valuable articles and illustrations intended to supplement Butler's big textbook.*

New Hope for Soundness
(2001) by Gene Ovnicek.
Wild Horse Publishing www.whpublishing.com
67 CR 142 Florence, CO 81226

A detailed paperback explaining the Natural Balance trimming and shoeing approach which is based on concepts derived from observation of captured mustangs. Includes information about the Equine Digital Support System which can be used in therapeutic horseshoeing.

Selected Resources: Books.

Color Atlas of the Horse's Foot
(1995) by Christopher C. Pollitt
Times Mirror International Publishers Ltd.
Lynton Hse., 7-12 Tavistock Square, London WC1H 9LB, UK

This book features an astonishing assortment of high-quality color photographs. Specimens are detailed from the electron-microscopic level on up. There are enough images of extreme hoof and leg pathologies here to fill a lifetime of farriers' nightmares. You may own this book for some time before you see past the images to realize the value of the text that goes with them.

On the Horse's Foot, Shoes and Shoeing:
the Bibliographic Record;
and a Brief Timeline History of Horseshoeing
(1990) by Henry Heymering.
St. Eloy Publishing
8621A Hunters Drive, Frederick, MD 21701

A complete bibliographic record of farrier science from 430 BC through AD 1990. Time line history from 4000 BC through AD 1990. This is simply the ultimate text for those interested in the history and development of farriery.

The Army Horseshoer
(1912) US War Department
Washington, DC   War Department Document #423

"A manual prepared for the use of the training school for farriers and horseshoers by the training school instructors."

Before the rise of Butler's textbook, the Army Manuals were a primary reference for many horseshoeing students in America.
(Selections from this one are included in the Historical Reference appendix.)

Selected Resources: Books.

A Handbook of Horse-Shoeing
with
Introductory Chapters on the Anatomy and Physiology of the Horse's Foot
(1898) by Dollar & Wheatly.
D. Douglas - Edinburgh / W.R. Jenkins - New York

A very detailed treatment of farrier science, complete with outstanding illustrations. It is interesting to see how many of the "revolutionary new" concepts and products of today were already familiar in the 19th Century.

(Selected illustrations from this book are included in the Historical Reference appendix.)

A Text-Book of Horseshoeing
for Horseshoers and Veterinarians
(1884) by A. Lungwitz
Dresden

This is one of the most historically significant texts on horseshoeing, featuring a great deal of technical information and detailed anatomical illustrations.

Unfortunately, like too many books on the subject, it was written by a veterinarian with little or no personal understanding of applied farriery, and is the source of some misconceptions that plague us to this day.

Horse-Shoes and Horse-Shoeing
Their Origin, History, Uses, and Abuses.
(1869) by George Fleming
Chapman and Hall   193 Piccadilly, London

Exactly what it says on the tin. Well-researched and thorough. Includes an overview of the many fads and trends in horseshoeing in the mid-to-late 19th Century.

(The first chapter of this book is included in the Historical Reference appendix.)

cclx

Selected Resources: Periodicals.

American Farriers Journal
www.lesspub.com
P.O. Box 624 Brookfield, WI 53008

The leading farrier's trade journal in America, in publication since 1975.

Farriers Journal
www.farriersjournal.com
Diasse SPRL - Rue d'Opprebais 16 - 1360 Malèves-Sainte-Marie

Formerly the **European Farriers Journal**, published in various multilingual formats since 1986. Now distributed in seven languages to sixty-eight countries. Also known as **Infor Maréchalerie, Der Huf, El Herrador, Infor Mascalcia, Hovslagarmagasinet, De hoef**, and **Kopyta**.

Crúdóir
www.crudoir.com
Bex Cothran   Lockeford, California

Free subscription, advertising-supported farrier magazine slated for launch in Spring 2012.

Available by mail in the US and by email PDF worldwide. Apparently an English language publication. The unusual title being a reference to the publisher's Scottish heritage.

cclxii

. . .

Selected Resources: Internet.

www.horseshoes.com   www.farriers.com
The Farrier & Hoofcare Resource Center
Worldwide Farriers Directory

The newly combined Internet megasite for all things pertaining to farriery. Includes a vast library of articles, an array of active discussion bulletin boards, an enormous farrier product and supply marketplace, and much more.

www.hoofblog.com   www.hoofcare.com
Fran Jurga's Hoofcare & Lameness Journal

The most active and in-depth online news source for farriery and hoofcare-related topics.

Also a good source for farrier science books, especially the high-end volumes that are hard to find elsewhere.

www.dougbutler.com
Doug Butler Enterprises

Online connection to Butler's publications, horseshoeing courses, blog, and extensive article archive.

www.forgeandfarrier.co.uk
Forge and Farrier

Online farrier magazine and resource site. Oriented towards farriers in the United Kingdom.

www.centaurforge.com
Centaur Forge

Books, videos, and more.

www.farrier-giles.co.uk
Giles Holtom

A small site with articles, opinions, and message boards. Worth mentioning here because the articles and opinions are those of a farrier with well over a half century of professional experience and the rare F.W.C.F. credential.

cclxiv

. . .

MILLWATER PUBLISHING

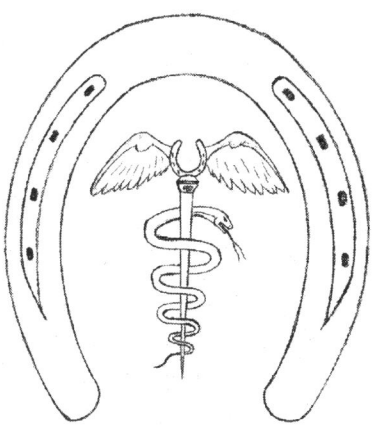

www.MillwaterPublishing.com

Our website includes a secure, online store featuring ***Millwater's Farriery***, other publications and products designed for farriers and horseowners.

MillwaterPublishing.com is also home to the free online archives of the *Carolina Farrier's Open Forum & Idea Exchange*, and *Equestrian Quarterly* periodicals, as well as selected articles and essays.

MILLWATER Lexicon Project History.

Millwater's Farriery:
The Illustrated Dictionary of Horseshoeing and Hoofcare
Version 3.0.1 / 3.0.2
(Mural trade paperback / deluxe hardcover) 2012

New Dictionary of Farrier Terms and Technical Language
Version 2.7.2 / PB
(Black pod coil / perfect bound) 2010

New Dictionary of Farrier Terms and Technical Language
Version 2.7.1
(Brown pod coil) 2008

New Dictionary of Farrier Terms and Technical Language
Version 2.7.0
(Brown pod coil) 2006

New Dictionary of Farrier Terms and Technical Language
Version 2.6.0
(Blue pod coil) 2004

New Dictionary of Farrier Terms and Technical Language
Version 2.5.1
(White pod coil) 2003

New Dictionary of Farrier Terms and Technical Language
Version 2.5.0
(White slick saddle) 2003

Virtual Dictionary of Farrier Terms II
Version 2.4.0
(HTML-based) Unreleased

Virtual Dictionary of Farrier Terms
Version 2.3.0
(Macintosh Application) 1997

New Dictionary of Farrier Terms / F&HRC Glossary
Version 2.2.0
(Original website glossary text content.) 1996

New Dictionary of Farrier Terms and Technical Language
Version 2.1.0
(Beige saddle) 1996

New Dictionary of Farrier Terms and Technical Language
Version 2.0.0
(Gray saddle) 1995

Pocket Dictionary of Farrier Terms and Technical Language
Version 1.0.0
(Gray saddle) 1994

MILLWATER'S FARRIERY:
THE ILLUSTRATED DICTIONARY OF FARRIERY AND HOOFCARE

and

MILLWATER PUBLISHING

are now represented on

Amazon
FaceBook
Google+
Blogspot
Twitter
YouTube
Squidoo
and
MySpace.

go to
http://www.MillwaterPublishing.com/
for links

cclxviii
. . .

Printed in Great Britain
by Amazon